ALSO BY JAMES BRADLEY

Flags of Our Fathers
Flyboys

THE
IMPERIAL
CRUISE

A SECRET HISTORY
OF EMPIRE AND WAR

JAMES BRADLEY

LITTLE, BROWN AND COMPANY

LARGE PRINT EDITION

Little, Brown and Company
Hachette Book Group
237 Park Avenue, New York, NY 10017
www.hachettebookgroup.com

First Large Print Edition: November 2009

Little, Brown and Company is a division of Hachette Book Group, Inc. The Little, Brown name and logo are trademarks of Hachette Book Group, Inc.

Maps by George W. Ward

ISBN 978-0-316-02461-7
LCCN 2009935165

10 9 8 7 6 5 4 3 2 1

RRD-IN

Printed in the United States of America

For Michelle, Alison, Ava, Jack

CONTENTS

THE
IMPERIAL
CRUISE

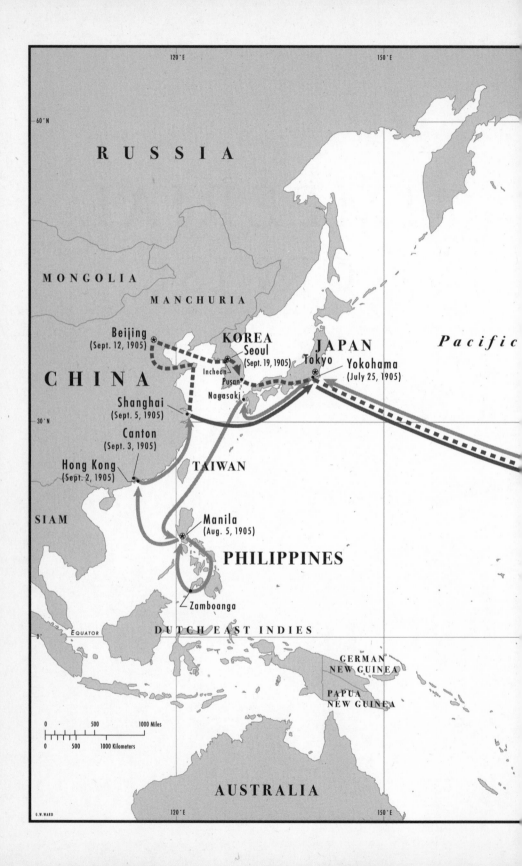

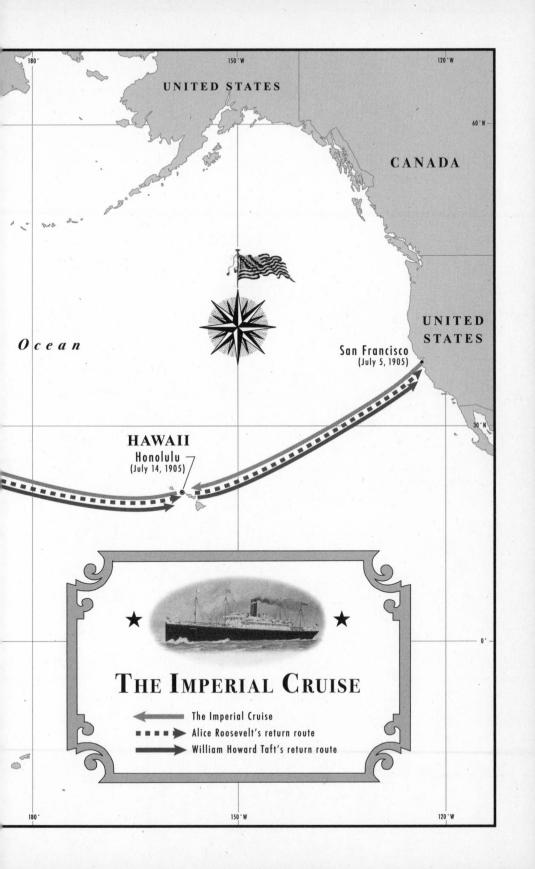

UNITED STATES

CANADA

UNITED
STATES

San Francisco
(July 5, 1905)

Ocean

HAWAII
Honolulu
(July 14, 1905)

THE IMPERIAL CRUISE

The Imperial Cruise
Alice Roosevelt's return route
William Howard Taft's return route

Chapter 1

ONE HUNDRED
YEARS LATER

---

*"I wish to see the United States the dominant
power on the shores of the Pacific Ocean."*[1]
—THEODORE ROOSEVELT, OCTOBER 29, 1900

When my father, John Bradley, died in 1994, his hidden memory boxes illuminated his experience as one of the six men who raised the flag on Iwo Jima. A book and movie—both named *Flags of Our Fathers*—told his story. After writing another book about World War II in the Pacific—*Flyboys*—I began to wonder about the origins of America's involvement in that war. The inferno that followed Japan's attack on Pearl Harbor had consumed countless lives, and believing there's smoke before a fire, I set off to search for the original spark.

In the summer of 1905, President Theodore Roosevelt—known as Teddy to the public—dispatched the largest diplomatic delegation to Asia in U.S. history. Teddy sent his secretary of war, seven senators, twenty-three congressmen, various military and civilian officials, and his daughter on an ocean liner from San Francisco to Hawaii, Japan, the Philippines, China, Korea, then back to San Francisco. At that time, Roosevelt was serving as his own secretary of state—John Hay had just passed away and Elihu

President Theodore Roosevelt. (Library of Congress)

Root had yet to be confirmed. Over the course of this imperial cruise, Theodore Roosevelt made important decisions that would affect America's involvement in Asia for generations.

The secretary of war, William Howard Taft, weighing in at 325 pounds, led the delegation, and

The secretary of war, William Howard Taft. President Roosevelt wrote Taft, "I have always said you would be the greatest President, bar only Washington and Lincoln, and I feel mighty inclined to strike out the exceptions!" (Library of Congress)

to guarantee a Roosevelt name in the headlines, the president sent his daughter Alice, the glamorous Jackie Kennedy of her day, a beautiful twenty-one-year-old known affectionately to the world as "Princess Alice." Her boyfriend was aboard, and Taft had promised his boss he would keep an eye on the couple. This was not so easy, and on a few hot tropical nights, Taft worried about what the unmarried daughter of the president of the United States was up to on some dark part of the ship.

Theodore Roosevelt had been enthusiastic about

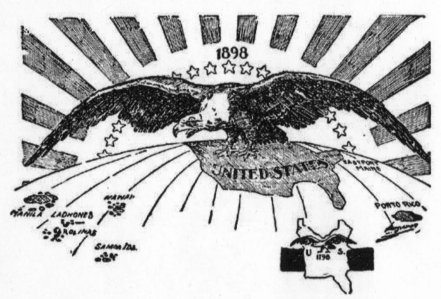

Ten thousand miles from tip to tip.—Philadelphia Press.

"Ten Thousand Miles from Tip to Tip." The map of a small United States in 1798 contrasts with the American eagle's 1898 spread from the Caribbean to China.
(Library of Congress)

American expansion in Asia, declaring, "Our future history will be more determined by our position on the Pacific facing China than by our position on the Atlantic facing Europe."[2] Teddy was confident that American power would spread across Asia just as it had on the North American continent. In his childhood, Americans had conquered the West by eradicating those who had stood in the way and linking forts together, which then grew into towns and cities. Now America was establishing its naval links in the Pacific with an eye toward civilizing Asia. Hawaii, annexed by the United States in 1898, had been the first step in that plan, and the Philippines was considered to be the launching pad to China.

Teddy had never been to Asia and knew little about Asians, but he was bully confident about his plans there. "I wish to see the United States the dominant power on the shores of the Pacific Ocean," he announced.[3]

Theodore Roosevelt stands as one of America's most important presidents and an unusually intelligent and brave man. His favorite maxim was "Speak softly and carry a big stick." This book reveals that behind his Asian whispers that critical summer of 1905 was a very big stick—the bruises from which would catalyze World War II in the Pacific, the Chinese Communist Revolution, the Korean War, and an array of tensions that inform our lives today.

The twentieth-century American experience in Asia would follow in the diplomatic wake first churned by Theodore Roosevelt.

IN THE SUMMER OF 2005—exactly one hundred years later—I traveled the route of the imperial cruise.

In Hawaii, I rode the Waikiki waves like Alice had, saw what she had seen, and learned why no native Hawaiians had come to greet her.

Today the United States is asking Japan to increase its military to further American interests in the North Pacific, especially on the Korean peninsula, where both the Chinese and the Russians seek influence. In the summer of 1905, clandestine diplomatic messages between Tokyo and Washington, D.C., pulsed through underwater cables far below the surface of the Pacific Ocean. In a top-secret meeting with the Japanese prime minister, Taft—at Roosevelt's direction—brokered a confidential pact allowing Japan to expand into Korea. It is unconstitutional for an American president to make a treaty with another nation without United States Senate approval. And as he was negotiating secretly with the Japanese, Roosevelt was simultaneously serving as the "honest broker" in discussions between Russia and Japan, who were then fighting what was up to that time history's largest war. The combatants would sign the Portsmouth Peace Treaty in that summer of 1905, and one year later, the president would become the first American to be awarded the Nobel Peace Prize. The Nobel committee was never made aware of Roosevelt's secret negotiations, and the world would learn of these diplomatic cables only after Theodore Roosevelt's death.

ON JULY 4, 1902, Roosevelt had proclaimed the U.S. war in the Philippines over, except for disturbances in the Muslim areas. In 1905, the imperial cruise steamed into the port city of Zamboanga, a Muslim enclave 516 miles south of Manila. Princess Alice sipped punch under a hot tropical sun as "Big Bill" Taft delivered a florid speech extolling the benefits of the American way.

A century later I ventured to Zamboanga and learned that the local Muslims hadn't taken Taft's message to heart: Zamboangan officials feared for my safety because I was an American and would not allow me to venture out of my hotel without an armed police escort.

The city looked peaceable enough to me and I thought the Zamboangan police's concern was overdone. One morning I was sitting in the backseat of a chauffeured car with my plainclothes police escort as we drove by city hall. The handsome old wooden building had once been headquarters of the American military. The U.S. general "Black Jack" Pershing had ruled local Muslims from a desk there, and the grassy shaded park across the street was named after him.

"Can we stop?" I asked the driver, who pulled to the curb. I got out of the car alone to take pictures, thinking I was safe in front of city hall. After all, here I was in the busy downtown area, in broad daylight, with mothers and their strollers nearby in a park named after an American.

My bodyguard thought otherwise. He jumped out of the car, his darting eyes scanning pedestrians, cars, windows, and rooftops, and his right hand hovered over the pistol at his side.

It was the same later, indoors at Zamboanga's largest mall. I was shopping for men's trousers, looking through the racks. I glanced up to see my bodyguard with his back to me eyeing the milling crowd. The Zamboangan police probably breathed a sigh of relief when I eventually left town.

Muslim terrorists struck Zamboanga the day after I departed. Two powerful bombs maimed twenty-six people, brought down buildings, blew up cars, severed electrical lines, and plunged the city into darkness and fear. The first bomb had cratered a sidewalk on whose cement I had recently trod, while the second one collapsed a hotel next door to Zamboanga's police station—just down the street from the mall I had judged safe.[4] Police sources told reporters the blasts were intended to divert Filipino and American army troops from their manhunt of an important Muslim insurgent.[5]

Just as President Teddy was declaring victory in 1902, the U.S. military had been opening a new full-scale offensive against Muslim insurgents in the southern Philippines.[6] Pacifying Zamboanga had been one of the goals of that offensive. A century later American troops were still fighting near that "pacified" town.

TODAY TRADE DISPUTES DOMINATE the United States–China relationship. In China, I strode down streets where in 1905 angry Chinese had protested Secretary Taft's visit. At the time, China had suspended trade with the United States and was boycotting all American products. Outraged Chinese were attending mass anti-American rallies, Chinese city walls were plastered with insulting anti-American posters, and U.S. diplomats in the region debated whether it was safe for Taft to travel to China. Teddy and Big Bill dismissed China's anger. But that 1905 Chinese boycott against America sparked a furious Chinese nationalism that would eventually lead to revolution and then the cutting of ties between China and the United States in 1949.

IN 2005, I STOOD in Seoul, where, in 1905, Princess Alice had toasted the emperor of Korea. In 1882, when Emperor Gojong* had opened Korea to the outside world, he chose to make his first Western treaty with the United States, whom he believed would protect his vulnerable country from predators. "We feel that America is to us as an Elder Brother," Gojong had often told the U.S. State Department.[7] In 1905, the emperor was convinced that Theodore Roosevelt would render his kingdom a square deal. He had no idea that back in Washington, Roosevelt often said, "I should like to see Japan have Korea."[8] Indeed, less than two months after Alice's friendly toasts to Korea-America friendship, her father shuttered the United States embassy in Seoul and abandoned the helpless country to Japanese troops. The number-two-ranking American diplomat on the scene observed that the United States fled Korea "like the stampede of rats from a sinking ship."[9] America would be the first country to recognize Japanese control over Korea, and

---

*Also King Kojong, King Gojong, or Emperor Kojong. He ruled from 1863 to 1907. Before 1897 he was King Gojong and after 1897 he was Emperor Gojong.

when Emperor Gojong's emissaries pleaded with the president to stop the Japanese, Teddy coldly informed the stunned Koreans that, as they were now part of Japan, they'd have to route their appeals through Tokyo. With this betrayal, Roosevelt had green-lighted Japanese imperialism on the Asian continent. Decades later, another Roosevelt would be forced to deal with the bloody ramifications of Teddy's secret maneuvering.

SINCE 1905, THE UNITED States has slogged through four major wars in Asia, its progress marked best not by colors on a map but by rows of haunting grave-stones and broken hearts. Yet for a century, the truth about Roosevelt's secret mission remained obscured in the shadows of history, its importance downplayed or ignored in favor of the myth of American benev-olence and of a president so wise and righteously muscular that his visage rightly belongs alongside Washington, Jefferson, and Lincoln in Black Hills granite. A single person does not make history, and in this case, Roosevelt did not act alone. At the same time, by virtue of his position and power, as well as by virtue of his *sense* of virtue, Teddy's impact was stag-gering and disastrous. If someone pushes another off a cliff, we can point to the distance between the edge of the overhang and the ground as the cause of injury.

But if we do not also acknowledge who pushed and who fell, how can we discover which decisions led to which results and which mistakes were made?

The truth will not be found in our history books, our monuments or movies, or our postage stamps. Here was the match that lit the fuse, and yet for decades we paid attention only to the dynamite. What really happened in 1905? Exactly one hundred years later, I set off to follow the churned historical wake in Hawaii, Japan, the Philippines, China, and Korea. Here is what I found. Here is *The Imperial Cruise*.

Chapter 2

CIVILIZATION FOLLOWS THE SUN

*"The vast movement by which this continent
was conquered and peopled cannot be rightly
understood if considered solely by itself.
It was the crowning and greatest achievement
of a series of mighty movements, and it must
be taken in connection with them. Its true
significance will be lost unless we grasp,
however roughly, the past race-history of the
nations who took part therein."*[1]
—THEODORE ROOSEVELT, 1889

They headed west, following the sun.

On July 1, 1905, the secretary of war, William Howard Taft, Alice Roosevelt, seven senators, and twenty-three congressmen—together with wives and aides—boarded a transcontinental train in Washington, D.C. Recalled Alice, "It was a huge Congressional party, a 'junket' if ever there was one. We left from the old Baltimore and Ohio Station that stood on what is now part of the park between the Capitol and the Union Station.... The Taft party was, I should say, about eighty strong."[2] Alice noted, "It was the first time I had ever been farther west than the Mississippi and I had a little Atlas that I used to read...as though it were a romance. I would look at it and think I—I am actually here at this place on the map. Those were the days when Kipling made Empire and far-flung territory dreams to dazzle."[3]

Princess Alice was traveling in style. "The luggage that I thought necessary for the trip included three large trunks and two equally large hat boxes, as well as a steamer trunk and many bags and boxes."[4] For his part, Taft brought along several trunks of clothes and a Black valet to help him dress. Both Big Bill and the Princess had their own private railroad carriages.

The two were not alone in their high style, and some taxpayers worried about the cost of the trip. The federal government then had much tighter purse strings than in later years. Only government officials had their fares paid, and everyone, including senators and even Big Bill, was required to pay for his own meals and personal expenses. Nor would Uncle Sam foot the bill for female accompaniment: Alice, like the other women in the party, paid her own way.

Regardless the source of cash, a *San Francisco Examiner* article entitled "Why Taft Pleases Steamer and Rail Folk" pointed out that this was "one of the most lucrative special parties ever hauled across the continent by the overland roads. The railroad fares totaled $14,440, which includes something like $2,100 for dining car service." Added to that would be the "very snug sum" of twenty-eight thousand dollars for almost three months on the passenger ship *Manchuria,* not including tips estimated to total "$1,800...it being taken for granted they will observe the usual tipping custom aboard Pacific liners."[5] These were big numbers to the average U.S. workingman in 1905, who earned between two hundred and four hundred dollars a year.

ALICE ROOSEVELT WAS A novelty, the twentieth century's first female celebrity. Like an early Madonna or Britney, newspaper readers knew her by her first name and even the illiterate recognized her photo. President Roosevelt realized that when Alice went somewhere, the crowds and press followed. She was the very first child entrusted to represent a president.

Teddy had been correct when he had calculated that with Alice on the imperial cruise, the world's newspapers would have more reason to print the family name. Reporters fluttered around her, eager to learn what the shapely girl wore, who sat near her, to whom she spoke, and what she said. Readers particularly loved it when Alice acted bolder than a twenty-one-year-old "girl" should, like when she welcomed the 1905 Fourth of July with a bang, going out to a car on the rear of the train after breakfast and taking potshots with her own revolver at receding telegraph poles. No one thought to ask why the president's young daughter was packing her own pistol. Americans expected such risqué behavior from their Princess.

Alice's public rambunctiousness was an outward reaction to her deep inner hurt over her cold and distant relationship with her domineering father. Her cousin Nicholas Roosevelt later wrote that Theodore Roosevelt's relationship with his daughter "subtly warped the development of this brilliant but basically unhappy person."[6] Alice masked her pain by developing a tough and flamboyant outer layer.

Alice seemed doomed from the start. Before she was born, the future president and a woman named Edith Carow had been sweethearts as adolescents. They quarreled and broke up, but Edith continued to love Teddy. A few years later, Roosevelt married Alice Lee, who birthed Alice Lee Roosevelt on February 12, 1884. Two days later, Teddy's wife died in her husband's arms from complications resulting from her daughter's birth. A year later, Teddy married Edith.

Alice never heard her father acknowledge her natural mother. After his presidency, Roosevelt wrote in his autobiography about the joys of family life and love between men and women, but he would not admit to having had a first wife. As Alice later explained, "My father didn't want me to be . . . a guilty burden . . . on my stepmother. He obviously felt guilty about it, otherwise he would have said at least once that I had another parent. The curious thing is that he never seemed to realize that I was perfectly aware of it and developing a resentment."[7] A relative wrote, "The only rational explanation that I have heard is that T.R.'s determination to regard his first marriage and his life with Alice Lee as a chapter never to be reread was so great that he deliberately buried it in the recesses of his memory forever."[8] Added Alice: "He never even said her name, or that I even had a different mother. . . . He didn't just never mention her to me, he never mentioned her to anyone. Never referred to her again."[9]

Wrote the Pulitzer Prize–winning biographer

Edmund Morris of Alice's stepmother: "Edith struck most strangers as snobbish.... 'If they had our brains,' she was wont to say of servants, 'they'd have our place.' "[10]

Theodore Roosevelt left to Edith the emotionally challenging job of dealing with the rebellious child. Edith responded by bluntly telling Alice that if she did not stop being so selfish, the family would stop caring for her.

Teddy and Edith had five children of their own: Theodore III, Kermit, Ethel, Archibald, and Quentin. Young Alice often felt like an outcast as her brothers teased her about not having the same mother. Her brother Ted told Alice that Edith said that it was good that Alice Lee had died, because she would have been a boring wife for Teddy. Alice later said of Edith, "I think she always resented being the second choice and she never really forgave him his first marriage."[11]

Alice was frequently shunted off to relatives, with whom she often spent more time than with her father and stepmother. Carol Felsenthal writes in *Alice: The Life and Times of Alice Roosevelt Longworth:* "Theodore Roosevelt gave few signs that he cared much about his oldest child."[12] In one letter to Edith, Teddy wrote affectionately about all the children except Alice. And, as Alice confided to her diary, "Father doesn't care for me.... We are not in the least congenial, and

Edith Roosevelt. She said of the servants, "If they had our brains, they'd have our place." (Stringer/MPI/Getty Images)

if I don't care overmuch for him and don't take any interest in the things he likes, why *should* he pay any attention to me or the things that I live for, except to look on them with disapproval."[13]

Among the things Alice rejected was her father's devout faith. As a little girl Alice informed her father that his Christian beliefs were "sheer voodoo" and that she was "a pagan and meant it."[14] She would be the only one of his six children not to be confirmed.

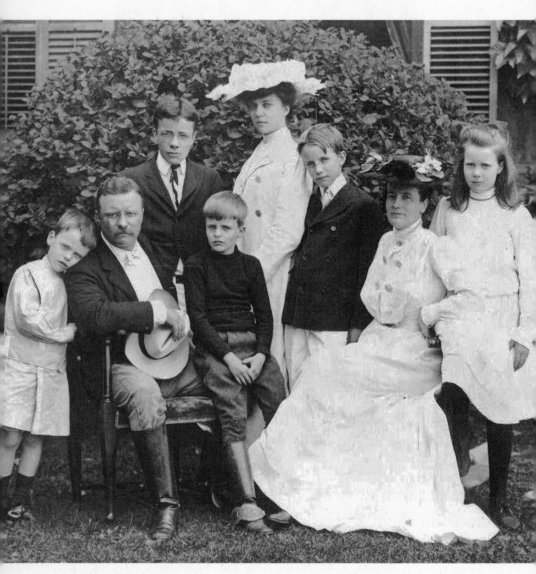

The Roosevelt family. Quentin, Theodore,
Theodore III, Archie, Alice, Kermit, Edith, and Ethel.
(Library of Congress)

Alice's rebellious nature was far from private. She violated White House etiquette by eating asparagus with gloved fingers at an official dinner. She daringly used makeup, bet on horse races, and dangled her legs from grand pianos. Alice once appeared in public with a boa constrictor curled around her neck, and to one "dry" dinner party Alice smuggled small whiskey bottles in her gloves. At a time when automobiles were rare, Alice drove her car unchaperoned around Washington and was ticketed at least once for speeding. Alice wrote that Edith and Teddy requested "that I should not smoke 'under their roof,' [so] I smoked on the roof, up the chimney, out of doors and in other houses."[15] (She was even "asked to leave Boston's Copley Plaza Hotel for smoking in the lobby."[16]) A friend called Alice "a young wild animal that had been put into good clothes."[17] Roosevelt once exclaimed to a visitor, "I can be President of the United States, or I can attend to Alice. I can't do both!"[18]

Yet Roosevelt—who became president after a twenty-year career as a best-selling author and student of public relations—could not help but notice how the media loved this presidential wild child and how useful that might be. He asked his seventeen-year-old daughter to christen Prussian Kaiser Wilhelm's American-made yacht "in the glare of international flashbulbs," and the French ambassador noted it "was

*Alice Roosevelt as a debutante, 1902. A friend called Alice
"a young wild animal that had been put into good clothes."
(Stringer/Hulton Archive/Getty Images)*

a means by which to reduce the hostility in the public
sentiment between the two countries."[19] Pleased with
her performance, Teddy then dispatched her to America's newly acquired Caribbean possessions, Cuba and
Puerto Rico. Although the teenager had once written, "I care for nothing except to amuse myself in a

charmingly expensive way,"[20] she took a serious interest in what she was shown: "As the daughter of the President, I was supposed to have an intelligent interest in such things as training schools, sugar plantations and the experiments with yellow fever mosquitoes."[21] Teddy wrote her, "You were of real service down there because you made those people feel that you liked them and took an interest in them and your presence was accepted as a great compliment."[22]

Having proved useful, Alice was asked by her father to serve as the hostess on Secretary Taft's Pacific voyage. She would not only be a convenient distraction, but an ocean away. After leaving Washington, Alice wrote, "My parting from my family...was really delicious, a casual peck on the cheek and a handshake, as if I was going to be gone six days. I wonder if they really care for me or I for them."[23]

Among those on the trip was Congressman Nicholas Longworth of Ohio. At thirty-four years of age, Nick was thirteen years Alice's senior and only eleven years younger than her father. He had qualified for the trip because of his seat on the House Foreign Affairs Committee and because of his particular interest in Hawaii and the Philippines.

Nick was the fourth generation of Longworths in Cincinnati, a rich aristocrat who grew up on an estate, toured Europe, learned French and the classics, and summered in Newport, Rhode Island. He'd won election to Congress in 1902 and, being wealthy and dashing, was a big attraction for Alice.

The elder Roosevelts did not know the details of Alice and Nick's romance, but if they had, it is likely they would have strongly disapproved. Edith warned Alice, "Your friend from Ohio drinks too much."[24] He was also a gambler and womanizer, known to frequent Washington brothels and enjoy the prostitutes

Congressman Nicholas Longworth aboard the Manchuria, *1905. (Collection of the New-York Historical Society)*

of K Street. Yet here the two were, setting off on a voyage that would take months and remove them both from Teddy's supervision.

THE ARRIVAL OF THE train to the three-day stay in and the subsequent sailing from the city by the bay was perhaps San Francisco's biggest news story since the gold rush. "It was San Francisco before the fire," Alice later wrote. "I shall never forget those days. There was an exhilarating quality in the air, the place, the people, that kept me on my toes every moment of the time there."[25]

The *San Francisco Chronicle*'s page-one headline on July 5, 1905, was "San Francisco Welcomes President's Daughter."[26] At the time, there were no bridges connecting San Francisco to the mainland, so Alice detrained at the Oakland railroad terminus and took the ferryboat *Berkeley* across the bay to San Francisco's Ferry Building. The press was surprised: the sophisticated Alice they'd known only from pictures looked like a schoolgirl in person. When reporters on the ferry tried to get close to her, Nick told them she did not wish to be interviewed, but eventually she relented, stating, "I am simply on a pleasure trip and I must refer all questions to Mr. Taft."[27]

"There was a great curiosity to see Alice Roosevelt,"

Big Bill noted in an understatement.[28] Indeed, the public couldn't get enough. Eager San Franciscans lined the streets for hours just to glimpse their Princess. Alice was followed everywhere, from the Palace Hotel, where she and Taft dined, to the University of California–Berkeley campus, where she was briefly overcome: "The wildest rumors were at once afloat," reported the *San Francisco Chronicle,* "one story being to the effect that the President's daughter had a sunstroke. The truth is that she was not unwilling to find an excuse to snatch a few hours of quiet."[29] One photo caption read "Miss Alice Roosevelt and Congressman Nicholas Longworth of Ohio, Who Is Very Attentive to the President's Daughter."[30]

THE PRESS TREATED TAFT with great respect, one local paper commenting, "Secretary Taft has certainly made a great many friends since his arrival, and in the hotel corridors one now hears him frequently spoken of as a Presidential possibility."[31] Taft had first come to national attention as governor of the Philippines. As ruler of America's largest colony, he had been in charge of America's first attempt at nation building far from home. But recent reports from Manila had Taft "alarmed that the political edifice he had left behind was collapsing."[32] The cruise would be a good chance for him to check on things personally in the

Philippines. In consultation with Roosevelt, Taft also took on presidential assignments in Japan, China, and Korea.

The official highlight of Big Bill's San Francisco visit was an elaborate all-male banquet thrown in his honor at the Palace Hotel. The *San Francisco Chronicle* reported, "Three hundred and seventy-six guests sat down to the repast, among them being representatives of the leading interests of the Pacific Coast."[33] When it came his turn to address the tuxedoed banqueters, Taft first praised those traveling with him to the Philippines:

> I consider it a great triumph, that we have been able to enlist the interest and the sympathy of seven distinguished United States senators and twenty-three representatives of the House of Representatives of the United States, who have been willing at a very considerable cost to each person and also at a very considerable cost of time to devote a hundred days to going out into those islands in a season when we must expect storm and rain, in order that they may know the facts concerning them. I think it is an exceptional instance of the degree of self-sacrifice to which our legislators and those who are responsible to us for government are willing to make.[34]

Taft referred to the Filipinos as "those wards of ours ten thousand miles away from here," declaring that America had "a desire to do the best for those people."[35] (The term *wards* was laden with meaning: former judge Taft and his audience knew that the United States Supreme Court had defined American Indians as "wards" of the federal government.) The problem—which he did not mention—was that the Filipino "wards" didn't agree with the American sense of what was "best" for them.

In 1898, Filipino freedom fighters had expected that America would come to their aid in their patriotic revolution against their Spanish colonial masters. Instead, the Americans short-circuited the revolution and took the country for themselves. Related American military actions left more than two hundred fifty thousand Filipinos dead. Over the next seven years, many Filipinos came to associate Americans with torture, concentration camps, rape and murder of civilians, and destruction of their villages. But in San Francisco's Palace Hotel, Taft assured his audience that the real problem was the Filipinos themselves:

The problem in the Philippines is the problem of making the people whom we are to govern in those islands for their benefit believe that we are sincere when we tell them that we are there for their benefit, and make them patient while we are instructing them in self-government. You cannot make them patient unless you convince them of your good intentions. I am confronted with the repeated question, Shall we grant them independence at once or are we right to show them that they cannot be made fit for independence at once? They are not yet ready for independence and if they talk of independence at the present time it is mere wind.[36]

When Big Bill said that Filipinos were not "fit for independence," he could be confident that those in attendance understood why. A majority of Americans—young and old, the unschooled and the highly educated—believed that, over the millennia, succeeding generations of Whites had inherited the instincts of the superior man. The day before his Palace Hotel speech, Taft had told a Berkeley university audience, "Filipinos are not capable of self-government and cannot be for at least a generation to come."[37] The young men listening understood that this was not a political judgment, but an organic truth, as Taft reminded the students, "it takes a thousand years to build up...an Anglo-Saxon frame of liberty."[38]

Teddy Roosevelt had built a dual career as a best-selling author and wildly popular president upon his image as a muscular White Christian man ready to civilize lesser races with the rifle. Like many Americans, Roosevelt held dearly to a powerful myth that proclaimed the White Christian male as the highest rung on the evolutionary ladder. It was the myth that "civilization follows the sun." The roots of this belief could be found in a concoction of history, fable, and fantasy.

ONCE UPON A TIME, the story went, an "Aryan race" sprang up in the Caucasus Mountains north of what is now Iran. (The word *Iran* derives from the word *Aryan*.) The Aryan was a beautiful human specimen: white-skinned, big-boned, sturdily built, blue-eyed, and unusually intelligent. He was a doer, a creator, a wanderer, a superior man with superior instincts, and, above all, a natural Civilizer. In time, the Aryan migrated north, south, east, and west. The ancient glories of China, India, and Egypt—indeed, all the world's great civilizations—were the product of his genius.

During this era of great enlightenment and prosperity, the bright light of White Civilization blazed throughout the world. But over time came a fatal error: the pure White Aryan mixed his blood with non-White Chinese, Indian, and Egyptian females. The sad result of this miscegenation was plain to see:

dirt and deterioration. History then recorded the long decline of those mongrelized civilizations.

Not all was lost, though. A group of Aryans had followed the sun westward from the Caucasus to the area of northern Europe we now call Germany. This Aryan tribe did not make the mistake of their brethren. Rather than mate with lesser-blooded peoples, these Aryans killed them. By eradicating the Others, the Aryans maintained the purity of their blood.

Through many mist-shrouded centuries in the dark German forests, the myth continued and the pure Aryan evolved into an even higher being: the Teuton. The clever Teuton demonstrated a unique genius for political organization. He paid no homage to kings or emperors. Instead, the Teuton consulted democratically among his own kind and slowly birthed embryonic institutions of liberty that would later manifest themselves elsewhere.

The original documentation of the Teuton was the book *Germania* (circa AD 98) by the Roman historian Caius Cornelius Tacitus. In *Germania,* Tacitus wrote that long ago "the peoples of Germany [were] a race untainted by intermarriage with other races, a peculiar people and pure, like no one but themselves [with] a high moral code and a profound love of freedom and individual rights; important decisions were made by the whole community."[39]

Eventually the Teuton—with his Aryan-inherited civilizing instinct—spread out from the German forests. Those who ventured south invigorated Greece, Italy, and Spain. But these Teuton tribes made the same mistake as the earlier Aryans who founded China, India, and Egypt: instead of annihilating the non-White women, they slept with them, and the inferior blood of the darker Mediterranean races polluted the superior blood of the White Teuton. Thus the history of the Mediterranean countries is one of dissolution and nondemocratic impulses.

The Teutons that furthered the spread of pure Aryan civilization were the ones who continued to follow the sun to the west. They marched out of Germany's forests and ventured to Europe's western coast. Then they sailed across what would later be called the English Channel and landed in what would become the British Isles.

Lesser races already populated those islands, and had the Teuton bred with these non-Aryans, their pure blood would have been sullied and the great flow of civilization would have come to a halt.* But luckily for world civilization, these Teutons obeyed their instincts. By methodical slaughter of native men, women, and children, they kept themselves pure. As

---

*In 1906 Theodore Roosevelt wrote, "The world would have halted had it not been for the Teutonic conquests in alien lands."[40]

these Germanic tribes spread westward and northerly, they gradually became known as Anglo-Saxons (a compound of two Germanic tribal names).

The Anglo-Saxon myth of White superiority hardened in the 1500s when King Henry VIII broke with the pope to create the Church of England. Royal propagandists blitzed the king's subjects with the idea that the new Anglican Church was not a break with tradition, but a *return* to a better time: Henry promoted the Church of England to his subjects as a reconnection to a purer Anglo-Saxon tradition that had existed before the Norman conquest of 1066. The success of the king's argument is revealed by an English pamphleteer writing in 1689 that those seeking wisdom in government should look "to Tacitus and as far as Germany to learn our English constitution."[41] Henry was long gone, but the myth had been reinforced and reinvigorated.

Thus, centuries of Aryan and Teuton history revealed the three Laws of Civilization:

1. The White race founded all civilizations.
2. When the White race maintains its Whiteness, civilization is maintained.
3. When the White race loses its Whiteness, civilization is lost.

A glance revealed the truth of these declarations: The Anglo-Saxons were a liberty-loving people who spawned the Magna Carta, debated laws in Parliament, produced exemplars like Shakespeare, and tinkered the Industrial Revolution to life. But woe to those who ignored civilization's rules and went south to Africa or east to Egypt, India, and China. The Anglo-Saxon in those benighted countries were but small rays of light overwhelmed by the more populous dark races. There were just too many Africans, Indians, and Chinese to slaughter in order to establish superior civilizations. The best that could be hoped for was an archipelago of White settlement and the exploitation of local primitives in order to produce greater European riches.

Given such constraints, civilization and democracy could reach the next level of evolution only if the Anglo-Saxon moved westward. Progress sailed across the Atlantic with the White Christians who followed the sun west to North America. And once again—emulating their successful Aryan and Teuton forebears—the American Aryans eliminated the native population. From Plymouth Rock to San Francisco Bay, the settlers slaughtered Indian men, women, and children so democracy could take root and civilization as they understood it could sparkle from sea to shining sea.

REGINALD HORSMAN WRITES IN *Race and Manifest Destiny: The Origins of American Racial Anglo-*

Saxonism that Whites in the New World believed "that they were acting as Englishmen—Englishmen contending for principles of popular government, freedom and liberty introduced into England more than a thousand years before by the high-minded, freedom-loving Anglo-Saxons from the woods of Germany."[42] American colonists studied Samuel Squire's *An Enquiry into the Foundation of the English Constitution* and learned "the ideas of Tacitus [and] the invincible love of liberty" that existed amidst the democratic Teutons.[43] One of the favorite sayings in Colonial America quoted Bishop Berkeley, the eighteenth-century philosopher:

> *Westward the course of empire takes its way*
> *The first four acts already past*
> *A fifth shall close the drama with the day*
> *Time's noblest offspring is the last.*[44]

Charles-Louis de Secondat, baron de La Brède et de Montesquieu, was the "most frequently quoted authority on government and politics in colonial pre-revolutionary British America."[45] (It was Montesquieu who recommended the separation of powers now so central to the U.S. government.) Tacitus was one of Montesquieu's favorite authors, and the Frenchman was inspired by "that beautiful system having been devised in the woods."[46]

While visiting Colonial America, another European observed: "An idea, strange as it is visionary, has entered into the minds of the generality of mankind, that empire is traveling westward; and everyone is looking forward with eager and impatient expectation to that destined moment when America is to give law to the rest of the world."[47]

He was not alone. Thomas Jefferson—who persuaded the trustees of the University of Virginia to offer the nation's first course in the Anglo-Saxon language—justified Colonial America's breaking its ties with Mother England as a return to a better time when his Aryan ancestors had lived in liberty. In 1774, he wrote *A Summary View of the Rights of British America,* a series of complaints against King George, which foreshadowed by two years his 1776 Declaration of Independence. Jefferson refers to "God" twice, but invokes England's "Saxon ancestors" six times. In calling for a freer hand from the king, Jefferson writes of their shared "Saxon ancestors [who] had...left their native wilds and woods in the north of Europe, had [taken] the island of Britain...and had established there that system of laws which has so long been the glory and protection of that country." Jefferson argued that since the original Saxons were ruled by "no superior and were [not] subject to feudal conditions," the king should lighten his hold on his American colonies.[48]

Two years later, in 1776, Jefferson wrote that he envisioned a new country warmed by the Aryan sun: "Has not every restitution of the ancient Saxon laws had happy effects? Is it not better now that we return at once into that happy system of our ancestors, the wisest and most perfect ever yet devised by the wit of man, as it stood before the 8th century?"[49]

On the original Fourth of July—July 4, 1776—the Continental Congress tasked Benjamin Franklin, John Adams, and Thomas Jefferson with suggestions for the design of the Great Seal of the United States. (For centuries nations had used seals to authenticate treaties and official documents.) Franklin suggested the image of Moses extending his hand over the sea with heavenly rays illuminating his path. Adams preferred young Hercules choosing between the easy downhill path of Vice and the rugged, uphill path of Virtue. Jefferson suggested the two Teuton brothers who had founded the Anglo-Saxon race. Adams wrote to his wife, Abigail, that Jefferson had proposed "Hengst and Horsa, the Saxon chiefs from whom we claim the honor of being descended, and whose political principles and form of government we have assumed."[50] (Congress rejected all three recommendations, and committees eventually worked out the present Great Seal of the United States.)

Meanwhile, the laws of the new nation followed the path of White supremacy. The legislation defining who could become an American citizen, the Naturalization Act of 1790, begins: "All free white persons..." While Congress debated whether Jews or Catholics could become citizens, "no member publicly questioned the idea of limiting citizenship to only 'free white persons.'"[51]

Many Americans concluded that if the course of empire was westward and the United States the westernmost home of the Aryan, they were a chosen people with a continental, hemispheric, and global racial destiny. Even when the United States was a young country hugging the Atlantic, many envisioned the day the American Aryan would arrive on the Pacific coast. From there he would leap across the Pacific and fight his way through Asia, until he reached the original home of his Aryan parents in the Caucasus and a White band of civilization would bring peace to the world. Senator Thomas Hart Benton—a powerful early-nineteenth-century Washington figure who served on the Senate's Military and Foreign Affairs committees—wrote of that happy time:

> All obey the same impulse—that of going to the West; which, from the beginning of time has been the course of heavenly bodies, of the human race, and of science, civilization, and national power following in their train. In a few years the Rocky Mountains will be passed,

and the children of Adam will have completed the circumambulation of the globe, by marching to the west until they arrive at the Pacific Ocean, in sight of the eastern shore of that Asia in which their first parents were originally planted.[52]

Such sentiments were reinforced throughout popular culture. Jedidah Morse wrote the most popular geography books in the early 1800s, proclaiming: "It is well known that empire has been traveling from east to west. Probably her last and broadest seat will be America... the largest empire that ever existed.... The AMERICAN EMPIRE will comprehend millions of souls, west of the Mississippi."[53] Walt Whitman's most enduring work, *Leaves of Grass,* includes the poem "Facing West from California's Shores," with the lines: "Now I face home again, very pleas'd and joyous... round the earth having wander'd... Facing west from California's shores... towards the house of maternity... the circle almost circled."[54] In his groundbreaking *The Descent of Man,* Charles Darwin wrote, "All other series of events—as that which resulted in the culture of mind in Greece, and that which resulted in the empire of Rome—only appear to have purpose and value when viewed in connection with, or rather as subsidiary to... the great stream of Anglo-Saxon emigration to the west."[55]

The great transcendentalist Ralph Waldo Emerson was also under the Aryan spell:

> It is race, is it not? That puts the hundred millions of India under the dominion of a remote island in the north of Europe. Race avails much, if that be true, which is alleged, that all Celts are Catholics, and all Saxons are Protestants; that Celts love unity of power, and Saxons the representative principle. Race is a controlling influence in the Jew, who for two millenniums, under every climate, has preserved the same character and employments. Race in the Negro is of appalling importance. The French in Canada, cut off from all intercourse with the parent people, have held their national traits. I chanced to read Tacitus 'On the Manners of the Germans,' not long since, in Missouri, and the heart of Illinois, and I found abundant points of resemblance between the Germans of the Hercynian forest, and our Hoosiers, Suckers, and Badgers of the American woods.[56]

Emerson was far from alone in such sentiments. Most scholarly American intellectuals of his time followed the sun. The 1800s saw the emergence of "social sciences" in America. Not surprisingly, they validated Aryan supremacy. One after another, White

Christian males in America's finest universities "discovered" that the Aryan was God's highest creation, that the Negro was designed for servitude, and that the Indian was doomed to extinction. The author Thomas Gossett, in his thoughtful book *Race: The History of an Idea in America,* writes, "One does not have to read very far in the writings of nineteenth-century social scientists to discover the immense influence of race theories among them. In studying human societies, they generally assumed that they were also studying innate racial character."[57]

One of the social sciences popular in America for much of the nineteenth century was phrenology, the study of skulls. White Christian phrenologists observed that the Caucasian skull was the most symmetrical, and "since the circle was the most beautiful shape in nature, it followed that this cranium was the original type created by God."[58] Samuel Morton of Philadelphia, America's leading phrenologist, amassed the world's largest skull collection. To calculate brain size he sealed all but one of a skull's openings and filled it with mustard seed, then weighed the seed. He then correlated the amount of mustard seed with intelligence, morality, cultural development, and national character. Morton's experiments proved that "eighty-four cubic inches of Indian brain had to compete against, and would eventually succumb before, ninety-six cubic inches of Teuton brain [which] comforted many Americans, for now they could find God's hand and not their own directing the extinction of the Indian."[59] In fact, the White skulls Morton examined "nearly all belonged to white men who had been hanged as felons. It would have been just as logical to conclude that a large head indicated criminal tendencies."[60] (Morton replied that the skulls of noncriminal Whites would be even larger.)

One of the "bibles" of American scientific thought in the nineteenth century was the best-selling book *Types of Mankind*. Published to acclaim in 1854, it went through twelve printings and was used as a standard text into the twentieth century. *Types of Mankind* held that only the White race was civilized and that "wherever in the history of the world the inferior races have been conquered and mixed in with the Caucasians, the latter have sunk into barbarism."[61] The resulting barbaric races "never can again rise until the present races are exterminated and the Caucasian substituted."[62] Describing Native Americans, the book stated:

He can no more be civilized than a leopard can change his spots. His race is run, and probably he has performed his earthly mission. He is now gradually disappearing, to give place to a higher order of beings. The order of nature must have its course.... Some are born to rule, and others to be ruled. No two distinctly marked races can dwell together on equal terms. Some races, moreover, appear destined to live and prosper for a time, until the destroying race comes, which is to exterminate and supplant them."[63]

This best-selling science textbook argued that exterminating the Indian was philanthropic: "A great aim of philanthropy should be to keep the ruling races of the world as pure and wise as possible, for it is only through them that the others can be made prosperous and happy."[64]

Such beliefs ruled America. As the California governor, Peter Burnett, put it in his 1851 Governor's Message, "That a war of extermination will continue to be waged between the two races until the Indian race becomes extinct must be expected.... The inevitable destiny of the [White] race is beyond the power and wisdom of man to avert."[65] Lewis Morgan, president of the American Association for the Advancement of Science, a member of the National Academy of Sciences, and the founder of anthropology in the United States, observed, "The Aryan family represents the central stream of progress, because it produced the highest type of mankind, and because it has proved its intrinsic superiority by gradually assuming control of the earth."[66]

*　　*　　*

BIG BILL'S SAN FRANCISCO audiences were proud to be descendants of history's master race. The crowds that greeted Taft were far from alone in this conceit: the myth was embedded in children's books, tomes of science and literature, sermons from the pulpit, speeches in the halls of Congress, and in everyday conversations at the kitchen table.

And how could the idea be creditably challenged? The White British had the largest seagoing empire, and the Russians—a White race—controlled the world's most extensive land empire. Europe's "scramble for Africa" had made Black Africans subjects to the White man. And the president of the United States firmly believed the myth to be an essential truth, a law of nature no less universal than gravity. During the Roosevelt administration, the center of world commerce and power was shifting from one Anglo-Saxon city—London—to another—New York. Westward went the sun indeed.

On its way from Washington, D.C., to California, Alice's train had rumbled across a continent that had recently heard the thunder of buffalo hooves. The Indian survivors of the American race–cleansing were locked up as noncitizen, nonvoting prisoners in squalid reservations. And while Lincoln had technically freed the slaves, by 1905 disenfranchisement and restrictive Jim Crow laws invisibly reshackled the American Black man, and the local lynching tree had plenty of branches left.

IN HIS YOUTH AND later in college, Theodore Roosevelt had imbibed the Aryan myth. As a famous

Theodore Roosevelt, 1905. Long before Ronald Reagan and George W. Bush used their ranches for photo shoots, Theodore Roosevelt set the manly standard. As Roosevelt wrote, "You never saw a photograph of me playing tennis. I'm careful about that. Photographs on horseback, yes. Tennis, no." (National Park Service)

author he explained American history as part of the Aryan/Teuton/Anglo-Saxon flow of westering civilization. Then he fashioned a winning political persona as a White male brave enough to vanquish lesser races. Roosevelt, with impressive public-relations acumen, had publicly embraced the manly strenuous life. He was photographed more than any other president up to his day, and if you visit the many historical touchstones of his life or peruse the numerous biographies, you will see many images depicting him with a rifle in hand or on horseback. Though President Teddy installed the first White House tennis court and frequently played, he allowed no photographs of himself dressed in his custom tennis whites, fearful that such images might undermine efforts to portray him as utterly masculine.

THEODORE ROOSEVELT JR. WAS born in a New York City mansion on October 27, 1858, among the seventh generation of Roosevelts to be born on Manhattan island. His father, Theodore Sr., was a wealthy New York aristocrat.

The first Roosevelt—Klaes Martenszen von Rosenvolt—had immigrated to New Amsterdam (later New York City) from Holland in 1649.[67] Klaes and his descendants acquired vast tracts of land in the Hudson River valley north of Manhattan, which was

Theodore Roosevelt Sr. He prescribed the Bible for his sons'
minds and barbells for their bodies.

worked by slaves. By the time of Teddy's birth two
hundred years later, the Roosevelt financial empire
included vast holdings of stock, real estate, insurance,
banking, and mining. Roosevelts had been elected as
congressmen and appointed as judges. The family's
time and money helped create such storied New York
institutions as Chemical National Bank, Roosevelt
Hospital, Central Park, the American Museum of
Natural History, the Metropolitan Museum of Art,
and the Children's Aid Society.

The Roosevelts were true aristocrats. Uniformed servants padded quietly about the family mansion, made beds, laid out their masters' clothes, cleaned, and cooked. Teddy ate from fine china emblazoned with the family crest. The Roosevelts dressed for dinner, and finger bowls were only a tinkle of the server's bell away.

Yet noble Theodore Sr. worried that his well-born sons might be doomed by this life of luxury, threatened by something called "overcivilization." The theory was that the Aryan race evolved in successive stages, just as people grew from childhood to old age. The first stage was the savage. The savage was disorganized, and useless chaos reigned. The second stage was the barbarian. The barbarian made a valuable contribution to civilization because it was in this Genghis Khan–like stage that the "barbarian virtues" were formed. Barbarian virtues were the fighting qualities by which a race advanced and protected its flank. In 1899 governor Theodore Roosevelt of New York wrote to psychologist G. Stanley Hill: "Over-sentimentality, over-softness... and mushiness are the great dangers of this age and this people. Unless we keep the barbarian virtues, gaining the civilized ones will be of little avail."[68] The third and most desired stage was the civilized man, who loved peace but when provoked could manifest his barbarian virtues. The fourth evolutionary stage was a step over the cliff: overcivilization.

Overcivilization existed when the barbarian virtues were replaced by the easy life, and many believed that modern American life was getting "soft." Instead of chopping wood, wrestling a heavy plow, and hunting for dinner, the modern American Aryan warmed himself with coal, worked at a desk, and ate hearty meals in cushy restaurants.

To combat this threatening condition, Theodore Sr. preached "muscular Christianity" that stressed "healthiness, manliness, athletic ability and courage in battle."[69] Young Teddy learned from his father that Christ himself was not gentle, saintly, and

Theodore Roosevelt, age eleven. "The older races of the city made the mould into which the newer ones were poured," wrote Manhattanite Teddy at the age of thirty-three in 1891.

long-suffering, but a soldier of vigor and righteousness. (During this era, muscular Christians founded the Young Men's Christian Association [YMCA] and composed the virile religious anthem "Onward Christian Soldiers.") Theodore Sr. dispensed his Christian duty by lecturing lower-class boys at the Children's Aid Society and the Newsboys' Lodging House, as well as teaching Sunday school. Teddy often tagged along, listening as his tall, bearded father prescribed Bibles for the boys' minds and barbells for their bodies.

Muscular Christianity was one solution to the bane of overcivilization. The other was "the nature cure"—romps in the woods that would make a boy manlier and therefore purer. Theodore Sr. took his children to the great outdoors for exercise and helped the Children's Aid Society export ninety thousand pauper children to the Midwest countryside. Such efforts not only circumscribed Teddy's childhood but would define his broader sense of the world.

TEDDY'S MOTHER, MARTHA BULLOCH Roosevelt, a Southern belle whose family owned an enormous plantation, further defined the future president's worldview. Roswell, Georgia, from where she hailed, was founded in 1839 on land that had been seized from the Cherokee nation, which was uprooted by

Martha Bulloch, Teddy's mother, in her early twenties.
Martha grew up in Bulloch Hall near Atlanta. Some
speculate that Martha and her mansion were Scarlett and
Tara in Margaret Mitchell's book Gone With the Wind.

U.S. Army troops and marched forcibly to Oklahoma
in the brutal journey now infamous as the "Trail of
Tears." Unable to adjust to chilly northern climes, her
stern husband's ways, and New York society, Martha
was usually ill and required constant care. From her
sickbed she captured young Teddy's imagination by

telling him stories of the thickheaded Bulloch slaves and the military exploits of her Bulloch relatives.

In story after story, the young boy heard about Martha's forebears and their courage under fire, their fearlessness, and their willingness to kill if need be. In Martha's accounts, two things became clear: first, that Teddy was part of a superior race; and second, that the most masculine men didn't need barbells to prove their manliness—they had rifles.

His mother's tales excited young Teddy, but her own fragility also reinforced the danger posed by weakness: Martha herself seemed a clear example within the Roosevelt home of the overcivilized woman. Unfortunately, young Teddy appeared to be a prime example of an overcivilized boy: a scrawny, sickly specimen who needed eyeglasses to see his own hands and who suffered from terrifying asthma attacks that at times left him an invalid. After one particularly severe attack, Theodore Sr. gathered up his sickly son, ran down the stairs and into the Roosevelt rig, then sped through the dark Manhattan streets, forcing a rush of air into Teddy's tiny lungs.

Theodore Sr. installed gymnastic equipment on the back piazza of the Roosevelt mansion, but Teddy's health was too fragile for a full regimen. Theodore Sr. even discussed sending his son west to Denver to cure his asthma. When Teddy was eight, his father dressed him in a velvet coat and sent him and his brother to an outside tutor. While Elliott flourished, sickly and nervous Teddy couldn't undertake even this minor effort and had to be schooled from home. With his mother, he visited such fashionable health resorts as New Lebanon, Saratoga, Old Sweet Springs, and White Sulphur Springs. But many saw these elite watering holes as places where the effete became even more overcivilized.

Teddy was so frail that the Roosevelt family physician, Dr. John Metcalfe, recommended that he see the famous neurologist Dr. George Beard. (Beard would go on to write the best-selling book *American Nervousness,* which warned that overcivilization threatened the country's future.) After examining the sickly lad, Beard gave Teddy to his partner, Dr. Alphonso Rockwell, who was known for treating high-strung, refined young aristocrats. Rockwell said Teddy suffered from "the handicap of riches" and told Beard that the youngster "ought to make his mark in the world; but the difficulty is, he has a rich father."[70]

Teddy was ten years old by now and must have been alarmed to hear doctors and his parents speak of him this way. And he must have been even more alarmed when Rockwell attached electrical equipment to his head, feet, and stomach and sent a jolt through his body to restore the boy's "vital force" and cure his overcivilization.

Isolated, homebound, and often bedridden, young

Teddy read widely and began to dream that he could fight and explore side by side with his literary heroes. The dime novels Teddy devoured were full of racial stereotypes: The Blacks were dim-witted, subservient, and comical. The Indians were treacherous, immoral creatures. The heroes were inevitably blond, blue-eyed frontiersmen who stood for righteousness. In his autobiography, Theodore Roosevelt mentioned the author Mayne Reid's books five times, writing that he had "so dearly loved" them as a child. Reid's works—among them *The Scalp Hunters, The Boy Hunters, The War Trail,* and *The Headless Horseman*—were tales of gruesome combat to the death. In one, a mother helplessly watches an alligator kill her daughter, then uses her body as bait in order to take revenge on the reptile who murdered her child.

Teddy also thrilled to "The Saga of King Olaf," a poem in which Longfellow celebrated Teutonic White supremacy. As a young teenager Roosevelt read *Nibelungenlied*—the German *Iliad*—which extolled Teutonic virility. Roosevelt quoted the work for the rest of his life, and the author Edmund Morris thought the *Nibelungenlied* so central to Teddy's life that he used phrases from it as aphorisms to begin each chapter of his first Roosevelt biography.

In 1872, when Teddy was a scrawny boy of thirteen, his father's patience wore out. He ordered Teddy to embrace manhood and thwart overcivilization with a rigorous bodybuilding program. Roosevelt later claimed that this cured his asthma. The truth was far different. After his death, his sister Corinne told a Teddy biographer: "I wish I could tell you something which really cured Theodore's asthma, but he never did recover in a definite way—and indeed suffered from it all his life."[71] The confinement and dread had a major impact on his personality. As Roosevelt scholar Kathleen Dalton writes, "Theodore grew up encased in iron cages of Victorian thought about cultural evolution, overcivilization, race suicide, class, mob violence, manliness and womanliness. As a child and a teen he was incapable of bending open those iron cages."[72] Overcompensating, Teddy became increasingly aggressive. Family members noticed a righteous ruthlessness as he advocated his ideas of right and wrong.

Cosseted in the family mansion with little contact with the outside world, Teddy never attended a grade school or high school—private tutors came to him. As a result, Harvard was the first school Roosevelt attended. When he made his way north from his Manhattan home in 1876 at the age of eighteen, some family members worried that he couldn't endure winter in Cambridge.

At Harvard, Teddy's anatomy professor, William

James, urged his students to regard manliness as their highest ideal. But for Teddy, that ideal was elusive. He was still hobbled by asthma and complained in letters about missing schoolwork due to persistent sickness. (His classmate Richard Weiling watched him grapple with weights in a gym and thought Roosevelt was a "humble-minded chap . . . to be willing to give such a lady-like exhibition in such a public place."[73])

The young Manhattan aristocrat was very conscious of his status as a "gentleman," cautious in his choice of friends, and quick to join socially prominent campus organizations. Roosevelt carefully researched the backgrounds of potential friends and considered only a few to be gentlemen. Writes Edmund Morris: "The truth is that Roosevelt from New York was much more at home with the languid fops of Harvard than his apologists would admit. He not only relished the company of rich young men, but moved immediately into the ranks of the very richest, and the most arrogantly fashionable."[74]

At Harvard, Roosevelt was in "an intellectual atmosphere pervasive with racially oriented topics and a campus dominated by intellectuals who subscribed to racially deterministic philosophies."[75] Warren Zimmermann, a former U.S. ambassador and author of *First Great Triumph,* writes, "Hierarchical racial theories helped shape the intellectual formation of virtually every American who reached adulthood during the second half of the century. Without even trying, well-educated American politicians carried into their careers large doses of Anglo-Saxonism administered to them in their universities."[76]

Francis Parkman graduated from Harvard in 1845 and taught there. His best-selling histories were translated into many languages and illustrated by famous artists. Theodore Roosevelt would dedicate his The Winning of the West book series to Parkman, who had once written, "The Germanic race, and especially the Anglo-Saxon branch of it, is peculiarly masculine and therefore, peculiarly fitted for self-government. It submits its action habitually to the guidance of reason and has the judicial faculty of seeing both sides of a question."[77]

Teddy's favorite Harvard professor was Nathaniel Southgate Shaler. Shaler founded Harvard's Natural History Society, of which Teddy was elected vice president. Professor Shaler, "one of the most respected professors on the faculty, taught white supremacy based on the racial heritage of England, [finding] non-Aryan peoples lacking in the correct 'ancestral experience' and impossible to Americanize."[78]

THERE WAS A TRADITION among highborn, wealthy college graduates to take off on a thrilling adventure, like a sea voyage, and turn it into a book. Teddy had become a millionaire at age twelve when his grand-father C. W. S. Roosevelt had died, and more inheritance came his way when Theodore Sr. died in 1878.[79] But Teddy had no personal history upon which to capitalize. He couldn't write about his father, ashamed that he had bought his way out of the Civil War. His maternal Bulloch uncles had been Confederate secret agents, another unpromising angle; still, those uncles were the most compelling men in Theodore Roosevelt's life, especially the older and more experienced Uncle Jimmie Bulloch. The U.S. Government considered Jimmie Bulloch to be a traitor to his country as a result of his anti-Union activities in the Civil War. He faced arrest in the United States and evaded American justice by living in England, where he is buried. He had served fourteen years in the U.S. Navy before the Civil War, a period when the War of 1812 stood alone as America's biggest naval conflict. Uncle Jimmie's tales about how the U.S. Navy bested England and the necessity of naval preparedness had made an indelible impression on Teddy. While still an undergraduate, Roosevelt began writing *The Naval War of 1812,* though he graduated from Harvard in 1880 with the manuscript incomplete.

With college finished, wealthy and idle Teddy headed off on vacation. As a child, Roosevelt had shot animals in a number of eastern states, in Europe, and in Egypt. Recently engaged to Alice Lee, he now

Alice Lee Roosevelt, Teddy's first wife and Princess Alice's mother. Father and daughter never discussed her. Roosevelt whitewashed his first wife's memory from his life story, not even mentioning her in his autobiography.
(Library of Congress)

went on a luxury hunting excursion in the Dakota Territory with his brother, Elliott. The idea of investing in the Dakota Territory was on rich men's minds everywhere, and with the Roosevelt family fortune at hand, getting in was easy. Teddy invested "ten thousand dollars in the Teschmaker and Debillier Cattle Company, then running a herd on the ranges north of Cheyenne.[80]

Further travel soon followed. Roosevelt married Alice on his twenty-second birthday, October 27, 1880. Several months later, in May of 1881, the newlyweds left for a costly five-month honeymoon in Europe. Teddy brought his draft chapters with him, and *The Naval War of 1812* was finally published in 1882.

Roosevelt's first book was a bold amalgam of a call for naval preparedness and Harvard's follow-the-sun dogma. In its first chapter, Teddy made clear the "Racial Identity of the Contestants."[81] He noted differing levels of ability among combatants according to the purity of their Aryanized blood. Norsemen—very Teutonic—made "excellent sailors and fighters." The non-Teutonic Portuguese and Italians "did not, as a rule, make the best kind of seamen [because] they were treacherous, fond of the knife, less ready with their hands, and likely to lose either their wits or their courage when in a tight place."[82] The finest sailors of all were the ones who had followed the sun farthest west: "the stern school in which the American was brought up forced him into habits of independent thought and action which it was impossible that the more protected Briton to possess.... He was shrewd, quiet and...rather moral.... There could not have been better material for a fighting crew."[83]

The Naval War of 1812 made Teddy a nationally

Professor John Burgess of Columbia University, who taught that only White people could rule because the Teuton had created the idea of the state. In 1910, ex-president Theodore Roosevelt wrote Burgess: "Your teaching was one of the formative influences in my life. You impressed me more than you'll ever know."

recognized advocate of a muscular navy, but it was a navy book with a narrow readership. Greater fame was still to come.

RETURNED FROM HIS EUROPEAN vacation, Roosevelt headed to Columbia University to study law under Professor John Burgess. Today Columbia University's website informs us that "Burgess ranks not only as the 'father' of American political science, but among the truly great figures in history who will be remembered for his work in founding and building up the school of Political Science at Columbia University."[84] Professor Burgess's political science course was Teddy's favorite class at Columbia. Burgess remembered that Roosevelt "seemed to grasp everything instantly, [and] made notes rapidly and incessantly."[85] For his part, Roosevelt "had an immense admiration and respect for Burgess."[86]

Burgess taught that "the United States Constitution...was the modern expression of Anglo-Saxon-Teutonic political genius—a genius which had originated in the black forests of Germany, spread through England and North America and expressed itself in the Magna Carta, the Glorious Revolution and the American Revolution."[87] Burgess taught that it was the mission of the White man to spread democracy around the world, and that since the state was an invention of the Teuton, the organs of state should be controlled only by those with Teutonic blood—no dark Others need apply.

At Columbia, as at Harvard, Teddy absorbed a scholarly, reasoned case for American world domination based upon the color of his skin and thus had acquired the prism through which he would judge people, events, and nations. As Thomas Dyer writes in *Theodore Roosevelt and the Idea of Race:*

> [Theodore Roosevelt] viewed the entire breadth of the American past through a racial lens. With constant, almost compulsive attention to underlying racial themes, he researched, analyzed, and synthesized the raw materials of history. The force of race in history occupied a singularly important place in Roosevelt's broad intellectual outlook. In fact, race provided him with a window on the past through which he could examine the grand principles of historical development. None of human history really meant much, Roosevelt believed, if racial history were not thoroughly understood first.[88]

In May of 1883, Alice told her twenty-five-year-old husband she was pregnant. Rich, restless, anxious to invest money, and worried about what fatherhood would mean, Teddy went to the Dakota Territory in September for a second time. Almost as soon as he arrived, he wrote Alice, "There was a chance to make a great deal of money, very safely, in the cattle business."[89] Already having invested in a cattle company, he now bought a ranch as a business venture. The investment in this case was with public image in mind; Roosevelt told one of his ranch hands that his goal was to "try to keep in a position from which I may be able at some future time to again go into public life, or literary life."[90]

With his golden name and backed by family money, Teddy ran for New York State assemblyman from Manhattan County. He was elected in 1883 when he was twenty-three years old, the youngest person still to this day to be elected assemblyman in New York State. Roosevelt's constituents were well-to-do Manhattanites, and Teddy allied himself with rich Protestants who looked down upon Catholics, Germans, and Irish and thought the Chinese were a dangerous contagion.

Teddy was an oddity in nineteenth-century Albany. Politics at that time was a game played by beer- and whiskey-drinking men, not aristocrats. To New York's political press and players, Teddy was a shrimp-size dandy, dressed in tight-fitting, tailor-made suits, a rich daddy's boy who read books and collected butterflies. Teddy made a bad first impression when he appeared on the assembly floor dressed

New York assemblyman Theodore Roosevelt. Other politicians mocked him as effeminate when he appeared on the New York assembly floor dressed in a purple satin suit and speaking in a high-pitched voice. To change that image, Roosevelt galloped west.

in a purple satin suit, speaking in a high-pitched, Harvard-tinged voice. The other assemblymen took one look at the rich kid and laughed.

In 1880s Albany, it would have been acceptable to be wanting in areas of intelligence or legislative ability. But being seen as effeminate was a death sentence for an aspiring politician. This was, after all, forty years before American women were even allowed to vote. Roosevelt's assembly colleagues hung the demeaning nickname "Oscar Wilde" on him, a mocking reference to the disgraced British homosexual. One newspaper went further, speculating whether Theodore was "given to sucking the knob of an ivory cane."[91]

During the years 1884 to 1901—from the time young Teddy thought of how to reform his effeminate image to when he became a manly man president—William Cody's extravaganza *Buffalo Bill's Wild West* was the leading cultural sensation in the United States. At twenty-six years of age, William Cody had left the West, headed east, and "was the subject of a vast literature: fictionalized biographies by the score, dime novels, dramatic criticism, puff pieces extolling the heroism of Buffalo Bill [and he was] starring as himself in New York theatrical dramas about his life."[92] Drawing millions of spectators in America and Europe, Cody's spectacle (three trains were required to transport the cast, staff, props, and livestock; the staging required almost twenty-three thousand yards of canvas and twenty miles of rope) helped create a lasting myth of the American frontier. The impact was global—Pope Leo XIII had personally blessed Cody's entourage, and in England a grieving Queen

Victoria made her first public appearance in twenty-five years to witness Cody's magic.

The full title of Cody's show was *Buffalo Bill's Wild West: A History of American Civilization.* Buffalo Bill was the embodiment of the blond Aryan who sowed civilization as he race-cleansed his way west. The show's program touted "the rifle as an aid to Civilization [without which] we of America would not be today in possession of a free land and united country."[93] The rifle's bullet was "the pioneer of civilization [which] has gone hand in hand with the axe that cleared the forest and with the family bible and the schoolbook."[94]

Recognizing that a frontier adventure of his own could remedy his wimpish reputation, Roosevelt galloped west, following Buffalo Bill's tracks. Thus began one of America's great political makeovers. After returning to Manhattan in 1884, Teddy boasted to the *New York Tribune:* "It would electrify some of my friends who have accused me of presenting the kid-glove element in politics if they could see me galloping over the plains, day in and day out, clad in a buck-skin shirt and leather chaparajos, with a big sombrero on my head."[95] Wrote Roosevelt, "For a number of years I spent most of my time on the frontier, and lived and worked like any other frontiersman. . . . We guarded our herds of branded cattle and shaggy horses, hunted bear, bison, elk, and deer, established

"Buffalo Bill's Wild West and Congress of Rough Riders of the World." William Cody, as Buffalo Bill, was the world's most famous man. Cody created the American idea of the West. His Buffalo Bill character was the prime example of a White manly man who civilized savages. Theodore Roosevelt borrowed from Cody twice: his Ranchman Teddy persona and the "Rough Riders" moniker. Roosevelt was not the first nor the last to be influenced by the power of Cody's imagery. Gene Autry, John Wayne, and Clint Eastwood walked through celluloid landscapes first conjured in the nineteenth-century mind of William Cody. (Library of Congress)

civil government, and put down evil-doers, white and red...exactly as did the pioneers."[96]

In fact, Roosevelt had commuted west aboard deluxe Pullman cars, staying for short periods of time to check on his investments and gather material for his books. Ranchman Teddy was to Theodore Roosevelt what Buffalo Bill was to William Cody: a spectacular fiction concocted with an audience in mind.

When Alice died in 1884, Roosevelt's first inclination was to flee, as he always had when troubled, and he again headed west. The next year, Teddy published *Hunting Trips of a Ranchman*. Three years later, he published *Ranch Life and the Hunting Trail*. Both books were action packed, beautifully illustrated adventure tales about the "real" West. Roosevelt wrote of hunting and bronco busting and described his rough-hewn ranch house with elk horns lining the walls and the buffalo robes he used to keep warm:

Civilization seems as remote as if we were living in an age long past.... Ranching is an occupation like those of vigorous, primitive pastoral peoples, having little in common with the humdrum, workaday business world of the nineteenth century; and the free ranchman in his manner of life shows more kinship to an Arab sheik than to a sleek city merchant or tradesman.... [The Ranchman] must not only be shrewd, thrifty, patient and enterprising, but he must also possess qualities of personal bravery, hardihood and self-reliance to a degree not demanded in the least by any mercantile occupation in a community long settled.[97]

Even though Teddy spent much more time writing about the frontier than experiencing it, with these books he became a principal historian of the cowboy and a chief interpreter of the wild Western life.

UNTIL HIS DEATH, TEDDY would repeat these mythical accounts of his Western adventures, passing them along as fact. But despite his claims to the contrary, Roosevelt spent the majority of his "Western years" in Manhattan. Notes John Milton Cooper Jr. in *The Warrior and the Priest*, "His commitment to western ways was neither permanent nor deep. Between the summers of 1884 and 1886 he spent a total of fifteen months on his ranch. He did not stay for an entire winter in either year; his longest stretch there came between March and July 1886. The rest of the time he shuttled back and forth to the East Coast."[98]

Teddy would later dissemble that he had lived out West "for three years," or the "major part of seven years and off and on for nearly fifteen years."[99] But in 1884 he made only three trips to his ranches and lived more than two-thirds of the year in Manhattan, and in 1885 the proportion was about the same. The lone exception was in 1886 when he took two prolonged trips, visiting the West for twenty-five weeks. But except for sporadic hunting trips, after 1886 he became a full-time easterner again. Teddy's "Western years" were career-building errands.

And he was hardly a pioneer. Teddy's two friends—the author Owen Wister (*The Virginian*) and the sculptor Frederic Remington—were also rich East Coast kids who went west via elegant Pullman coach and Grand Hotel and then spun their short sojourns into careers as interpreters of the West. As Aspen is to a rich college graduate today, so the Dakota Territory was to young nineteenth-century mansion dwellers. "The number of Harvard graduates alone that appeared on the cattle frontier," Edward White writes in *The Eastern Establishment and the Western Experience,* "is ample testimony to the fact that long hours were spent in the Hasty Pudding Club by scions of wealthy families romanticizing the West as a place for adventure."[100] (Cowpokes laughed when Roosevelt ordered one of his men to round up a stray cow with a patrician "Hasten forward quickly there."[101])

Teddy's ranches went bust within two years and he finally abandoned the West. By the end of 1886, half his inheritance was gone. Teddy knew his ranching days were over. John Milton Cooper Jr. writes:

In his subsequent career on the national scene, no aspect of Roosevelt's life except his war service made him more of a popular figure than his western sojourn. Nothing did more to make him appear a man of the people. He himself liked to recount how ranching had augmented politics in ridding him of all snobbish inclinations. Actually, his experience was more complicated. In going west, Roosevelt was following a well-beaten track among the upper crust on both sides of the Atlantic. One of his Dakota neighbors was a French marquis, while two others maintained dude ranches for scions of the best British and American families.[102]

Teddy's frontier life was more soft blankets than barbwire, but Roosevelt skillfully projected a different reality. Hermann Hagedorn—the first director of the Theodore Roosevelt Association—describes Teddy's author photo for *Hunting Trips of a Ranchman:*

He solemnly dressed himself up in the buckskin shirt and the rest of [his] elaborate costume...and had himself photographed. There is something hilariously funny...The imitation grass not quite concealing the rug beneath, the painted background, the theatrical (slightly patched) rocks against which [Roosevelt] leans gazing dreamily across an imaginary prairie… with rifle ready and finger on the trigger, grimly facing dangerous game which is not there.[103]

William Cody's "Buffalo Bill" (left) was a hunter. Theodore Roosevelt's "Ranchman Teddy" (above) was a rancher, the next step up on the evolutionary ladder as understood in the agrarian nineteenth century: the hunter (Buffalo Bill) secures the wilderness and the rancher tames it. Theodore Roosevelt was not the only rich easterner who went west in pursuit of fame. The author Owen Wister (The Virginian) *and the sculptor Frederic Remington were also rich East Coast men who went west via elegant Pullman coaches and grand hotels and then spun their short visits into careers as Western manly men. (Bettmann/Corbis)*

Yet the danger had been there—the danger that without sufficient masculinity, Teddy's political career was doomed.

In 1886—one year into the creation of the Ranchman myth—Roosevelt ran for mayor of New York. Newspapers hailed the "blizzard-seasoned constitution" of the "Cowboy of the Dakotas."[104] He began writing advice columns for men, such as "Who Should Go West?" in *Harper's Weekly*.

In his two *Ranchman* books, Teddy established himself as a civilized man with barbarian virtues. In his next four books—a series entitled The Winning of the West—Teddy drew upon the civilization-follows-the-sun myth to glorify how the American Aryan civilized his continent.

In the very first sentence of his very first The Winning of the West book, Roosevelt declared his theme: "During the past three centuries the spread of the English-speaking peoples over the world's waste spaces has been not only the most striking feature in the world's history, but also the event of all others most far-reaching in its effects and its importance."[105] "English-speaking peoples" was Teddy's euphemism for the White inheritors of the Aryan tradition; "waste spaces" refers to where non-White Others lived or had lived until their righteous extermination. And Roosevelt certainly meant it when he wrote of "the world's history": "The vast movement by which

75

this continent was conquered and peopled cannot be rightly understood if considered solely by itself. It was the crowning and greatest achievement of a series of mighty movements, and it must be taken in connection with them. Its true significance will be lost unless we grasp, however roughly, the past race-history of the nations who took part therein."[106]

Elsewhere the books are full of commentary in line with Aryan mythology:

> *The persistent Germans swarmed out of the dark woodland east of the Rhine and north of the Danube [to conquer] their brethren who dwelt along the coasts of the Baltic and the North Atlantic.*[107]
>
> *There sprang up in conquered southern Britain...that branch of the Germanic stock which was in the end to grasp almost literally worldwide power, and by its over-shadowing growth to dwarf into comparative insignificance all its kindred folk.*[108]
>
> *After the great Teutonic wanderings were over, there came a long lull, until, with the discovery of America, a new period of even vaster race expansion began.*[109]

Roosevelt wrote that Indians' "life was but a few degrees less meaningless, squalid and ferocious than that of the wild beasts[110] [who] seemed to the White settlers devils and not men."[111] Originally Teddy had planned to write a fifth The Winning of the West book, but just four years after the publication of his fourth, he became president.

ON JULY 8, 1905, the first morning rays of sun in the San Francisco harbor revealed busy *Manchuria* crew members scurrying about. They polished the twenty-seven-thousand-ton behemoth—it was sixty-five feet wide and the length of two football fields. Three thousand excited Californians came to the docks to

SS Manchuria. *In 1905 this Pacific & Ocean liner carried the largest delegation of American officials to Asia in U.S. history. (Courtesy of Jonathan Kinghorn)*

see the American delegation off. Big Bill was aboard by midmorning. It was easy for the throng ashore to pick out the rotund 325-pound secretary of war as he mingled on deck with passengers and guests.

The Princess and her party reached the dock about noon. Alice was "attired in a simple traveling dress of gray, trimmed with dashes of deep blue here and there [with] an Eton jacket to match.... Her hat was of deep red straw."[112] Noted the *San Francisco Chronicle,* "She ascended the gang plank alone, the crowd drawing back to allow her ample room. Just before stepping aboard, she paused, looked over her shoulder and beckoned to Representative Longworth to come to her side. Together they stepped on board and many romance-loving souls wondered if the incident foreshadowed the beginning of a yet pleasant voyage by these same fellow travelers."[113]

Alice "found her spacious staterooms filled with a wealth of beautiful flowers."[114] On a table was an expensively produced souvenir guidebook entitled *From Occident to Orient, Being the Itinerary of a Congressional Party Conducted to the Far East by Secretary of War Taft, 1905, as Guests of the Philippine Government.* It was "handsomely illustrated with photographic scenes of the countries and three excellent maps showing the route to be traveled."[115]

Alice then joined Big Bill on deck. The *San Francisco Bulletin* observed, "For a half hour she looked down upon the throng of 3,000 people on the dock, all of them straining to see the president's daughter. As the whistles sounded at 1 o'clock, the hawsers of the big liner were cast loose and, in command of Captain Saunders, the *Manchuria* gracefully departed. In response to the cheer that went up, Miss Roosevelt waved her handkerchief and threw a kiss."[116]

And then they headed west. Following the sun.

Chapter 3

BENEVOLENT INTENTIONS

---

*The people of the Island of Cuba are, of
right ought to be, free and independent. . . .
The United States hereby disclaims any
disposition or intention to exercise sovereignty,
jurisdiction, or control over said Island except
for the pacification thereof, and asserts its
determination, when that is accomplished,
to leave the government and control of
the Island to its people.*[1]
—THE TELLER AMENDMENT TO THE U.S. DECLARATION
OF WAR AGAINST SPAIN, 1898

The imperial cruise ventured out into the Pacific
Ocean, the largest single physical feature on the
planet. Within the past seven years, the United States

had made that enormous body of water an American lake. It had taken more than a century for the American Aryan to fill out its continental area as the U.S. Army's forts became cities. But as the nineteenth century had come to a close, the U.S. Navy had quickly secured the naval links that the Aryan would need to continue westward and capture Asia's riches.

The U.S. thrust into the Pacific had been the work of President William McKinley and his administration. As assistant secretary of the Navy, Theodore Roosevelt had been a key cheerleader for this naval expansion, and later, as vice president and president, he defended America's military actions in Asia as a positive example of the White Christian spreading civilization. The whys and wherefores of American expansion into the Pacific would occupy the thoughts of presidents McKinley, Roosevelt, and Taft. And all three would come to doubt the wisdom of dipping America's toe into that lake.

IN 1844, AMERICA ELECTED James Polk to the presidency. At the time of his election, the United States was a small country with states exclusively east of the Mississippi. The Louisiana Purchase territory was unorganized. Great Britain claimed the Oregon Territory in the Northwest, and Mexico held what would later be Texas, New Mexico, Colorado, Utah, Nevada, and California.

At the end of his inauguration day, Polk told his secretary of the Navy, George Bancroft, that one of his main goals was to acquire California. The U.S. Navy had surveyed the Pacific coast in the early 1840s and reported that San Francisco was "one of the finest, if not the very best, harbour in the world."[2] Writes University of Virginia professor Norman Graebner in *Empire on the Pacific:*

> It was American commerce with the Far East primarily that focused attention on the harbor of San Francisco. This bay was regarded the unqualified answer to American hopes of commercial greatness in the Pacific area. Geographically, its location opposite Asia would give it a commanding position; its intrinsic advantage would make that position fully effective. Prevailing westerly winds had located this extraordinary harbor on the direct route of traffic between India, China, and Manila and the Pacific ports of Mexico and Central and South America.[3]

For its part, the Oregon Territory held world-class ports such as Seattle and Portland. Indeed, one sunfollower declared, "the nation that possesses Oregon will not only control the navigation of the Pacific, the trade of the Pacific and Sandwich Islands, but the trade of China itself on the Pacific."[4] Congressman William Fell Giles of Maryland announced the Aryans' intention: "We must march from ocean to ocean... straight to the Pacific Ocean, and be bounded only by its roaring wave.... It is the destiny of the white race, it is the destiny of the Anglo-Saxon race."[5]

Polk quickly picked diplomatic fistfights with the British and Mexicans. But while Britain ceded Oregon, Mexico held on to its precious Pacific frontage.

Mexico was a nation of seven million that had won independence from Spain in 1821 and had modeled its constitution after America's. The internationally recognized border between Mexico and the United States was the Nueces River in south Texas. President Polk decided it should instead be the Rio Grande, 150 miles to the south, and he ordered General Zachary Taylor into Mexican territory between the two rivers. Mexican historians refer to the U.S. Army's actions as "the American Invasion." American historians call it "the Mexican-American War."

Taylor's incursion was brutal, with massacres of Mexican civilians and rapes of local women. (The *New York Herald* wrote of the Mexican women assaulted by U.S. soldiers, "Like the Sabine virgins, she will soon learn to love her ravisher."[6]) Polk had initiated the invasion with seven thousand troops and thought the conflict would be over in days. It was a vast miscalculation; the war dragged on for three years, involved one hundred thousand U.S. soldiers, and resulted in thirteen thousand U.S. casualties and the deaths of countless Mexican civilians. Ulysses S. Grant—who served in Mexico as a young officer—wrote in his memoirs that he regarded the war "as one of the most unjust ever waged by a stronger against a weaker nation."[7]

With the eventual American victory, the United States could have claimed all of Mexico—but that would have meant absorbing too many non-Aryans. Argued the powerful Senator John Calhoun of South Carolina, "We have never dreamt of incorporating into our Union any but the Caucasian race....Ours, sir, is the Government of a white race."[8] Added Senator Lewis Cass of Michigan, "We do not want the people of Mexico, either as citizens or subjects. All we want is a portion of territory."[9]

IN 1872, THE ARTIST John Gast painted what would become the most popular visual euphemization of the American Aryan's westering. Gast named his masterwork *American Progress,* and prints of it became one of the best-selling American images of the second half of the nineteenth century.

Gast painted *American Progress* as a lingerie-clad

American Progress *by John Gast, 1872. Civilization
follows the sun across the American continent, bringing
order and prosperity as dark savages recede. This painting
became the most popular nineteenth-century depiction
of America's westward expansion. Painted at the height
of America's longest conflict—the Indian Wars—American
Progress doesn't depict the thousands of U.S. Army soldiers
who ethnic-cleansed the land of non-White
Others. (Library of Congress)*

beautiful blonde, pale skinned and voluptuous, floating westward. On her forehead is the "Star of Empire," and she holds in her right hand civilization's tome—a "School Book"—and from her left hand trails a telegraph wire. Below her, American civilization advances: farmers till land, pioneers ride in stagecoaches and ox-drawn wagons, miners with picks and shovels make their way, while the Pony Express and three transcontinental railways all head west. Between the Pacific and advancing American civilization stands savagery—a growling bear, wild horses, a bare-breasted Indian woman, one Indian warrior with his hatchet raised, another clutching his bow. Animals and Indians run from the American advance. No violence is depicted—no stacks of dead Indians or decimated buffalo herds. Only one rifle appears, held by a lone buckskin-clad frontiersman. The United States military is nowhere to be seen.

Much more representative of how the West was won is the 1890 photograph taken near Wounded Knee Creek in South Dakota. American Aryans stand triumphantly around a mass grave into which they dump frozen Indian carcasses. The "battle" (said the White victors) or "massacre" (said the Red losers) at Wounded Knee was the final grand drama of a quarter century of merciless warring upon the Indians—the longest conflict in America's history.

This was total war—here's a typical U.S. Army

*"Burial of Dead at Wounded Knee, 1890." How the
West was really won. The White victors called Wounded
Knee a "battle." The Indian losers called it a "massacre."
(Stringer/MPI/Getty Images)*

order during the Indian Wars: "Proceed south in
the direction of the Antelope Hills, thence toward
the Washita River, the supposed winter seat of the
hostile tribes; to destroy their villages and ponies,
to kill or hang all warriors, and bring back all
women and children."[10] General William Tecumseh

Sherman—who commanded the Indian Wars from 1866 to 1884—ordered his troops: "During an assault the soldiers cannot pause to distinguish between male and female, or even discriminate as to age."[11] They did not, and through the decades the Indian dead included uncounted thousands of mothers, children, and elderly, some killed merely for sport, their private parts sliced off and used to make prized wallets or to decorate hats, their scalps and their genitals displayed as trophies.

Theodore Roosevelt, then a U.S. civil service commissioner, visited South Dakota three years after the Wounded Knee Massacre. He wrote that the U.S. government had treated the Indians "with great justice and fairness."[12]

ONE OF THE HISTORIANS who arose to explain the success of American expansion was a University of Wisconsin professor named Frederick Jackson Turner. Turner too believed that the northern German forests had formed the Teuton, that the British Isles had formed the Anglo-Saxon, and that American greatness was part of the Aryan westering. "Forest philosophy," he wrote, "is the philosophy of American democracy [and] the forest clearings have been the seed plots of American character."[13]

By this time the United States was a continental

nation of seventy-six million people, spread across forty-five states. America occupied more land area than all other countries except Russia and Canada.

In 1893, the thirty-two-year-old Professor Turner, in a speech before the American Historical Association in Chicago, announced, "Now, four centuries from the discovery of America, at the end of a hundred years of life under the Constitution, the frontier has gone, and with its going has closed the first period of American history."[14]

The idea that America's frontier was gone stunned westering White Christians. Roosevelt was one of the first to sense the revolutionary qualities of Turner's thesis. As John Judis explains in *The Folly of Empire,* "For Roosevelt...the closing of the frontier [meant] the loss of those elements in national life that made Americans virile and vigorous, stimulated their taste and aptitude for competition, and gave them a strong and unifying sense of racial solidarity. Roosevelt worried that with the absence of battle, Americans would grow soft and overcivilized and unable to defend themselves against a new 'masterful race' that still carried within the fighting qualities of the barbarian."[15]

In addition to concerns about the end of the frontier, in 1893 the United States economy sank into its worst depression ever. Six hundred forty-two banks closed and an incredible sixteen thousand companies shuttered their doors. The most actively traded company on the New York Stock Exchange—National Cordage—went belly-up. Giant pillars of the economy such as the Northern Pacific Railway and the Union Pacific Railroad crumbled. America had experienced economic downturns before, but this was much bigger, lasting for four frightening years, from 1893 to 1898. At one point, four million workers were idle—more than one-fourth of a labor force of fifteen million—at a time of no government support for the unemployed.

Not surprisingly, anxiety about overcivilization increased. Kristin Hoganson, associate professor of history at the University of Illinois, writes in *Fighting for American Manhood,* "The depression of 1893 exacerbated anxieties about manhood, for unemployment resulting from the depression led to fears of male dependency. Rather than providing for their families, as men were expected to do, thousands failed to fulfill this basic male responsibility."[16]

Overseas expansion was seen as a cure-all for the triple whammy of overcivilization, economic depression, and the end of the frontier. Battling Others for their land would enhance the American male's barbarian virtues and secure profitable markets, and the United States would once again have a frontier in which to hone its Teutonic blade. For many, the sun was not setting on America, but rising on a new ocean of opportunities.

The United States was not the first White Christian country to the imperial feeding frenzy. By the end of the nineteenth century, Britain had fifty colonies, France thirty-three, and Germany thirteen. More than 98 percent of Polynesia was colonized, 90 percent of Africa, and more than 56 percent of Asia. Across this broad swath of the planet, only seven countries were still fully independent nations. Senator Henry Cabot Lodge expressed America's "empire envy": "The great nations are rapidly absorbing for their future expansion and their present defense all the waste places of the earth. It is a movement which makes for civilization and the advancement of the race. As one of the great nations of the world, the United States must not fall out of the line of march."[17]

The U.S. Army had brought the Aryan to the Pacific coast. It now passed the baton to the U.S. Navy. Captain Alfred Thayer Mahan, president of the newly founded Naval War College, lectured about the need for U.S. expansion "to seek the welfare of the country."[18] Captain Mahan published his collected lectures in an 1890 book entitled *The Influence of Seapower upon History, 1660–1783*. Overnight the groundbreaking book made Mahan the best-known American naval officer and the Naval War College an internationally respected institution.

The U.S. Navy's traditional approach had been defensive—the protection of America's borders.

Mahan preached an offensive mission: the U.S. Navy should seize strategic world ports, each "one link in the chain of exchange by which wealth accumulates."[19] The United States, he stated, could experience British-style imperial greatness by concentrating its naval power at the "links" or "pressure points" of international commerce. By striking quickly and sharply at any of these nerve centers, the United States could paralyze whole oceans. To bring Asian booty back to the United States, Captain Mahan said the U.S. Navy must establish links in the Pacific, cut a canal through Central America, and turn the Caribbean into an American lake.

In the *Atlantic Monthly,* a reviewer called Mahan's *The Influence of Seapower upon History* "distinctively the best and most important, also by far the most interesting, book on naval history which has been produced…for many a long year."[20] The reviewer's name was Theodore Roosevelt.

NOW THE AMERICAN ARYAN sought his naval links. By the 1890s, a generation of young nationalists had arisen around the globe to reclaim their homelands from the White Christian colonial powers. Spain was battling insurrections in both its Cuban and Philippines colonies.

Spain had a conventional Western-style army

trained to fight set battles with heavy armaments and many men. The Cuban freedom fighters had little money or arms, so they turned to guerilla warfare: Small bands burned sugar fields, mills, and plantations. They tore up telegraph lines, railroad tracks, and bridges and attacked Spanish forces to seize weapons.

To combat these guerilla tactics, the Spanish introduced a "reconcentrato" policy that "concentrated" Cuban civilians into concentration camps. (After World War II the term *concentration camp* has come to mean "extermination camp." But in the 1890s, concentration camps referred to areas where noncombatant civilians were held in order to deny material and moral support to the freedom fighters.) The Spanish put the entire island under martial law and gathered Cubans in central locations where they could be watched by the Spanish army. The concentration camps were roofless and virtually uninhabitable— pigpens, cattle pens, and barbwire-enclosed fields. Food was scarce and lacked nutritional value. Disrupted lives bred mental terror and sleeplessness, which soon gave way to hopelessness. Famine and disease felled thousands of innocent civilians.

By 1898, one-third of Cuba's population languished in these camps. At least 30 percent perished from lack of proper food, sanitary conditions, and medicines. More than four hundred thousand Cubans died. One reporter wrote, "In other wars men have fought with men, and women have suffered indirectly because the men were killed, but in this war it is the women, herded together in towns like cattle, who are going to die, while the men, camped in the fields and mountains, will live."[21]

The underdog Cuban freedom fighters received positive press coverage in the United States as a result of an excellent public-relations effort by expatriate Cubans based in New York City, who deftly spun the American press toward stories favorable to their revolutionary cause. The Yellow Press painted the greasy Spaniards as brutal villains who murdered, tortured, and raped innocent Cuban women and children— indeed, newspapers portrayed the entire island as a pure woman being raped by Spain. A New York stage production about the Cuban revolution featured a scheming Spanish villain who attempted to have his way with an attractive Cuban girl. And editorials presented the United States as a chivalrous man outraged at the brutal Spanish for assaulting the helpless Cubans.

Many Americans assumed that the Cubans were revolting to become more like America. Senator William Mason of Illinois said, "Cuban boys had come to our colleges, learned about George Washington and returned home to tell their compatriots."[22] On March 4, 1896, the *Chicago Times-Herald* wrote,

"The struggle Cuba is making for civil and political liberty is identical with the struggle the founders of the republic of the United States made against the selfishness and oppression of the crown of Great Britain."[23] Charles Kendall Adams, president of the University of Wisconsin, asked Madison's 1897 graduating class, "What has Spain ever done for civilization? What books, what inventions have come from Spain? What discoveries in the laboratory or in scientific fields? So few have they been that they are scarcely worth mentioning."[24]

IN 1895, ROOSEVELT RESIGNED as a civil service commissioner to become one of three New York City police commissioners on the civilian oversight board. In a letter to his sister Bamie, he complained, "The work of the Police Board is as grimy as all work for municipal reform over here must be for some decades to come; and it is inconceivably arduous, disheartening, and irritating."[25] Agitated, bored, and ambitious, Roosevelt quickly turned his sights to Washington.

The former governor of Ohio, congressman, and Civil War veteran William McKinley was the Republican Party's 1896 presidential nominee, and Teddy knew that if he worked to ensure McKinley's election, he might receive a high-level job in the new administration. Roosevelt campaigned in a number of states for McKinley, who won, and then enlisted powerful friends to help him lobby the president-elect for the post of assistant secretary of the Navy. McKinley was hesitant, confessing to one of Roosevelt's friends, "I want peace and I am told that your friend Theodore—whom I know only slightly— is always getting into rows with everybody. I am afraid he is too pugnacious."[26]

Roosevelt worried that if more time elapsed, McKinley might learn what a disaster the New York police board had become. Writes Edmund Morris: "By March 4, when William McKinley was inaugurated, the situation at Police Headquarters had become an open scandal. Newspapers that day carried reports of an almost total breakdown of discipline in the force, new outbreaks of corruption, tearful threats of resignation."[27] Knowing this, Roosevelt and his friends furiously lobbied for his appointment. "The only, absolutely the only thing I can hear adverse," Senator Henry Cabot Lodge wrote Teddy, "is that there is a fear that you will want to fight somebody at once."[28]

Eventually the lobbying paid off. On April 6, 1897, Theodore Roosevelt was nominated as assistant secretary of the Navy, at a salary of $4,500 a year. One New York City police commissioner laughed triumphantly and declared, "What a glorious retreat!"[29] Notes Morris, "An inescapable aura of defeat clouded

President William McKinley. He jump-started the national careers of Theodore Roosevelt and William Howard Taft. McKinley was the first president to advance the idea that the U.S. military invaded foreign countries with benevolent intentions. His logic struck a humanitarian chord and is still embraced today by the American public. (Library of Congress)

his resignation....No matter what he said about 'an honorable way out of this beastly job,' the fact remained that he was leaving a position of supreme responsibility for a subservient one."[30]

At the time, the hottest debates in Washington were about whether to annex Hawaii and whether to invade Cuba. The secretary of the Navy, John Long, was Roosevelt's boss, and Teddy had promised him that he would be entirely loyal and subordinate, though to his sister Roosevelt confided, "I am a quietly rampant 'Cuba libre' man."[31]

On April 26—after just one week in office—Roosevelt gave President McKinley a memo with four warnings of possible trouble with Cuba. This was just the beginning of his pro-war campaign. The nerve center of American strategic planning was the Naval War College. Assistant Secretary Teddy—in office only seven weeks—journeyed to Newport, Rhode Island, to address the War College planners. There, Roosevelt delivered a powerful "peace through strength" speech in which he said the word "war" sixty-two times, approximately once a minute.

Teddy's war cry caused a nationwide sensation when his speech was printed in major newspapers. Exclaimed the *Washington Post,* "Theodore Roosevelt, you have found your place at last!" The *Baltimore Sun* called it "manly, patriotic, intelligent and convincing."[32] The Naval War College planners got the message and, on June 30, 1897, submitted to Washington a plan to wage war on Spain that stated, "hostilities would take place mainly in the Caribbean, but the U.S. Navy would also attack the Philippines."[33]

In September of 1897—when Secretary Long was out of town—Roosevelt met with the president three times and gave McKinley a memorandum in which he advocated immediate war and recommended that the United States take and retain the Philippines. He also lobbied Congress. Representative Thomas Butler (Pennsylvania), a member of the House Naval Affairs Committee, remembered, "Roosevelt came down here looking for war. He did not care whom we fought as long as there was a scrap."[34] Teddy's private correspondence supported this: in a letter to a West Point professor, Roosevelt wrote, "In strict confidence... I should welcome almost any war, for I think this country needs one."[35]

AMERICA'S ORIGINAL NEMESIS IN the Philippines was Emilio Aguinaldo, the freedom-fighting general and first president, who would see his country's short independence snatched by the United States. His neighbors recognized his promise early—they elected him mayor of his hometown when he was only seventeen years old. A talented pupil who studied America's

Declaration of Independence and Constitution, Aguinaldo dreamed of his country throwing off its Spanish masters. By the 1890s, he was a leading freedom fighter, now General Aguinaldo of the Philippines Revolutionary Army. In 1896, he wrote of an independent Philippines: "The form of government will be like that of the United States of America, founded upon the most rigid principles of liberty, fraternity, and equality."[36]

Hoping to emulate America's War of Independence, on January 29, 1897, the Filipino freedom fighters appealed to the U.S. State Department: "Pray that help be extended to the Filipinos to expel the Spanish by force, just as the Emperor Napoleon helped America in the war of separation from England, by whose aid the Americans attained independence."[37] The United States turned a deaf ear to their pleas.

In battle after battle, the Philippines Revolutionary Army—consisting of motivated but poorly trained and meagerly armed fighters—beat back Spanish colonial forces. On December 14, 1897, the two sides signed a truce. The Spanish promised democratic reforms and asked Aguinaldo and other freedom fighters to leave the country temporarily as Spain made the transition. Aguinaldo established a government-in-exile in nearby Hong Kong, where he could keep a watchful eye on officials in Manila.

*   *   *

THE UNITED STATES' ROAD to war began with
two Spanish challenges to American manhood.
The Spanish minister to the United States, Enrique
Dupuy de Lôme, had written a letter to a friend in
Cuba describing a meeting with President McKinley.
A Cuba Libre sympathizer in the Havana post office
stole de Lôme's letter and forwarded it to newspaper
magnate William Randolph Hearst in New York,
who published it. Minister de Lôme had written that
President McKinley was "weak and catering to the
rabble, and besides, a low politician."[38] Hearst's *New
York Journal* called de Lôme's comments the "Worst
Insult to the United States in History,"[39] and rival
papers offered similarly outraged interpretations.

Less than a week after the de Lôme affair—at
9:40 p.m. on February 15, 1898—the USS *Maine*
exploded and sank in Havana harbor, killing more
than two hundred American sailors. It was the most
sensational American news event since President
Garfield's assassination in 1881. Not one shred of
evidence ever existed to suggest that the Spanish had
sunk the *Maine*.[40] (Captain Charles Dwight Sigsbee,
the *Maine*'s skipper, suspected that the explosion had
been caused by a fire in a coal bunker next to a reserve
magazine, which was a frequent mishap aboard
steam-driven warships.) Nevertheless, the February

General Emilio Aguinaldo, the George Washington of the Philippines. However, he wasn't White, and according to Professor Burgess of Columbia and most American political and intellectual leaders, this disqualified him from leading a state, a job restricted to those with Teutonic blood. Aguinaldo's biggest mistake was to believe that the United States would support independence for the non-White Filipinos. As president of the short-lived Philippines republic, Aguinaldo told his cabinet: "I have studied attentively the Constitution of the United States, and I find in it no authority for colonies, and I have no fear." (Library of Congress)

18, 1898, edition of Hearst's *Journal* ran the banner headline, "DESTRUCTION OF THE WAR SHIP MAINE WAS THE WORK OF AN ENEMY." Directly below was a boldface quote about a top U.S. government official supporting Hearst's sensational claim: "Assistant Secretary Roosevelt Convinced the Explosion of the War Ship Was Not an Accident." Hearst sold more than a million copies of his paper that morning.

Before any U.S. government body investigated the facts, Congress rushed through a fifty-million-dollar defense appropriation bill to put the country on an aggressive war footing. McKinley confided to an aide, "I have been through one war; I have seen the dead piled up, and I do not want to see another."[41] But the *Atlanta Constitution* ridiculed McKinley as a "goody-goody man," calling for a "declaration of American virility.... At this moment here is a great need of a man in the White House.... The people need a man—an American—at the helm." The *New York Journal* sought "any signs, however faint, of manhood in the White House," while a *New York World* editorial proclaimed, "There are manly and resolute ways of dealing with treachery and wrong. There are unmanly and irresolute ways." As other papers piled on, Assistant Secretary Roosevelt remarked to a friend, "McKinley has no more backbone than a chocolate éclair."[42]

New York Journal, *February 18, 1898. Front page. The USS* Maine *blew up in Havana harbor because of a ship malfunction. But the assistant secretary of the Navy, Theodore Roosevelt, wanted a war and, with not a shred of evidence, helped Yellow Press publisher William Randolph Hearst create the idea in the American mind that it "was the work of an enemy." Years later, President Franklin Roosevelt belatedly apologized to the government of Spain for American accusations.*

McKinley paced his Executive Mansion office by day and needed sleeping pills at night. He recalled to visitors the horrors he had witnessed in the Civil War and reiterated how he wanted to prevent any recurrence. With one friend he burst into tears as he voiced his fear of war. Nevertheless, on April 20, 1898, McKinley reluctantly signed the war resolution against Spain. A brilliant politician regarding domestic affairs, the president who had never paid much attention to the rest of the world now had to square the nation's conscience with its opposition to European-style imperialism. Initiating what would become a recurring Yankee tradition, McKinley contended that the U.S. military could invade other countries when Americans decided that their people needed help. McKinley conjured up the fantasy that when a U.S. soldier pointed a gun at a foreign Other, he was there to help. The Teller amendment to McKinley's war resolution declared these benevolent intentions:

> The people of the Island of Cuba are, of right ought to be, free and independent.... The United States does hereby demand, that the Government of Spain at once relinquish its authority and government in the Island of Cuba [and] the United States hereby disclaims any disposition or intention to exercise sovereignty, jurisdiction, or control over said Island except for the pacification thereof, and asserts its determination, when that is accomplished, to leave the government and control of the Island to its people.[43]

When McKinley called for volunteers, he authorized three regiments composed of frontiersmen with special qualifications as marksmen and horsemen. The secretary of war, Russell Alger, offered Teddy a regiment. Roosevelt turned down command but said he would serve as lieutenant colonel if his friend Leonard Wood commanded. Thus the "Rough Riders" (a name Roosevelt cribbed from Buffalo Bill) were born.

On June 14, 1898, American troops sailed from Tampa to free Cuba. Roosevelt's thoughts were of how he would help "score the first great triumph of a mighty world movement."[44]

In contrast to the American Revolutionary War, Cuban freedom fighters would have beaten the Spanish without foreign aid. (Indeed, impartial observers noted that U.S. troops could not have landed if the Cubans had not fought the Spanish back.) But Teddy saw things differently:

The Cuban soldiers were almost all blacks and mulattoes and were clothed in rags and armed with every kind of old rifle. They were utterly unable to make a serious fight, or to stand against even a very inferior number of Spanish troops, but we hoped they might be of some use as scouts and skirmishers. For various reasons this proved not to be the case, and so far as the Santiago Campaign was concerned, we should have been better off if there had not been a single Cuban with the army. They accomplished literally nothing, while they were a source of trouble and embarrassment, and consumed much provisions.[45]

Teddy's commander, Leonard Wood, wrote to the secretary of war that the Cuban Army was "made up very considerably of black people, only partially civilized, in whom the old spirit of savagery has been more or less aroused by years of warfare, during which time they have reverted more or less to the condition of men taking what they need and living by plunder."[46] English correspondent John Atkins remarked that "by far the most notable thing" about the Americans' reaction to the color of the natives "was their sudden open disavowal of friendliness towards the Cubans."[47] Before the invasion, the American press had portrayed the Cuban fighters as predominantly White men, "as brave as any who wear the blue."[48] Those newspapers reflected the military's disappointment that the Cubans were Black: the Cuban freedom fighters were now lazy, thieving, murderous bands.

Roosevelt, who as an author had crafted a winning persona as a manly Ranchman, had arranged for friendly photographers and correspondents to accompany the Rough Riders to Cuba, where they reported Teddy's courageous charge up Kettle Hill on the San Juan Ridge. Roosevelt's men had been waiting in trenches for orders when they began suffering serious casualties. Teddy decided to wait no longer and led his men to charge the Spanish positions above. Joined by several other brigades, Roosevelt successfully drove the Spanish away. Later, Roosevelt's men helped repel a counterattack on another hill. Awash in celebrity as a result of the press coverage, Roosevelt "became a walking advertisement for the imperialistic manhood he desired for the American race."[49]

The war in Cuba was brief, and on July 17, 1898, Spanish and American troops gathered in the city of Santiago for the surrender ceremony. In 1894, Teddy had penned an article entitled "National Life and Character" in which he wrote that Blacks were "a perfectly stupid race" and it would take "many thousand years" before the Black became even "as intellectual as the [ancient] Athenian."[50] Victorious American Aryans had no intention of handing a state to this inferior race. This was at a time when Professor Burgess's political science students at Columbia University were learning from him that only those Whites with Teutonic heritage were capable to control the organs of a state. Instead, the Americans informed shocked Cuban freedom fighters that the old Spanish civil authorities—White men—would remain in charge. No Cubans were allowed to confer on the

Theodore Roosevelt in his Rough Rider uniform. With almost twenty years of public-relations experience as a successful author, Roosevelt was a past master at using New York photo studios to create a lasting image. He cribbed the title "Rough Rider" from William Cody ("Buffalo Bill") and had his uniform tailored by Brooks Brothers. (Library of Congress)

surrender or to sign it. Down came the Spanish flag and, to the cheers of American soldiers, up went the Stars and Stripes.

As soon as the United States got control of Cuba, Congress passed the Platt Amendment, which canceled the benevolent intentions expressed in the original war resolution. Cuba was prohibited from making treaties with other countries and was forced to cede Guantánamo Bay to the United States for use as a naval base. After he became military governor of Cuba, Leonard Wood admitted to Roosevelt, "There is, of course, little or no independence left Cuba under the Platt Amendment."[51]

AMERICAN SUN-FOLLOWERS ALSO EYED naval links necessary for westward expansion across the Pacific. Filipino freedom fighters had been battling their Spanish colonial masters for years. But most Americans had never heard of the distant Philippines. Even fewer understood that it was experiencing its own revolution, just like Cuba. It was not until an 1898 article in the *North American Review*—"The Cuba of the Far East"—that there was a single public reference to the revolt in the Philippines.[52]

Indeed, early in his presidency, McKinley was asked the location of the Philippine Islands. "Somewhere away around on the other side of the world," he answered.[53] And the president later admitted, "When we received

The Philippine Islands

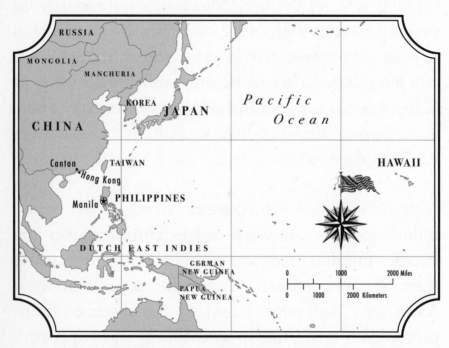

When asked the location of the Philippine Islands, President McKinley answered, "Somewhere away around on the other side of the world."

the cable from Admiral Dewey [Commodore at the time] telling of the taking of the Philippines I looked up their location on the globe. I could not have told where those darned islands were within 2,000 miles."[54]

ON FEBRUARY 15, 1898, when the *Maine* exploded in Havana, Cuba, Puerto Rico, Guam, and the Philippines were suddenly in play. Just as the U.S. Army had planted forts that facilitated westering, the U.S. Navy could now obtain the links necessary to circle Whitman's circle.

With Assistant Secretary Roosevelt beating the tom-toms in Washington, Admiral George Dewey in Hong Kong made plans to seize Manila. While the United States could defeat Spanish naval power, that was not the same as controlling the Philippines. Conquering territory required land troops, and the U.S. Army was on the other side of the world. Aguinaldo's soldiers had proven themselves against Spanish forces, and now Dewey imagined he could use them as a temporary rent-an-army.

Dewey solicited Aguinaldo's assistance several times. Within a month of the *Maine* explosion, he dispatched Commander Edward Wood to liaise with the Filipino leader. When he met with Wood, Aguinaldo naturally assumed that since he was dealing with an emissary of the top U.S. official in Asia, he was hearing the official American position on his revolution. Wood told him that the United States would support Filipino independence if the Filipino army teamed with the U.S. Navy against Spain. With his own Indians, the American Aryan had been quick to make treaties that Congress could later disregard. Now on the international stage, U.S. officials were more circumspect. When Aguinaldo asked whether the United States had designs of its own for the Philippines, Wood assured him, "The United States is a great and rich nation and needs no colonies."[55] When Aguinaldo suggested that he commit this in writing, Wood "replied that he would refer the matter to Admiral Dewey."[56]

In almost every meeting, Aguinaldo asked the U.S. officials for a signed agreement stating their intentions and obligations. According to Aguinaldo, the U.S. consul to Singapore, Spencer Pratt, assured him, "The Government of North America is a very honest, just, and powerful government. There is no necessity for entering into a formal written agreement because the word of the Admiral and of the United States Consul were in fact equivalent to the most solemn pledge, that their verbal promises and assurance would be fulfilled to the letter and were not to be classed with Spanish promises or Spanish ideas of a man's word of honour."[57]

Many historians maintain it is impossible to

ascertain precisely what the State Department and War Department representatives promised the Filipinos. They point to the lack of written agreements, the ambiguity of the verbal interchanges, the potential for misunderstandings between English-speaking Americans and their Spanish-speaking Filipino counterparts. But it is clear that the American emissaries gave Aguinaldo every encouragement. In hindsight, the Filipino leader should have heeded the warning of the Spanish governor-general of the Philippines, Basilio Augustín y Dávila:

A squadron manned by foreigners, possessing neither instruction nor discipline, is preparing to come to this archipelago with the ruffianly intention of robbing us of all that means life, honor, and liberty. Pretending to be inspired by a courage of which they are incapable, the North American seamen undertake, as an enterprise capable of realization, the substitution of Protestantism for the Catholic religion...to treat you as tribes refractory to civilization, to take possession of your riches as if they were unacquainted with the rights of property.[58]

The May 1 "Battle of Manila Bay" was actually not much of a fight. On May 1, Admiral Dewey's modern, steel ships steamed into Manila Bay. Spain's creaky, wooden ships were conveniently tied up in a row. It was a turkey shoot, American cannon pounding Spain's wooden relics into kindling. The conflict was so one-sided that Dewey had his sailors break for a sit-down morning meal. After the breakfast dishes had been washed and dried, the U.S. Navy resumed its attack.

Americans back home were elated by the stunning news. Newspaper front pages featured images of America's new high-tech navy hero, Admiral Dewey, who was blond and blue-eyed, the very picture of an Aryan. "Americans saw the white-haired Navy Military man as the paragon of American racial superiority, civilization and manhood,"[59] William Leeman writes in "America's Admiral: George Dewey and American Culture in the Gilded Age." Biographers "traced Dewey's heritage through Saxon royal lines as far back as the early centuries A.D."[60] Some went so far as to assert that he was a descendant of Thor, the Saxon hero-god of war and thunder. A young English author wrote in the *American Monthly Review of Reviews,* "[Admiral Dewey was] the logical result of a system which produces the best naval officers in the world . . . the American officer combines valuable qualities of his own with the necessary traits which are found in the English and other northern races."[61] The author's name was Winston Churchill.

Theodore Roosevelt proclaimed, "No man since

the Civil War, whether soldier or civilian, has added so much to the honorable renown of the nation or has deserved so well of it."[62] Recalled Dewey, "Towns, children, and articles of commerce were named after me. I was assured that nothing like the enthusiasm for a man and a deed had ever been known."[63] Dewey mania swept through America with Dewey days, Dewey songs, Dewey fireworks, Dewey parades, Dewey flags, Dewey portraits, Dewey mugs, Dewey hats, Dewey skirts, Dewey shorts, and baby boys named George in his honor. These babies chewed Dewey teething rings and shook rattles shaped like Dewey's body. Older children played with Dewey action figures. A St. Louis department store's newspaper ad offered "Dewey souvenir bargains in every department, in every aisle, on every counter."[64] Adults bought Dewey neckties, cuff links, canes, paperweights, letter openers, shaving mugs, napkins, commemorative plates and coins, miniature busts, candlesticks, replica navy hats, Dewey laxatives, and Dewey gum, called "Dewey's Chewies." Nationwide ads for the Pears' Soap Company featured a drawing of Admiral Dewey scrubbing his White hands whiter. Below Dewey's image, a White Christian missionary hands a bar of soap to a crouching "Pacific Negro"; the advertising copy reads: "The first step towards lightening The White Man's Burden is through teaching the virtues of cleanliness. Pears' Soap is a potent factor in brightening the dark corners of the earth as civilization advances, while amongst the cultured of all nations it holds the highest place—it is the ideal toilet soap."[65]

The Navy Department had ordered Dewey to attack Spanish naval power in Manila before he was able to secure his rent-an-army. Many in the United States assumed that Dewey's victory assured control of the Philippines, but the U.S. Navy held only Manila Bay; the American consulate operated from a bobbing ship. Spanish colonial forces held the walled city of Manila and its immediate environs. The Philippines Revolutionary Army had the rest of the country.

Dewey dispatched the USS *McCulloch* to Hong Kong to pick up the man who he hoped would align the Filipino freedom fighters with the U.S. Navy. Under the cover of darkness on the evening of May 16, the U.S. consul-general, Rounseville Wildman, shepherded General Emilio Aguinaldo through Hong Kong harbor, where together they boarded the *McCulloch* for Aguinaldo's return.

Just after noon on May 19 in Manila Bay, U.S. Navy officers saluted General Aguinaldo as he transferred from the USS *McCulloch* to Dewey's private launch for the trip to Dewey's command ship. The Filipino freedom fighter soon found himself face-to-face with the most famous military man in the world.

Aguinaldo grilled Dewey about the United States' past verbal assurances. According to Aguinaldo, Dewey explained that the United States was a humanitarian country that had dispatched its navy to help the Filipinos win their independence. When asked for a written commitment to Filipino independence, Aguinaldo recalled that Dewey said that "the United States would unquestionably recognize the Independence of the people of the Philippines, guaranteed as it was by the word of honour of Americans, which, he said, is more positive, more irrevocable than any written agreement."[66] Dewey pointed out that the United States was a rich nation with enough territory and no history of taking colonies. Historian Stanley Karnow observes: "The Americans' only preoccupation at that juncture was to defeat the Spanish. To achieve that goal, they sought the help of the Filipinos, indulging them with pledges that had no foundation in reality. Aguinaldo filtered Dewey's remarks through the prism of his own dreams, [and he] construed American attention to mean that he was now a U.S. ally in the struggle against Spain."[67]

U.S. sailors ferried the returning hero to the mainland, where thousands cheered as U.S. Marines turned rifles over to the freedom fighters. Addressing the crowd, Aguinaldo declared, "Divine Providence is about to place independence within our reach. The Americans have extended their protecting mantle

The first step towards lightening

The White Man's Burden

is through teaching the virtues of cleanliness.

Pears' Soap

is a potent factor in brightening the dark corners of the earth as
civilization advances, while amongst the cultured of all nations
it holds the highest place—it is the ideal toilet soap.

Pears' Soap advertisement, 1899. Admiral George Dewey
was the most famous military man in the world, the high-
tech Daniel Boone bringing bright, White civilization to
the dark savages. (First appeared in McClure's Magazine,
October 1899)

to our beloved country....The American fleet will prevent any reinforcements coming from Spain.... Where you see the American flag flying, assemble in numbers; they are our redeemers."[68]

For the first two months after Dewey splintered the Spanish fleet, American and Filipino military forces complemented each other: the U.S. Navy held the sea, and the Philippines Revolutionary Army beat Spanish forces into a humiliating retreat behind Manila's walls. But while Filipinos perceived the U.S. Navy as a benevolent force providing a protective canopy under which they fought for independence, Washington saw things differently. In his residence, President McKinley wrote a note to himself: "While we are conducting a war and until its conclusion we must keep all we get; when the war is over we must keep what we want."[69]

The Philippines' first Independence Day was celebrated on June 12, 1898. The main event was led by (now president) Aguinaldo in his hometown. He proudly unfurled the country's new flag, explaining that the banner's red, white, and blue colors were a salute to "the flag of the United States of America as a manifestation of our profound gratitude towards that Great Nation for the disinterested protection she is extending to us and will continue to extend to us."[70]

The Filipinos would not celebrate another Independence Day for sixty-four years.

*   *   *

ON JUNE 16, THE AMERICAN consul, Oscar Williams, wrote from Manila that "[Aguinaldo] has organized a government... and from that day to this he has been uninterruptedly successful in the field and

"Filipino's First Bath," Judge *magazine, June 10, 1899.*
President McKinley bathes a Filipino in civilization's waters like
St. John the Baptist. "Oh, you dirty boy," exclaims McKinley.
The artist was able to depict Filipinos as Africans because so few
*Americans knew the difference. (*Puck *magazine begat* Judge
magazine, which begat The New Yorker *magazine.)*

dignified and just as the head of his government."[71] But the future of the Philippines would be decided in the American Aryan's capital. The very idea that a Pacific Negro was capable of ruling eight million people was unthinkable. Instead of referring to the leader of the Philippines as President Aguinaldo, the *New York Times* called him "Chief Aguinaldo," or just "insurgent" or "unmoral infant."[72] Professor Theodore Woolsey of Yale Law School argued, "The so-called Filipino republic is but a body of insurgents against the sovereignty of the United States."[73]

On June 30, 1898, President Aguinaldo made the strategic error that marked the beginning of the end of Filipino nationhood: he allowed twenty-five hundred armed American soldiers to come ashore to prosecute the war with Spain. Aguinaldo told his cabinet, "I have studied attentively the Constitution of the United States, and I find in it no authority for colonies, and I have no fear."[74]

The half-starved Spanish held out behind Manila's walls. Aguinaldo's troops held the rest of the country. But one crucial element had become clear: the Spanish were White and the Filipinos were not. The Americans approached the Spanish with a deal: U.S. forces would pretend to attack Manila, the Spanish would pretend to defend, and, after a little noise, the Spanish would surrender the capital. The Americans would then claim a glorious victory, the Spanish—who had

HURRAH FOR THE FOURTH OF JULY.
We're Coming In on Independence Day Celebrations, Too.—July 2.

make the cartoon of Hawaii, Cuba and the Philippines coming in for an independence day cele-
bration. For two days we had had reports of furious fighting before Santiago. It was a Fourth

*"Hurrah for the Fourth of July! We're coming in on
independence day celebrations too."* Minneapolis Journal.
*President McKinley's premise that the U.S. military would
act with benevolent intentions convinced Americans
that the people of Cuba, Hawaii, and the Philippines
appreciated American invasions of their countries. (Charles
Bartholomew,* Cartoons of the Spanish-American War*)*

realized they could not win—a manly defeat without
casualties. Recalled Admiral Dewey, "The Governor-
General arranged with me that I was to go up and
fire a few shots and then I was to make the signal,
'Do you surrender?' and he would hoist the white flag
and then the troops would march in."[75] All of this
was kept secret from the Filipinos.

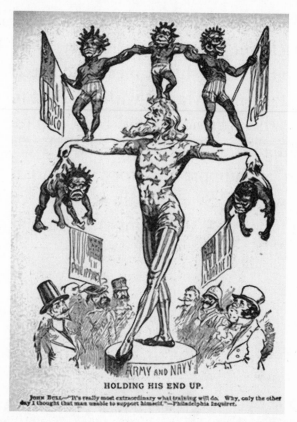

HOLDING HIS END UP.

JOHN BULL.—"It's really most extraordinary what training will do. Why, only the other day I thought that man unable to support himself."—Philadelphia Inquirer.

"Holding His End Up." Europeans gaze at a newly imperial Uncle Sam, who stands on an Army and Navy platform in 1898. Because Americans knew so little about their new possessions, the artist could portray Hawaiians, Cubans, and Filipinos as monkeylike Africans. (Philadelphia Inquirer, *1898*)

On August 13, the Americans and Spanish "fought" the sham Battle of Manila. Filipino troops tried to join their U.S. Army allies, but the Americans shot at them to prevent any but White troops from passing through Manila's thick walls.

For almost four months Aguinaldo's forces had beaten back the Spanish until they were huddled in the capital eating horse meat and rats. The U.S. Army waltzed into Manila with little wear and tear. And since the Americans had been careful to commit nothing in writing, Aguindalo had no documentation to support his story. Historian Ambeth Ocampo writes, "By nightfall, it had become painfully clear that the Americans transformed the 'ally' to 'enemy.'"[76]

U.S. Army soldiers on Manila's wall, August 13, 1898. The McKinley administration portrayed the Battle of Manila as a great military victory. The truth was that the United States and Spain agreed that Spain would surrender Manila to the Americans after a fake battle, which served the interests of both the U.S. and Spanish militaries and kept the non-White Filipinos from taking the capital.

The capture of Manila marked the end of the Spanish-American War and thrilled the expansionists who imagined that Manila (as the assistant secretary of the Navy, Theodore Roosevelt, had argued) would be a key strategic link for the United States. In his rush to war, Teddy apparently never asked himself the elementary question of why a merchant shipping goods from China would first ship them to nearby Manila.

The United States could have saved blood and treasure if Washington had just leased warehouses in Hong Kong rather than attempt the military conquest of a poor and inconvenient Asian backwater. Only years later would Roosevelt comprehend the enormity of America's blunder in the Pacific.

Theodore Roosevelt's Strategic Blunder

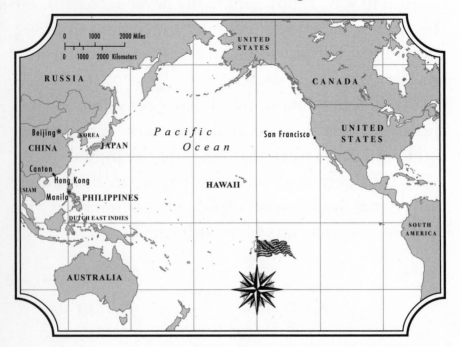

Assistant Secretary of the Navy Theodore Roosevelt imagined Manila to be a key American strategic link to China. Roosevelt never asked himself the elementary question of why merchants would detour to Manila on the U.S.-China trade route.

Chapter 4

PACIFIC NEGROES

---

*"We come not to make war upon
the Philippines, but to protect them in their
homes, in their employment, and in their
personal and religious rights."[1]*
—PRESIDENT WILLIAM McKINLEY, 1899

*"The people of the United States want us
to kill all the men, fuck all the women, and
raise up a new race in these Islands."[2]*
—ROBERT AUSTILL, SOLDIER IN THE PHILIPPINES, 1902

Textbooks present the debate over whether the United States would keep the Philippines as a titanic battle between imperialists and anti-imperialists. The anti-imperialist writings of Mark Twain and Andrew Carnegie give the impression that the United States was doing something new, that up to that point the country did not have a tradition of holding alien peoples as colonial subjects. But America already had a colonial policy. In 1832—when the United States government controlled only a small portion of the continent—the Supreme Court had designated White Christian males as "guardians" of their Indian "wards." As Professor Walter Williams writes in the *Journal of American History* article "United States Indian Policy and the Debate over Philippine Annexation":

> The imperialists believed that imperialism abroad was similar to past United States expansion over North America. The precedents to govern colonial subjects were clear and exact, based on the long road from independence to wardships for American Indians. There was an almost solid consensus among white Americans of the time that expansion over Indians was unquestionably right. White Americans generally did not believe that their past was criminal, they accepted the rightness of their actions in the Philippines. To admit doubt would have undercut the whole history of the nation.[3]

"Governing the Philippines is not a sign of a new policy, but the enlargement of a policy long pursued, wrote Professor Albert Bushnell Hart of Harvard, later president of the American Historical Association and the editor of *American Political Science Magazine*."[4] The *Atlantic Monthly* concluded that "the question is not whether we shall enter upon a career of colonization or not, but whether we shall shift into other channels the colonization which has lasted as long as our national existence."[5] Senator Orville Platt called westward Pacific expansion "the law of our national growth...the great law of our racial development."[6] As Theodore Roosevelt had written in the third volume of his Winning of the West series: "Many good persons seem prone to speak of all wars of conquest as necessarily evil. This is, of course, a shortsighted view. In its after effects a conquest may be fraught either with evil or with good for mankind, according to the comparative worth of the conquering and conquered peoples."[7]

Though the American Anti-Imperialist League—newly founded to oppose the annexation of the Philippines—threatened to gather ten million protests, "the petition drive died out at a miserable five thousand signatures."[8] The *Baltimore American* concluded, "It is the same old law of the survival of the fittest. The weak must bend to the strong and today the American race is the sturdiest, the noblest on earth."[9]

One of the most famous stories about McKinley is how the president confessed to a visiting delegation of Methodist ministers that he fell to his knees and prayed for enlightenment and that God told him it was his duty to uplift, civilize, and Christianize the Filipinos. The story might not be true, but it captures the benevolent intentions that McKinley injected into U.S. foreign policy. McKinley understood that to his electorate, imperialism was a dirty word, and so he made Americans believe that their nation's boldly imperial moves were instead efforts of great compassion and sacrifice. If the average American felt pity for Others, he had a Christian duty to help.

The Senate debate over retention of the Philippines was a clash between young bucks and old fogies. The American Anti-Imperialist League's president was over eighty years old; Senator George Hoar of Massachusetts was seventy-two; Andrew Carnegie and Mark Twain were comparative youngsters at sixty-three years of age. In contrast, Senator Henry Cabot Lodge was forty-eight and Theodore Roosevelt was forty. Thirty-six-year-old Senator Albert Beveridge of Indiana exclaimed, "The millions of young Americans with a virile manhood unequalled in the world will not admit or submit to the proposition that their flag is not to fly in the midst of the swiftly coming world events, so vast that all history have been but preparation for them."[10]

The British author Rudyard Kipling penned the poem "The White Man's Burden" to urge the senators

to emulate their Anglo-Saxon brethren. The subtitle
was "The United States and the Philippine Islands."

Take up the White Man's burden—
Send forth the best ye breed—
Go bind your sons to exile
To serve your captives' need;
To wait in heavy harness
On fluttered folk and wild—
Your new-caught, sullen peoples,
Half devil and half child.
. . . .
Take up the White Man's burden—
The savage wars of peace—
. . . .
Go mark them with your living,
And mark them with your dead!

Take up the White Man's burden—
And reap his old reward:
. . . .
Take up the White Man's burden—
Ye dare not stoop to less—
. . . .
Take up the White Man's burden—
Have done with childish days—
The lightly proffered laurel,
The easy, ungrudged praise.

Comes now, to search your manhood
Through all the thankless years,
Cold, edged with dear-bought wisdom,
The judgment of your peers![11]

On Admiral Dewey's orders, two American Navy men—W. B. Wilcox and L. R. Sargent—conducted a fact-finding mission on the Philippine island of Luzon from October 8 to November 20, 1898. Wilcox and Sargent documented a fully functioning Filipino government that was efficiently administering justice through its courts, keeping the peace, providing police protection, holding elections, and carrying out the consent of the governed. The two Americans recalled the moving, patriotic speech of a Philippines government official who promised that "every man, woman, and child stood ready to take up arms to defend their newly won liberty and to resist with the last drop of their blood the attempt of any nation whatever to bring them back to their former state of dependence."[12] When the burden-bearing men in the War Department realized Dewey's report had documented Aguinaldo's functioning democracy, they buried it.[13]

President McKinley imagined all would be well when the Pacific Negroes submitted and accepted America's kindness. On December 21, he instructed the U.S. military to act with benevolent intentions:

It should be the earnest and paramount aim of
the military administration to win the confidence, respect, and affection of the inhabitants
of the Philippines by assuring them, in every
possible way, that full measure of individual
rights which is the heritage of free peoples,
and by proving to them that the mission of the
United States is one of benevolent assimilation,
substituting the mild sway of justice and right
for arbitrary rule.[14]

On February 4, 1899, the U.S. military governor
of the Philippines—General Elwell Otis—suddenly
ordered U.S. lines to be extended out from Manila
into Philippines army territory and ordered sentries
to fire on Filipino "intruders." That evening, Private
William Grayson and Private Orville Miller were on
guard duty. Grayson peered into the darkness and saw
four Filipinos who were later found to be drunk and
unarmed. Grayson yelled, "Halt!" A Filipino shouted
back, "Halto!" Grayson recalled, "Well I thought the
best thing to do was to shoot him. He dropped. Then
two Filipinos sprang out of the gateway about 15 feet
from us. I called 'Halt' and Miller fired and dropped
one. Well I think I got my second Filipino that time.
We retreated to where six other fellows were and I
said, 'Line up fellows...the niggers are in here all
through these yards.'"[15]

All that had occurred was that four inebriated Filipinos lay dead. The army could have treated this as a minor event, but back at headquarters, General Robert Hughes ran up to General Otis and exclaimed, "The thing is on!"[16] Colonel Frederick Funston was asleep when an aide startled him awake: "Come on out here, Colonel, the ball has begun."[17] U.S. rifles crackled and cannons roared all along the ten-mile-long front separating American and Filipino forces. An Englishman who observed the coordinated American attack noted skeptically, "If the Filipinos were aggressors, it is very remarkable that the American troops should have been so well prepared for an unseen event as to be able to immediately and simultaneously attack, in full force, all the native outposts for miles around the capital."[18]

U.S. forces killed more than three thousand Filipino freedom fighters in twenty-four hours. Photos of Filipino corpses heaped in American-dug ditches recalled the U.S. Army's burial scene at Wounded Knee. In the annals of warfare, few remember that more Filipinos died defending their country in that first day's storm than Americans died storming the beaches of Normandy on D-Day in World War II.

Two days later, on February 6, the Senate ratified the Treaty of Paris, which ended the Spanish-American War, by one vote more than the required two-thirds majority. Reflected Colorado's Senator

Dead Filipino soldiers in a U.S. Army ditch, the day after the Americans' surprise attack ignited hostility, February 5, 1899. The ditch was circular and many more bodies lay outside the frame. Theodore Roosevelt saw an exact parallel between the Filipinos and the Apaches and the Sioux. (National Archives)

Thomas Patterson, "Senators who had stood against the treaty, incensed by what they were led to believe was a wanton, deliberate, and unprovoked assault upon the American Army by Aguinaldo's forces, changed their purposes and voted for ratification."[19] The American public learned that the treaty called for the United States to purchase the Philippines from Spain for twenty million dollars, seemingly a good deal at two dollars per Pacific Negro. Yet as Admiral Dewey later observed, "We were far from being in possession of the property which we had bought.... After paying twenty million for the islands, we must establish our authority by force against the very people whom we sought to benefit."[20]

As with Baghdad more than a century later, Americans assumed that the fall of a capital meant control of the country. The author Henry Adams wrote Theodore Roosevelt to express his alarm: "I turn green in bed at night if I think of the horror of a year's warfare in the Philippines [where] we must slaughter a million or two of foolish Malays in order to give them the comforts of flannel petticoats and electric railways."[21]

But challenging as the task appeared, the Americans had useful experience. The U.S. Army had waged race war in the American West, shooting civilians, executing prisoners, raping women, torturing captives, looting and burning villages, and herding the defeated into concentration camps. Now, it was assumed, they would chew through the preindustrialized, agricultural Philippines.

As Richard Welch Jr. writes of U.S. soldiers in the Philippines, "They were determined to prove their manhood by 'shooting niggers.' Removed from the inhibitions of small-town American folkways, they celebrated by burning barrios of nipa huts; stimulated with the instant authority granted by a uniform and a rifle, they saw civilians as inferior and short... as less than human."[22] The American journalist H. L. Wells observed in the *New-York Evening Post:* "There is no question that our men do 'shoot niggers' somewhat in the sporting spirit."[23]

The U.S. Army's attack on the village of Malabon was one of the first battles. A soldier wrote home: "Brutality began right off. At Malabon three women were raped by the soldiers.... Morals became awfully bad. Vino drinking and whiskey guzzling got the upper hand of benevolent assimilation."[24]

The third U.S. military governor of the Philippines, General Arthur MacArthur,[25] later justified these actions in testimony in front of the U.S. Senate:

Many thousand years ago our Aryan ancestors raised cattle, made a language, multiplied in numbers, and overflowed. By due process of expansion to the west they occupied Europe, developed arts and sciences, and created a great civilization, which, separating into innumerable currents, inundated and fertilized the globe with blood and ideas, the primary bases of all human progress, incidentally crossing the Atlantic and thereby reclaiming, populating, and civilizing a hemisphere.

As to why the United States was in the Philippines, the broad actuating laws which underlie all these wonderful phenomena are still operating with relentless vigor and have recently forced one of the currents of this magnificent Aryan people across the Pacific—that is to say, back almost to the cradle of its race—thus initiating a stage of progressive social evolution which may reasonably be expected to result in substantial contributions on behalf of the unity of the race and the brotherhood of man.[26]

When General MacArthur referred to Americans as descendants of the Aryan who were now using the U.S. military to expand back to the race cradle, no senator asked for clarification.

Early in the war, Filipinos shot and cut open the stomach of a U.S. soldier. General Loyd Wheaton ordered a massacre of civilians in retaliation. In a letter home, a soldier from Kingston, New York, recalled, "Immediately orders were received from General Wheaton to burn the town and kill every native in sight; which was done to a finish. About 1,000 men, women, and children were reported killed. I am probably growing hard-hearted, for I am in my glory when I can sight my gun on some dark skin and pull the trigger."[27] F. A. Blake of the American Red Cross visited the Philippines and reported, "American soldiers

General Arthur MacArthur, the third military governor of the Philippines and father of General Douglas MacArthur. In Senate testimony, General MacArther portrayed the U.S. Army's westward expansion to the Philippines as in the tradition of America's Aryan ancestors. (The U.S. Army Heritage and Education Center)

are determined to kill every Filipino in sight."[28] And there was "fun" to be had with the women: Captain Fred McDonald ordered every native killed in the hamlet of LaNog, save a beautiful mestizo mother, whom the officers repeatedly raped, before turning her over to enlisted men.

Typically, when the U.S. Army arrived, soldiers

rounded up the mayor, town officials, priests, and any other potential sources of information. "Water detail!" an officer would bark, and up came the torturers with their black tools. In the Philippines conflict, waterboarding was known as the "water cure." Former first lieutenant Grover Flint of the 35th Infantry served in the Philippines from November 1899

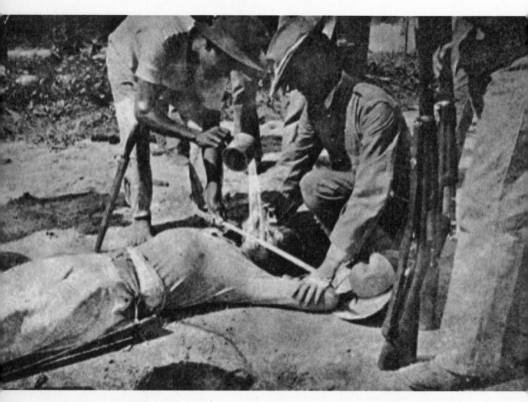

U.S. soldiers torturing a Filipino, 1901. When the U.S. military waterboarded Filipinos, the practice was accepted. When the Japanese later waterboarded U.S. personnel in World War II, America tried them for war crimes. (Ohio State University)

to April 1901 and later described the water cure to a Senate panel:

A man is thrown down on his back and three or four men sit or stand on his arms and legs and hold him down, and either a gun barrel or a rifle or a carbine barrel or a stick as big as a belaying pin...is simply thrust into his jaws and his jaws are thrust back, and, if possible, a wood log or stone is put under...his neck, so he can be held firmly...in the case of very old men I have seen their teeth fall out—I mean when it was done a little roughly. He is simply held down, and then water is poured into his face, down his throat and nose from a jar, and that is kept up until the man gives some sign of giving in or becoming unconscious, and when he becomes unconscious he is simply rolled aside and he is allowed to come to.... Well, I know that in a great many cases, in almost every case, the men have been a little roughly handled; they were rolled aside rudely, so that water was expelled. A man suffers tremendously; there is no doubt about that. His suffering must be that of a man who is drowning, but he can not drown.[29]

A popular U.S. Army marching song, "The Water Cure," gleefully described the process:

Get the good old syringe boys and fill it
  to the brim.
We've caught another nigger and we'll
  operate on him.
Let someone take the handle who can
  work it with a vim.
Shouting the battle cry of freedom.

Chorus:
Hurray. Hurrah. We bring the Jubilee.
Hurray. Hurrah. The flag that makes him
  free.
Shove in the nozzle deep and let him
  taste of liberty.
Shouting the battle cry of freedom.

We've come across the bounding main to
  kindly spread around
Sweet liberty whenever there are rebels
  to be found.
So hurry with the syringe boys. We've got
  him down and bound.
Shouting the battle cry of freedom.

Oh pump it in him till he swells like a toy
  balloon.
The fool pretends that liberty is not a
  precious boon.

But we'll contrive to make him see the
beauty of it soon.
Shouting the battle cry of freedom.

Keep the piston going boys and let the banner
wave.
The banner that floats proudly o'er the noble
and the brave.
Keep on till the squirt gun breaks or he
explodes the slave.
Shouting the battle cry of freedom.

Chorus:
Hurrah. Hurrah. We bring the Jubilee.
Hurrah. Hurrah. The flag that makes him
free.
We've got him down and bound, so let's fill
him full of liberty.
Shouting the battle cry of freedom.[30]

Ingenious Yankees employed a variety of other gruesome tortures, including flogging, scorching bound prisoners over open fires, and the "rope cure" (hanging trussed prisoners from the ceiling). A private from Utah summed things up in a letter home to his folks: "No cruelty is too severe for these brainless monkeys, who can appreciate no sense of honor, kindness or justice."[31] Roosevelt stiffened American resolve in the Philippines with a speech he called "The Strenuous Life":

> We cannot avoid the responsibilities that confront us in Hawaii, Cuba, Puerto Rico, and the Philippines. . . . I have scant patience with those who fear to undertake the task of governing the Philippines, and who openly avow that they do fear to undertake it, or that they shrink from it because of the expense and trouble; but I have even scanter patience with those who make a pretense of humanitarianism to hide and cover their timidity, and who cant about 'liberty' and the 'consent of the governed,' in order to excuse themselves for their willingness to play the part of men. Their doctrines, if carried out, would make it incumbent upon us to leave the Apaches of Arizona to work out their own salvation, and to decline to interfere in a single Indian reservation.[32]

Veteran soldiers told newspaper reporters, "The country won't be pacified until the niggers are killed off like Indians," and that it was necessary "to blow every nigger into a nigger heaven."[33] The Medal of Honor recipient Frederick Funston executed POWs, tortured civilians, and raped women and then stoutly defended these tactics: "I am afraid some people at home will lie awake nights worrying about the ethics of this war, thinking that our enemy is fighting for the right of self-government.... They are, as a rule, an illiterate, semi-savage people, who are waging war, not against tyranny, but against Anglo-Saxon order and decency."[34]

In war, many more combatants typically are injured rather than killed—the ratio from the U.S. Civil War and other conflicts was five to one. But a summary of Filipinos dead from February through July of 1899 found only 3,297 wounded to 14,643 killed, a ratio of one to four[35]; U.S. soldiers were killing four times more Filipinos than injuring them. General MacArthur explained: "Men of Anglo-Saxon stock do not succumb as easily to wounds as do men of 'inferior races.'"[36]

IN A DECEMBER 1899 essay called "Expansion and Peace," Teddy explained that "peace may come only through war."[37] But while Americans at home were led to believe that civilization was following the sun, the reality in the Philippines was different, as Leon Wolff recalls in *Little Brown Brother:* "New-comers from the States were astonished at the discrepancy between fact and fable. They had read and had been told that the fighting was over except for minor police actions. Instead they found that the 'quiet countryside' meant constant scouting parties, petty engagements, ambushes, and tense garrison duties in hundreds of far-flung villages."[38] Nevertheless, one year into a race war that the army had assumed would be a cinch, the U.S. military governor-general, Otis, told reporters: "I have held that opinion for some time that the thing is entirely over. I cannot see where it is possible for the guerillas to effect any reorganization, concentrate any force or accomplish anything serious."[39] On the day Otis spoke those words, Filipino freedom fighters killed nineteen U.S. soldiers in a fierce battle.

When he retired, the war "won," Otis made a victory lap of parades and banquets across the nation. In an interview with the popular *Frank Leslie's Weekly*, Otis insisted, "The war is already over. The insurrection ended some months ago, and all we have to do now is to protect the Filipinos against themselves and to give protection to those natives who are begging for it."[40] In Washington, President McKinley congratulated Otis on his victory. As more soldiers lost their lives in 1900 than the year before, a joint session of Congress cheered a new American hero.

AFTER MORE THAN A year of bloody fighting, the new American military governor, Arthur MacArthur, warned that the war was not winding down and that the guerilla warfare was intensifying. MacArthur concluded that the freedom fighters could resist only if civilians supported them, so like the Spanish had done in Cuba, he decided to "concentrate" the civilian population to better hunt the guerillas. The U.S. Army would post notices that in a few days, all civilians within a designated zone were to report to a concentration camp. The people could bring what they could carry; the remainder of their possessions were to be abandoned.

Inside the fetid and poorly supplied camps, many uprooted civilians died. Outside the camps, U.S. troops shot captured freedom fighters as common criminals because MacArthur had stripped them of their prisoner-of-war status. Officers set the example. General Frederick Funston ordered his regiment to take no prisoners, and he bragged to reporters that he had personally strung up thirty-five civilians. Major Edwin Glenn chimed in that he had forced forty-seven prisoners to kneel before him and repent their sins before they were bayoneted to death. Writing home, Private Clarence Clowe reported:

At any time I am liable to be called upon to go out and bind and gag helpless prisoners, to strike them in the face, to knock them down when so bound, to bear them away from wife and children, at their very door, who are shrieking pitifully the while, or kneeling and kissing the hands of our officers, imploring mercy from those who seem not to know what it is, and then, with a crowd of soldiers, hold our helpless victim head downward in a tub of water in his own yard, bind him hand and foot, attaching ropes to head and feet, and then lowering him into the depths of a well of water till life is well-nigh choked out, and the bitterness of a death is tasted, and our poor, gasping victims ask us for the poor boon of being finished off, in mercy to themselves.[41]

The president ruled the Philippines through his War Department, whose top man in the islands was the U.S. military governor of the Philippines, now MacArthur. In 1900, an election year, McKinley told voters that since the Filipino insurrection had been defeated it was safe to transfer power from a "military government" to a U.S. "civil government." It was critical that McKinley select just the right poster boy to lead the new civil government. On a cold January day in 1900, it was Judge William Howard Taft who stood in front of the president in his Executive Mansion office. Back in 1876, President Ulysses Grant had summoned Judge Alphonso Taft as his secretary of war, charged with assimilating the Indians at the height of the Indian Wars. Now President

McKinley was summoning Alphonso's son to be the War Department's benevolent assimilator of the Pacific Negroes.

Taft had no knowledge of the Philippines beyond that of any Cincinnatian who read the news. But when he learned what was on the president's mind, Taft immediately parroted the McKinley administration's rationale: that the Filipinos were incapable of ruling themselves, that America had to exert itself to help its Pacific wards, and that America was "doing them great good" by building them a nation. McKinley subsequently announced the formation of the Taft Commission to study conditions in the Philippines, with Big Bill the lead commissioner.

For forty-nine days in the spring of 1900, Commissioner Taft steamed across the wide Pacific, dreaming of how he would mold the Pacific Negroes into a "self-governing people" and build them a shiny new nation. Big Bill imagined that if he and the other nation builders demonstrated their benevolent intentions, the Filipinos would naturally want to become just like their American masters. He called this his "policy of attraction." Wrote Taft: "We expect to do considerable entertaining and especially of Filipinos, both ladies and gentlemen. We are advised that the army has alienated a good many of our Filipino friends...and given them the impression...that they regard the Filipino ladies and men as 'niggers' and as

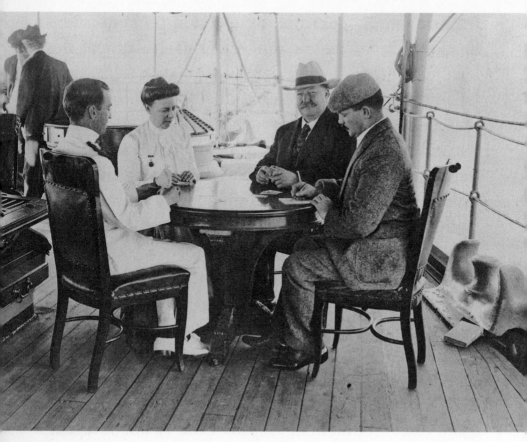

The U.S. commissioner to the Philippines, William Howard Taft, and Mrs. Helen "Nellie" Taft en route to Manila, 1900. On this trip Taft decided to implement a "policy of attraction." He reasoned that if U.S. colonial rulers were benevolent, the Filipinos would over time desire to be like Americans. (Library of Congress)

not fit to be associated with. We propose, so far as we are able, to banish this idea from their mind."[42]

The McKinley administration had so successfully hidden the military reality that even the commission was unaware of the intensity of the fighting and that hundreds of thousands of Filipinos lay rotting in their early graves. When he sailed into Manila Bay on June 3, 1900, Commissioner Taft noted in surprise, "The populace that we expected to welcome us was not there."[43] After observing Big Bill's arrival, an American newspaperman wrote, "We ought to ship this splendid fellow back. It's a shame to spoil his illusion that folks the world over are just like the folks he knows out in Ohio."[44]

PERHAPS WILLIAM HOWARD TAFT'S most famous utterance is that the Filipinos were his "little brown brothers." Yet immediately upon his arrival, Commissioner Taft cabled opinions with little brotherly love: "The population of the islands is made up of a vast mass of ignorant, superstitious people, well-intentioned, lighthearted, temperate, somewhat cruel, domestic and fond of their families, and deeply wedded to the Catholic Church. . . . These people are the greatest liars it has been my fortune to meet, in many respects nothing but grown up children. . . . They need the training of fifty or a hundred years before they shall even realize what Anglo-Saxon liberty is."[45]

With the presidential election just months away, Taft's cables reinforced the president's claims: "The backbone of the revolt as a political war is broken."[46]

Yet while Taft wrote superbly optimistic reports, General MacArthur described a depressing quagmire where the U.S. Army controlled only 117 square miles out of a total of 116,000 square miles, a hostile country where Americans could not venture out alone, and a shell-shocked populace whose hatred for their oppressors grew each day.

MCKINLEY NEEDED TO PICK a running mate for the 1900 election and Teddy got the job. For two decades as a famous author, Roosevelt had urged America to follow the sun, and in the case of America's latest expansion, he had toed the administration's line. "The insurrection in the Philippine Islands has been overcome," he boldly declared to the New York State Republican Party in April of 1900.[47] Impressed with Rough Rider Teddy's magnetism and public relations, the Republican Party nominated the forty-one-year-old for vice president. The campaign's slogan was "The American flag has not been planted in foreign soil to acquire more territory but for humanity's sake."

On the campaign trail, Roosevelt demonstrated little knowledge regarding the Philippines but great skill in framing the debate in terms of the sun-following imperative. "It is unthinkable," he proclaimed, "that the United States would abandon the Philippines to

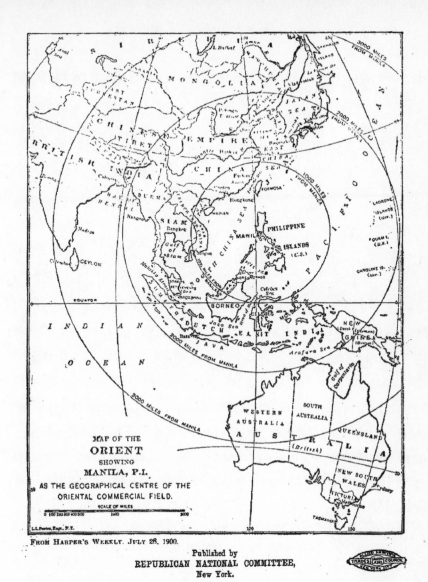

Map of the Orient showing Manila as the geographical center of the Oriental Commercial Field. Republican National Committee presidential campaign advertisement, published in Harper's Weekly, *July 28, 1900. In the 1900 presidential campaign, William McKinley and Theodore Roosevelt portrayed the expensive military acquisition of the Philippines as a good investment for America's trading future in Asia, a claim that rested upon the voting public's ignorance of Asian geography. Roosevelt later realized that taking the Philippines was a mistake.*

"The Administration's Promises Have Been Kept"
(Republican campaign poster, 1900). The McKinley-
Roosevelt ticket portrayed the U.S. military's invasions as
benevolent: "The American flag has not been planted in
foreign soil to acquire more territory but for humanity's
sake." This humanitarian justification for military action
still resonates with the American public.

their own tribes. To grant self-government...under
Aguinaldo would be like granting self-government to
an Apache reservation under some local chief."[48]

The Democratic presidential candidate, William
Jennings Bryan, tried to paint American activity in
the Philippines as imperialistic, but to no avail. On
election day, November 6, 1900, voters handed the

Republicans their biggest victory since Ulysses Grant's triumph in 1872. Upon hearing of the result, Robert Austill, a soldier in the Philippines, concluded: "The people of the United States want us to kill all the men, fuck all the women, and raise up a new race in these Islands."[49] With the contest now decided, McKinley presented a whopping request of $400 million for the War Department. Some wondered why, if the islands were, as McKinley and Roosevelt claimed, becoming peaceful, so much more money was necessary. In the course of hearings on the War Department appropriations, General MacArthur's pessimistic military assessment came to light. The *Springfield* (Massachusetts) *Republican* forlornly asked, "Why did all this truth telling become available only after the election?"[50]

ON MARCH 23, 1901, the U.S. Army captured President Aguinaldo in his mountain lair. After two months in General MacArthur's custody in Manila, the Philippines' founding father declared, "There has been enough blood, enough tears, enough desolation.... I cannot refuse to heed the voice of a people longing for peace ... by acknowledging and accepting the sovereignty of the United States throughout the Philippine Archipelago.... I believe that I am serving thee, my beloved country."[51] The *New York Times*— which had pilloried Aguinaldo as a lying thief—now described America's captive as "a warm, friendly, intelligent, trustworthy, and reasonable person—a man of honor with the best interest of his countrymen at heart."[52]

President McKinley made the most of the news with a victory lap across the country to "heal the sharp divisions" created by the conflict. "At Harvard University, he called upon Americans to forget their past differences over the Philippines and unite in peace to carry out the task assigned to them by Providence: to bring the benefits of American civilization to the Filipinos." The president's tour ended in San Francisco. As Stuart Creighton Miller writes in *Benevolent Assimilation:* "Climbing a nearby sand dune, McKinley gazed at the Pacific in the manner of the conquistador Balboa and claimed that vast ocean for American freedom."[53]

ON JULY 4, 1901, the United States pulled off one of the most remarkable shell games in colonial history. Textbooks recall that on that day the U.S. ended "military government" in the Philippines and initiated "civil government." In a flowery ceremony in Manila, a mostly White Christian audience applauded as General MacArthur—the outgoing military governor—handed over the reins to William Howard Taft, the incoming civil governor. Before this, the majority of the War Department's men, supplies, and money had flowed to the military in the Philippines, while few men and much less money went to the civil arm. After the ceremony, it would be exactly the same. Governor Taft's government was "a military regime under a civil name."[54]

Governor Taft lived in the Malacañang Palace, the elegant whitewashed home of the Spanish governors. His wife, Helen, wrote, "We are really so grand now that it will be hard to descend to common doings. We have five carriages and two smaller vehicles, and fourteen ponies, a steam launch and dear knows how many servants."[55]

Outside Manila, the U.S. military was still herding civilians into concentration camps, vultures grew too fat to fly as they feasted on the corpses of dead Filipinos, torture was routine, and the smoke of burnt towns hung in the air. In Manila, Governor Taft met with Americans and those Filipinos who would collaborate with his rule, setting a pattern that would bedevil future U.S. nation builders from Saigon to Kabul. Taft's correspondence reveals he had little respect for his collaborators—educated and wealthy Filipinos who spoke English and wore top hats—but for the fact that they scratched his back by telling him what he wanted to hear. In return, Taft funneled money and power to these elite few, cementing the oligarchy that still controls the Philippines.

The governor of the Philippines, William Howard Taft, on a carabao. Filipino farmers used carabaos as beasts of burden to plant and harvest rice, their main crop. U.S. military action reduced the population of carabaos by 90 percent, which contributed to mass hunger throughout the Philippines archipelago. (U.S. Army Military History Institute)

Democracies usually build themselves up from the bottom—the masses that vote— and thus have a wide foundation. Taft tried to build from the top down, with the few elite that he nursed in his governmental kindergarten. He approved the formation of the Federal Party (*Partido Federal*), which was made up of his rich collaborator buddies and heralded by the McKinley administration as a democratic step forward, but Taft prevented the formation of competing parties. He allowed only 3 percent of the upper crust to vote, and those elections were only for lower-level offices; Americans held all the top posts. Explained Taft, "The masses are ignorant, credulous, and childlike [so] the electoral franchise must be much limited, because the large majority will not, for a long time, be capable of intelligently exercising it."[56] The Yale-educated governor never considered that Filipinos could master higher education like Whites; instead they would be processed through schools modeled on Alabama's Tuskegee Institute, where good Blacks learned how to work with their hands and say "yes, sir" at every opportunity. Taft wrote privately, "In this system we must beware the possibility of overdoing the matter of higher education and unfitting the Filipino for practical work. We should heed the lesson taught us in our reconstruction period when we started to educate the negro."[57] Taft put out a call for American teachers to help build the nation and lavished U.S. taxpayer money on the building of schools. After just three months in the Philippines, one of the American teachers grew frustrated: "I find this work very monotonous, trying to teach these monkeys to talk."[58] A Radcliffe graduate looked on the bright side: "I suppose with patience and perseverance they will progress little by little until within two or three hundred years they may be quite Americanistic."[59]

ON SEPTEMBER 14, 1901, Governor Taft got a new boss, as Theodore Roosevelt was sworn in as president after McKinley succumbed to an assassin's bullet. Just two weeks into his presidency, Teddy was confronted with the nation's worst military crisis since Custer's Last Stand at Little Bighorn. U.S. soldiers had tried

General Jake Smith
General Smith ordered U.S. troops to kill all
Filipino men over the age of ten: "I want no prisoners.
I wish you to kill and burn, the more you kill and burn
the better you will please me."

to benevolently assimilate the residents of Balangiga, a tiny fishing village on the island of Samar. On September 28, the villagers revolted and killed fifty-one Americans. An untested president awoke to headlines proclaiming the "Balangiga Massacre."

General Jake Smith was put in charge of disciplining Balangiga and the island of Samar. Smith had built his career over decades as an Indian hunter out West. On October 23, the U.S. Navy ship *New York* bobbed off the west coast of Samar. Major Littleton Waller, a battle-hardened marine who had fought in Asia, the Middle East, and Cuba, came aboard to receive his orders from Smith for the subjugation of the island. Smith ordered Waller, "I want no prisoners. I wish you to kill and burn, the more you kill and burn the better you will please me. I want all persons killed who are capable of bearing arms in actual hostilities against the United States."[60]

WALLER: "I would like to know the limit of age to respect, sir."
SMITH: "Ten years."
WALLER: "Persons of ten years and older are those designated as being capable of bearing arms?"
SMITH: "Yes."[61]

Smith gave the entire population of Samar Island—two hundred fifty thousand people spread over five thousand square miles of inhospitable jungle—ten days to abandon their homes and enter U.S. concentration camps or be shot dead on sight. In field reports, Major Waller enumerated the many Filipino civilians he had slain. There were no American casualties.

Whispers about the orgies of violence in the Philippines gradually made their way back to the United States. Congressman Thomas Selby of Illinois asked, "What American ever dreamed that within four years...our generals in the Philippines would be following the notable and brutal methods of that Spanish dictator?"[62] Added Congressman Joseph Sibley of Pennsylvania, "This is not civilization. This is barbarism."[63] In his 1901 Message to Congress, Roosevelt explained that the problem was simply that the Filipinos had not followed the sun:

> The Philippines...are very rich tropical islands, inhabited by many varying tribes, representing widely different stages of progress towards civilization. Our earnest effort is to help these people upward along the stony and difficult path that leads to self-government. [Americans] are now successfully governing themselves, because for more than a thousand years they have been slowly fitting themselves, sometimes consciously, sometimes unconsciously, toward this end. What has taken us thirty generations

to achieve we cannot expect to see another race accomplish out of hand.[64]

Realizing that another brutal military campaign might create a backlash that could seriously damage his presidential chances in 1904, Roosevelt reined his army in, but it was too late: Congress was bestirred by soldiers' letters and press reports so at odds with the president's benevolent line.[65] A January 15, 1902, *New York Times* headline was the first sign of potential trouble: "Senior Massachusetts Senator Wants to Question Gov. Taft About the Administration of the Islands." Senator George Hoar, the article explained, "spoke at length regarding the unreliability of statements which have been made from time regarding the situation in the Philippines."[66] The Republican-controlled Senate was subsequently forced to hold hearings, an enormous threat to the accidental president, in office less than six months. Fortunately for Teddy, Senator Henry Cabot Lodge, the president's best friend in the Senate, installed himself as chairman of the Philippine Investigation Committee. Lodge then chose Senator Albert Beveridge—famous for his eloquent speeches supporting Aryan expansion—to run the hearings and tamp down the noise.[67] Relieved, Roosevelt wrote Lodge, "With the Philippines, I feel tolerably safe under your management."[68]

The U.S. Senate's hearings on the Philippines

began on January 31, 1902. First up to be grilled about the unreliability of the administration's statements was Governor Taft, who had authored so many of them. In almost two months of testimony, Taft hewed to the benevolent line, only once inadvertently straying to admit routine American torture: "That cruelties have been inflicted; that people have been shot when they ought not to have been; that there have been... individual instances of water cure, that torture which I believe involves pouring water down the throat so that the man swells and gets the impression that he is going to be suffocated and then tells what he knows... all these things are true."[69] A popular magazine called the slip "a most humiliating admission that should strike horror in the mind of every American."[70]

Back in the White House, Roosevelt's monocle must have fallen from his eye. Realizing his mistake, Taft repeated the benevolent intentions line: "It is my deliberate judgment that there never was a war conducted, whether against inferior races or not, in which there were more compassion and more restraint and more generosity, assuming that there was a war at all, than there have been in the Philippine Islands."[71]

Unfortunately for Roosevelt, Taft was followed by an avalanche of embarrassing testimony that belied Teddy's claims that the United States condemned torture and that it was done by only a few low-level, bad-apple soldiers. In one letter that surfaced, a soldier had written that he had personally waterboarded 160 Filipinos, of which 134 died.[72] Other evidence made it undeniably clear that atrocity warfare was condoned and encouraged from the top. Suddenly confronted by an indignant press, Roosevelt rushed a memo to Lodge claiming his intolerance of uncivilized warfare. Teddy listed forty-four officers and soldiers who had been tried "for violation of orders forbidding cruelty, looting and like crimes."[73] Thirty-nine of these cases had resulted in convictions, but Senate investigators discovered that those convictions had mysteriously been reduced to "reprimands" and that these convicted felons were now commanding soldiers in the Philippines. One by one, most of Roosevelt's assertions to the Senate were proven untrue.

However, the truth made little difference. Americans so embraced the benevolent intentions myth that they ultimately could not accept the idea that their humanitarian military was capable of atrocities. In the hearings, Senator Joseph Rawlins of Utah asked General Robert Hughes if exterminating whole Filipino families was "within the ordinary rule of civilized warfare?" Replied General Hughes, "These people are not civilized."[74]

There were a few who saw through this. Senator Edward Carmack of Tennessee, in a speech on the floor of the Senate, blamed the U.S. military's bloodlust on Roosevelt, who habitually demeaned Filipinos as "savages," "barbarians," "a savage people," "a wild and ignorant people," "Apaches," "Sioux," and "Chinese Boxers."[75] On May 22, 1902, Senator Hoar assailed the president: "You have devastated provinces. You have slain uncounted thousands of peoples you desire to benefit. You have established reconcentration camps. . . . You make the American flag in the eyes of a numerous people the emblem of sacrilege in Christian churches, and of the burning of human dwellings, and of the horror of the water torture."[76] The two-time presidential candidate William Jennings Bryan declared himself disgusted: "The country must purge itself of the guilt of the Republican crimes against the innocent people of the Philippines!"[77]

Roosevelt told Americans not to expect much from those who hadn't followed the sun: "The slowly-learned and difficult art of self-government, an art which our people have taught themselves by the labor of thousands of years, cannot be grasped in a day by a people only just emerging from conditions of life which our ancestors left behind them in the dim years before history dawned."[78]

On June 28, 1902, Senator Lodge ordered Senator Beveridge to adjourn the Philippines Investigation Committee. Beveridge did a cut-and-paste job on the final report, suppressing any slander contradicting American benevolence in the Philippines. On July 4, 1902, Roosevelt tried to make the Philippines conflict disappear into history with a wave of his hand, declaring that "the insurrection against the authority and sovereignty of the United States is now at an end, and peace has been established in all parts of the archipelago except in the country inhabited by the Moro tribes."[79] Roosevelt's claim did not impress the Filipino freedom fighters, who battled on. By then the war had cost American taxpayers more than six hundred million turn-of-the-twentieth-century dollars,[80] 4,234 Americans were dead, 2,818 had been wounded, and many soldiers who returned home would perish of related diseases and wounds.[81] Most American history books claim that U.S. forces killed about twenty thousand freedom fighters and two hundred thousand to three hundred thousand Filipino civilians; other sources estimate that the U.S. military sent one million to three million to their early graves. Even with a lowball number, this represents serious slaughter: three hundred thousand Filipinos killed in forty-one months. The United States later fought World War II over a period of fifty-six months with approximately four hundred thousand American deaths. So Adolf Hitler and Hideki Tojo, with their mechanized weaponry, killed about the same per month—seventy-two hundred—as American civilizers did in the Philippines.

And that was up until only 1902. At the moment President Roosevelt declared mission accomplished, his army was simultaneously launching a full-scale offensive near Zamboanga in the southern Philippines, where U.S. troops remain today.

FOR ALMOST TWENTY YEARS as a best-selling author, Roosevelt had euphemized the Aryan's westering as civilized. Now, as president, his actions in the Philippines were seen by many as barbaric. The cover of a popular magazine depicted a U.S. Army officer supervising two soldiers as they waterboarded a barefoot Filipino prisoner thrown on the ground with his hands and feet bound. One soldier points a pistol at the Pacific Negro's head and shoves a funnel into his mouth. Another soldier forces water into the victim from a U.S. Army pail. In the background a group of Europeans laugh mockingly, saying, "Those pious Yankees can't throw stones at us any more."

The *New York Evening Journal* featured an editorial cartoon of a U.S. Army firing squad executing blindfolded, barefoot Filipino boys. The caption read: "Kill Every One Over Ten—Criminals Because They Were Born Ten Years Before We Took the Philippines."

And one morning, Roosevelt awoke to an inconvenient story in the *Washington Post* about how the U.S. Army had systematically executed thirteen hundred Filipino prisoners of war in just one camp. The

Life *magazine, May 22, 1902. American soldiers waterboarding a Filipino. Europeans in the background gloat that Americans no longer hold the moral high ground: "Those pious Yankees can't throw stones at us any more."*

Americans had brought in a native priest to hear the condemned prisoners' last confessions. U.S. soldiers marched the Filipino prisoners to the killing ground and, after making them dig their own graves, shot them in the head. The body of the priest swung from a noose overhead.

Roosevelt, in a brilliant public-relations maneuver, decided to rescue his reputation as a civilized man by substituting pictures of American atrocities with imagery of Pacific Negroes being benevolently assimilated by Americans. Understanding that humanitarian U.S. voters still dimly perceived the distant islands, Roosevelt would recreate a mini Philippines in the middle of America.

The 1904 St. Louis World's Fair was the biggest international fair ever, double the size of the 1893 Chicago World's Fair. (The fair's official name was the Louisiana Purchase Exposition, celebrating President Jefferson's purchase of the Louisiana territory

"Kill Everyone Over Ten." A U.S. Army firing squad executing blindfolded, barefoot Filipino boys. "Criminals because they were born ten years before we took the Philippines." (New York Evening Journal, *May 5, 1902)*

one hundred years earlier.) Almost ninety million people would view exhibits from forty-five countries. The fair was so huge that the 1904 Olympics, the first held in the United States, was staged in just one small part of the grounds. With government funds, Roosevelt commandeered the largest part of the fairgrounds to create a make-believe Philippines, where fairgoers would see benevolent assimilation come to life.

Teddy cleverly distanced himself, declaring that he didn't want to exploit the event for political purposes in an election year. Instead, he managed his race fair through Taft, by now his assistant president. Roosevelt called his zoo-like freak show the Philippines reservation. In case anyone didn't grasp the significance of the name, it was located next to the Indian reservation.

Roosevelt had his minions search the wilds of the Philippines and ship twelve hundred Filipinos to St. Louis, where he presented them as creatures closer to monkeys than human beings. The Filipinos had no input into how their country was represented.

The fair's chief of the Department of Anthropology was William McGee, who was also president of both the National Geographic Society and the American Anthropological Association. The esteemed anthropologist proclaimed that "white and strong are synonymous terms.... It is the duty of the strong man

WORLD'S FAIR. ST. LOUIS. 1904.
CELEBRATING THE CENTENNIAL OF ACQUISITION OF LOUISIANA TERRITORY.
OPENS APRIL 30, 1904.   CLOSES DEC. 1, 1904.

*The 1904 St. Louis World's Fair was the largest
international fair to date, double the size of the 1893
Chicago World's Fair. The official name was the Louisiana
Purchase Exposition. President Roosevelt portrayed
President Jefferson's purchase of the Louisiana territory one
hundred years earlier as similar to the recent acquisition
of the Philippines. Roosevelt commandeered the largest
part of the fairgrounds for his Philippines reservation, an
election-year Potemkin Philippines, where fairgoers could see
benevolent assimilation come to life. (Library of Congress)*

*"Missing Link." President Roosevelt presented
Filipinos as monkey-men in need of American benevolence.
(Library of Congress)*

to subjugate lower nature, to extirpate the bad and
cultivate the good among living things...and in all
ways to enslave the world for the support of humanity and the increase of human intelligence."[82] To
reinforce the idea that the uncivilized Filipinos were
headed toward extinction, Smithsonian scientists

named one of them "Missing Link." Yet there was hope for some of Teddy's Others; as the fair program noted, "scientists have declared that with the proper training they are susceptible of a high stage of development, and, unlike the American Indian, will accept rather than defy the advance of American civilization."[83]

Smithsonian Institution scientists exhibited the Filipinos on a scale from barbaric to civilized. Loinclothed dog eaters in fenced-in enclosures squatted over a roasted canine. American observers quickly understood why such savages needed to be held in barbwired concentration camps. One fairgoer wrote his wife, "I went up to the Philippine village today and I saw the wild, barbaric Igorots, who eat dogs, and are so vicious that they are fenced in and guarded by a special constabulary.... They are the lowest type of civilization I ever saw and thirst for blood."[84] Farther on, visitors came upon the more reassuring scene of fresh-scrubbed Filipino children dressed in Western clothes reciting their lessons in a model American school. After that, fairgoers admired the most civilized of all: natty Filipino military men in shiny boots, smartly twirling their rifles, obeying the commands of a White American officer.

The official brochure of the Philippines reservation made the benevolent assimilation process clear. The cover featured a scary-looking savage in a bird-feather headdress. The back cover featured the end result of American uplift: a close-shaven Filipino standing ramrod-straight, dressed in his U.S. Army–supplied uniform.

As a keepsake souvenir to take home to the kids, fairgoers could purchase an "Album of Philippine Types." Each Filipino type was represented by two photographs that looked like mug shots, which they were—Roosevelt's scientists had searched Bilibid Prison in Manila to find "typical" Pacific Negroes.

Front and back covers of the official Philippines reservation pamphlet. The front features an uncivilized Filipino. The back features the end result of President Roosevelt's benevolent assimilation. (National Archives)

Fairgoers viewed more than one thousand photographs depicting a Philippines populated by robbers, murderers, and rapists.

The Philippines reservation was by far the most visited part of the St. Louis World's Fair, with approximately 18.5 million visitors.[85] (The population of the entire United States at that time was approximately 83 million.) Those who witnessed the display were some of America's leading citizens, teachers, politicians, and businessmen, who then spread Teddy's race message throughout the country's institutions and across its kitchen tables: like Jefferson's Louisiana Purchase, the Philippines would become Americanized and civilized. Two Christian missionaries wrote: "[The Philippines reservation] has strengthened our confidence in the wisdom of our government's general policy respecting the Philippines and their people, and in the hopeful outlook for the Filipinos under American jurisdiction."[86] When Princess Alice visited the Philippines reservation on May 27, the press had a field day contrasting her civilized White Christian bearing with the uncivilized dog eaters.

When a delegation of leading Filipinos had met with Secretary of State Root to discuss the possibility that the Philippines might become an American state, Root had responded, "Statehood for Filipinos would add another serious problem to the one we have already. The Negroes are a cancer in our body politic, a source of constant difficulty, and we wish to avoid developing another such problem."[87] In 1904, as Teddy's race fair reframed the debate about Pacific Negroes, candidate Roosevelt bragged to voters that the number of Negroes employed by the U.S. federal government, "which was insignificant even under McKinley, has been still further reduced."[88]

Roosevelt celebrated his victory by taking his family on a luxury train trip to St. Louis two weeks after the election. The Roosevelts strolled through the Philippines reservation to see the Filipino monkeymen in need of U.S. help and came upon the model

"Crack archers of the Negrito village," Philippines reservation pamphlet. President Roosevelt helped Americans imagine Filipinos as wild African-looking peoples in need of benevolent assimilation. (National Archives)

American school. Teddy watched with fascination as a classroom of smiling Filipino children welcomed him by singing, "My Country, 'Tis of Thee." Teddy flashed his famous smile and exclaimed, "It is wonderful. Such advancement and in so short a time!"[89]

Chapter 5

HAOLES

"Nineteenth-century democracy needs no more complete vindication for its existence than the fact that it has kept for the white race the best portions of the new world's surface."[1]
—Theodore Roosevelt, 1897

Helen "Nellie" Taft did not accompany her husband on his 1905 Pacific cruise. Rather than sweat through another South Pacific summer, she took the children to England. At an English train station, Helen tried to get the stationmaster to hold a train long enough to load her luggage. "I am Mrs. William Howard Taft of Washington," she told the stationmaster. "My husband is the Secretary of War of the United States." The man looked at her blankly. Helen tried again: "You must have heard of him. He's traveling now with Miss Alice Roosevelt." The stationmaster sprang to attention, held the train, and accompanied Helen, her children, and her luggage aboard.[2]

Aboard the Manchuria, *summer of 1905. Secretary of War William Howard Taft (center), Alice Roosevelt (below Taft), and Congressman Nick Longworth (to Alice's left). (Collection of the New-York Historical Society)*

On the second night out at sea the Americans threw a party. To create a dance-floor setting, they partitioned off a section of the ship with hanging flags and, for traction, sprinkled cornmeal on the deck. The ship's captain had a Victor Talking Machine (a primitive phonograph) that provided the music. A correspondent on board reported, "Secretary Taft was nearly always on the floor and the surprise was not that he danced beautifully but that he could dance at all. But he can, fat as he is."[3] Alice later wrote, "I do not think that I have ever known any one with the equanimity, amiability, and kindliness of Mr. Taft. During all that summer, I never once saw him really cross or upset. He was always beaming, genial, and friendly, through all his official duties, and the task of keeping harmony among his varied and somewhat temperamental army of trippers."[4] Added a St. Louis newspaperman aboard the *Manchuria,* "Secretary Taft either designedly, or from natural good nature, has put the entire party at ease. He is an early riser and is not in a hurry to retire at night. He is at home on the promenade deck, in the smoking room, at the dinner table, or anywhere else. His good nature seems to become him."[5]

Such was invariably the take on Taft: a reliable Mr. Nice Guy with a beaming smile and hearty chuckle. As the author Stephen Hess notes:

If one were to plot Taft's career on a graph, the line would rise sharply and steeply, without a single dip, until it marked the summit of American political life. He became assistant prosecutor of Hamilton County, Ohio, at the age of twenty-three. Collector of Internal Revenue in Cincinnati two years later, judge of the state superior court at twenty-nine. Solicitor General of the United States at thirty-two, a federal circuit-court judge at thirty-four, first U.S. Civil Governor of the Philippines at forty-two, Secretary of War in the Cabinet of Theodore Roosevelt at forty-six.... Each job seemed to be a logical outgrowth of the one before; each new opportunity seemed only to await the successful conclusion of the preceding episode.[6]

As secretary of war, Taft oversaw the testosterone heart of the Roosevelt presidency. He controlled an enormous budget and commanded a fast-growing military machine. Millions of people were subjects of the War Department, from Cuba through the Isthmus of Panama and out to Guam, Wake Island, and the Philippines.

Yet Taft's War Department was a dysfunctional place, with the boss frequently absent and subordinates constantly competing for power. Serving as Teddy's troubleshooter, dispatched to negotiate and smooth over political rough patches, Taft was absent from Washington more than any other cabinet member during his four-year tenure. At one point the War Department auditor received this written complaint: "As a taxpayer and citizen I beg to ask the following question: How many days, or if not days, hours, has Secretary of War William Taft spent at his desk in Washington?"[7]

Roosevelt managed the military himself, so Taft was not severely tested. In fact, the former judge knew little about military matters and admitted, "I have had so much outside work to do that I was entirely willing to turn the control all over to the chief of staff."[8]

As Judith Anderson writes in *William Howard Taft: an Intimate History*, "Roosevelt initiated and Taft assisted. . . . Taft, eager for affection and approval, agreed with Roosevelt even when it meant revising his own earlier views."[9] The Taft biographer Henry Pringle observed, "One searches in vain for a major issue on which Taft took a stand, even in private, against Roosevelt."[10] Not surprisingly, Roosevelt was fond of his likeable yes-man: "You know, I think Taft has the most lovable personality I have ever come in contact with. I almost envy a man possessing a personality like Taft's. One loves him at first sight."[11]

WHEN THE NEWLY APPOINTED secretary of war, Taft, was asked by an interviewer to explain his rapid ascent, he replied: "I got my political pull, first, through father's prominence."[12]

Alphonso Taft was born in Vermont in 1810. He cofounded Yale's secretive Skull and Bones society, and he graduated from Yale College at the age of twenty-three in 1833. In 1839, at the age of twenty-nine, Alphonso decided that he would make his mark in the frontier town of Cincinnati. Tafts have dominated Ohio politics since.

Alphonso was "Judge Taft" to the locals as he served on the superior court of Cincinnati and became the first president of the Cincinnati Bar Association. He was later appointed secretary of war by President Grant in March 1876, and three months later attorney general of the United States. He was made ambassador to Austria-Hungary in 1882 and ambassador to Imperial Russia from 1884 to 1885.

William Howard Taft was born in Cincinnati in 1857 in a house that is now part of the William Howard Taft National Historic Site. While Alphonso was the guiding patriarch, the Taft boys were products of a proud, strict, domineering mother. Louisa Taft's first child, Sammie, died in that house of whooping cough soon after his first birthday. Bill was Louisa's second child and she showered more attention on him than her other children. She also pressured him more to succeed. Instead of gentle hugs, Louisa issued sharp orders. A recent Taft biographer writes, "Taft never developed much confidence in himself or his abilities. He had been taught in early childhood that no matter how hard he strove, he would not succeed fully, that he had never done enough to merit full acceptance and approval."[13]

He was not the only one to suffer: Louisa Taft's pressure on Bill's half brother Peter was particularly intense. At first, he responded: Peter delivered the valedictory address to his high school class, and at Yale he scored the highest grades recorded up to that time. But after graduation he suffered a nervous collapse and died in a sanatorium.

From childhood through Yale to various appointive offices and then on to the presidency, Big Bill's weight increased in proportion to his stressors. Diet and exercise could never overcome his inner disharmony, and he ate compulsively from frustration and to better fill the roles into which he was pushed.

Taft's parents, hoping to model his career on his father's, declared that Bill would become a Cincinnati lawyer. Yet even after establishing his own Cincinnati practice, Taft still received written rebukes from his father: "I do not think you have accomplished as much this past year as you ought with your opportunities. Our anxiety for your success is very great and I know that there is but one way to attain it, & that is by self-denial and enthusiastic hard work."[14] And his taskmaster mother never loosened the reins. Up until her death, on the eve of his nomination as a candidate for president, Louisa followed each step of his career and often gave her son highly critical advice.

Taft set his sights early on a girl named Helen. Helen "Nellie" Herron's father, John, had been law partners with President Rutherford Hayes. In 1877, when she was seventeen years old, she spent several exhilarating weeks in Washington, living in the Executive Mansion with the president's family. Nellie wrote of "brilliant parties and meeting all manner of charming people," and she later admitted "that she fantasized becoming First Lady herself," vowing to marry a man "destined to be president of the United States."[15]

For his part, Big Bill saw Nellie as "his 'senior partner' for life [and] got what he felt he most needed in his life—a whip that would drive him to achieve."[16] Bill once wrote her, "I need you to scold me."[17]

Bill got the whip, but not much love. Nellie never did show as much interest in him as he did in her. For her, it was a union of ambition, not affection.

TAFT HAD BEEN ENJOYING his life in Cincinnati as a federal judge when, in 1890, President Benjamin Harrison nominated him to become solicitor general, the attorney who represents the federal government before the Supreme Court. Bill found the prospect

Mrs. William Howard Taft (Helen "Nellie" Herron Taft).
From childhood she yearned to be the wife of a president.
She willed her husband into the presidency but soon
suffered a stroke. (Library of Congress)

"rather overwhelming," but Nellie saw her husband's
contented Cincinnati life as "an awful groove" and
the opportunity to live in Washington as a welcome
"interruption...in our peaceful existence." Big Bill
hesitated, Nellie pushed, and Nellie won, proclaiming herself "very glad because it gave Mr. Taft an
opportunity for exactly the kind of work I wished
him to do."[18]

In 1891, Harrison nominated Taft to become a

judge of the Sixth Federal Circuit Court of Appeals. This meant a return to his beloved Cincinnati. Nellie feared the appointment would divert her from her goal of being a president's wife and warned her husband about accepting the offer. But because of the prestige of this presidential appointment, Taft—for once—got his way.

Campaigning in Ohio in 1899, President McKinley remarked to a local judge, "I am in need of a man who is strong, tactful, and honest, for an executive in the Philippines."[19] Days later Taft opened a telegram from the president that read, "I would like to see you in Washington on important business within the next few days."[20]

McKinley now offered Taft an appointment as commissioner to the Philippines, but Taft demurred. "Why I am not the man you want," he told the president. "To begin with, I have never approved of keeping the Philippines." McKinley was not put off by his answer, explaining, "We have got them and in dealing with them I think I can trust the man who didn't want them better than I can the man who did." McKinley added that if he accepted posting to the Philippines, the president would appoint Taft to the Supreme Court if any opportunity arose.[21]

Taft now faced a dilemma. To please the president by going to the Philippines, he might displease Nellie, who yearned for Washington. "I dreaded meeting

Nellie," Taft later wrote. "She met me at the door and her first question was, 'Well, are we going to Washington?'"[22] But when Big Bill explained McKinley's offer, Nellie realized that this executive-branch assignment could put her back on the road to becoming a First Lady, and she enthusiastically recommended that he accept.

Big Bill was sworn in as governor of the Philippines on the Fourth of July, 1901. Nellie—married to the ruler of an island nation—was thus a First Lady, famed throughout the territory, living on a vast estate and attended to by innumerable servants. Later that year, Roosevelt succeeded the assassinated McKinley. Teddy offered Taft several nominations to the Supreme Court, but he turned them down despite being no fan of the hot and humid climate he now found himself in, as Nellie had no inclination to leave the islands and regress to the life of a justice's wife.

On March 27, 1903, an offer came from Washington that suited Nellie's tastes and ambitions: Teddy offered Taft the powerful cabinet post of secretary of war. Big Bill took stock of his personal skills and wrote Nellie of his concern that he was not qualified: "I do not know how much executive ability I have and I very much doubt my having a great deal."[23] But Nellie felt that a cabinet post was "in line with...the kind of career I wanted for him and expected him to have," and she got her way.[24] Taft wrote, "It seems strange that with an effort to keep out of politics and with my real dislike for it, I should thus be pitched into the middle of it."[25]

EARLY ON THE MORNING of July 14, 1905, the *Manchuria* steamed into Honolulu harbor. Recalled Alice:

> I was wakened by the plaintive singing voices and musical instruments of the natives who had come out to meet the steamer. It was before Hawaiian tunes and ukuleles had become as hackneyed as they now are. I had never heard anything like it before.... My eyes were open and my head was out of the porthole simultaneously, to see the lovely mass of the island of Oahu lying off-side in the early dawn light, mountains and valleys in cloudy green down to the line of the white beach. The entire population seemed to be on the wharf to meet us and garland us with leis of heavy, perfumed flowers, gardenias and ginger blossoms.[26]

Marines from the USS *Iroquois* fired a seventeen-gun salute, accompanied by "whistles all over the city, on factories, locomotives, and steamers."[27] When Alice appeared on deck, to more cheers, Taft placed a lei about her neck, formally welcoming her to Hawaii.[28]

At 7:40 a.m., Alice and Big Bill led the passengers down the gangplank, where the acting governor and the welcoming committee greeted them. Taft and the governor got into the lead horse carriage, with Alice and Nick behind. A dozen carriages moved through crowds held back by U.S. Army troops and local police. A Honolulu newspaper reported, "The outer wharf was crowded with people, who had braved the early morning hours just to catch a glimpse of the great war secretary and the president's daughter. It must be confessed that Miss Alice Roosevelt was really the cynosure of all eyes. 'There she is,' was the general murmur as the cavalcade moved on."[29]

The party drove out of Honolulu on a country road cut through the Nuʻuanu Valley's moist green mountain walls. They rode past hibiscus flowers, mango trees hanging low with fruit, stands of gleaming green bamboo, white gardenia flowers, and waterfalls leaping off the mountainsides. They continued until they reached the magnificent Pali lookout.

A local reporter recalled the scene: "A series of 'Ohs!' and 'How wonderful!' and 'Would you believe it!' were heard from all sides. Miss Roosevelt strode over to the rail which marked the beginning of the 1000 foot precipice and gazed in silence over the great expanse of landscape which has been, and was so pronounced yesterday as one of the most beautiful views in the world."[30]

The party returned to Honolulu, where they boarded a train to tour a sugar plantation—the heart of the modern Hawaiian economy. "On the way through the cane [the train] went slowly in order that the guests might see the steam plows at work and the process of planting, irrigating and cutting cane."[31] Japanese laborers served lemonade and cookies and a Hawaiian troupe performed what Alice called "a rather expurgated Hula."[32] Bare midriffs were considered too risqué, so the hula dancers were asked to cover up "in American costume."[33]

By 1:00 p.m. the group was back in Honolulu for a luncheon for 225 guests at a downtown hotel. Alice said she was "nearly suffocated" in thirty to forty leis "reaching from my neck to almost my knees—and for politeness sake I couldn't take them off."[34]

Taft began his luncheon speech in jovial spirits: "The welcome that we have received today was no surprise, for the reputation of these islands for hospitality is known everywhere. We knew that even before you were annexed."[35] The appreciative audience laughed heartily.

Just seven years earlier the U.S. annexation had divested native Hawaiians of their kingdom. To the white sugar barons this was a source of amusement; to the native Hawaiians, a tragedy. Hawaii was now the property of pink-skinned Christians, whom the real Hawaiians called "Haoles." But Big Bill didn't have to worry about any party poopers at this luncheon: there were no native Hawaiians present. No dark frowning faces of disenfranchised Others would spoil the good time.

THE HAWAIIANS' WORLD BEGAN its downward slide when the first White Christian Haole—Captain James Cook—"discovered" the islands in 1778.

Observers on Cook's ships wrote that Hawaiians were "above the middle size, strong and well made and of a dark copper colour...upon the whole a fine handsome sett of People [whose] abundant stock of Children promised...a plentiful supply for the next Generation."[36] Microbiologists now know that before contact with Whites, "the Hawaiians were an exceptionally well nourished, strong and vigorous people...who were afflicted with no important infectious diseases [and that] it is now almost certain that Hawaiians in 1778 had life expectancies greater than their European contemporaries."[37] Cook and his crew were the first westerners to behold healthy Hawaiians—and they would be the last. Along with great White civilization, Cook brought the Great White Plague (tuberculosis) to Hawaii. Cook's sailors had been recruited from the lowest depths of

English society, then beset by rampant diseases. Back in England, "more than three out of four deaths were being caused by typhus, typhoid fever, measles, smallpox, bronchitis, whooping cough, tuberculosis and 'convulsions.'"[38] Indeed, when Cook shoved off from Tahiti toward Hawaii, more than half of his crew were too sick from venereal disease to work. Upon reaching Hawaii, Cook commandeered a sacred Hawaiian house of worship and converted it into a hospital, where the locals cared for the sick sailors.

Eventually, Captain Cook sailed away. Seven years passed. In 1786, the French frigate *LaBoussole* reached Hawaii. The ship's surgeon observed Hawaiians

covered with buboes, and scars which result from their suppurating, warts, spreading ulcers with caries of the bones, nodes, exostoses, fistula, tumors of the lachrymal and salival ducts, scrofulous swellings, inveterate opthalmiae, ichorous ulcerations of the tunica conjuctiva, atrophy of the eyes, blindness, inflamed prurient herpetic eruptions, indolent swellings of the extremities, and among children, scald head, or a malignant tinea, from which exudes a fetid and acrid matter....The greater part of these unhappy victims of sensuality, when arrived at the age of nine or ten, were feeble and languid, exhausted by marasmus, and affected with the rickets.[39]

Soon New England whalers and merchants visited the islands. Then American missionaries sailed to save the pagan Hawaiians. Missionary activity assumes the inferiority of its subject; for the missionary to bring civilization and light, there must be uncivilized darkness. As one American missionary wrote, the Hawaiians were "exceedingly ignorant; stupid to all that was lovely, grand and awful in the work of God; low, naked, filthy, vile and sensual; covered with every abomination, stained with blood and black with crime."[40] The missionaries soon forbade the Hawaiians' easy ways: the hula was too sensual; surfboarding—with the half-nude dark-skinned natives exposing themselves as they gracefully rode the waves—was judged indecent. A white sailor who revisited Honolulu in 1825 wrote, "The streets, formerly so full of animation, are now deserted. Games of all kinds, even the most innocent, are prohibited. Singing is a punishable offense, and the consummate profligacy of attempting to dance would certainly find no mercy."[41]

David Stannard of the University of Hawai'i's Social Science Research Institute estimates that the population of Hawaii in Captain Cook's time was probably more than a million people. Just two generations later, in 1832, the first missionary census found only one hundred thirty thousand survivors. Missionaries observed an astonishing demographic phenomenon: annual deaths were at least double the number of births, and few Hawaiian children survived their first years of life. But to the American missionaries—who came from a country in the midst of cleansing its own natives—the decline of a non-White race was thought to be God's will. One missionary wrote that Hawaiian deaths were like "the amputation of diseased members of the body."[42] Added one popular American magazine, "the experience of the Polynesians and of the American Indians has proved that the aboriginal races, under the present philanthropic system of Christianization, [were unable to] change their habits of life, as required by present Christian systems."[43] Missionaries took comfort in the fact that the doomed at least had had the good fortune of Christian conversion. Back in the United States, Mark Twain joked caustically that Hawaiians suffered from "various complicated diseases, and education, and civilization," and Twain "proposed to send a few more missionaries to finish them."[44]

Like so many colonial adventures, saving souls was ultimately a secondary consideration. Imperialism's great financial success story was the production of sugar from tropical sugarcane fields. From Jamaica to Jakarta, slaves had toiled under imperialism's lash to produce this profitable commodity. Haole settlers took note of Hawaii's fertile soil, constant sunshine, plentiful rain, and easy access to good ports and saw before them a sugar producer's dream. Large-scale sugar production required high-level financial and government contacts back in the United States. It would be the educated American missionaries who offered Hawaii to Washington and Wall Street.

In Hawaii there is a well-known saying that the missionaries "came to do good and stayed to do well." One who did just that was Reverend Amos Cooke. Born in Danbury, Connecticut, and educated at Yale, Reverend Cooke had followed the sun to Hawaii in 1837, where he ran the Royal School to educate the future kings and queens of Hawaii. In 1843, Cooke agreed to sit on the Hawaiian king's special board as an "unofficial adviser." This was ethically dubious because the American Board of Missionaries had rules against their missionaries' serving in government positions. In addition, the king had been Cooke's pupil.

Cooke's first step was getting title to valuable Hawaiian land. As Stephen Kinzer writes in *Overthrow,* "Buying it was complicated, since native Hawaiians had little notion of private property or cash exchange. They had great difficulty understanding how a transaction—or anything else, for that matter—could deprive them of land."[45]

Ever persistent, Cooke helped convince King Kamehameha III to institute a revolutionary land reform: whoever had money could buy as much land as he wanted. Soon the terms *missionary* and *planter* became synonymous.

In 1851, Cooke—along with fellow missionary Samuel Castle—founded the Castle & Cooke company. It quickly grew to become the third-largest company in Hawaii and went on to become one of Hawaii's biggest landowners, one of the world's largest sugar producers, and one of the infamous "Big Five" companies that controlled the Hawaiian government with an iron fist throughout much of the twentieth century.

Sugar plantations required many workers, and the Hawaiians with their casual ways were considered by the Whites to be poor candidates for hard labor. If Hawaii had been settled in the eighteenth rather than the nineteenth century, slaves could have been imported. But with changing times, the Whites brought in "contract laborers" from China and Japan who were bound to serve at fixed wages for three to five years.

The importation of Asian laborers created a demographic challenge. On the American mainland, it was possible to kill Indians, enslave Blacks, and still speak of "democracy" and "spreading freedom" because the majority (understood as White males, women being subordinate) were free. Hawaii was tiny, and relatively few white Haoles had moved there. The small community that came to control the land (about five thousand White Haoles) were soon outnumbered up to twenty times by the combined populations of the native Hawaiians and imported Chinese and Japanese. Therefore, Haoles opposed democracy for Hawaii, realizing that suffrage—even just male suffrage—would produce a government of non-Whites.

THE NAVY DEPARTMENT described Hawaii as the "crossroad of the Pacific," a link to the commerce of Asia: "With a supply of coal well guarded at Pearl Harbor, our war-ships and merchantmen can cross the Pacific at maximum speed, or concentrate at distant points at high speed."[46] The Reciprocity Treaty of 1875—forced down the throats of native Hawaiians—eliminated tariffs on Hawaiian sugar and included a provision that granted the United States exclusive rights to maintain military bases in Hawaii.

When the treaty was formally approved, Hawaiians took to the streets in protest, just as they had done when the agreement had first been announced; it had taken 220 armed soldiers and eight days to restore order. Now the protests again turned violent and the king requested American protection. The United States provided 150 marines and the protestors were swatted away.

Sugar exports soared over the next decades, and with great wealth came increased economic power and political influence. A Haole observed, "Nearly all important government positions are held by Americans, and the islands are really an American colony."[47]

Imbued with the belief that only the White man could efficiently rule, the Haoles sought to overthrow the monarchy as a form of Aryan patriotism. Referring to themselves as a "morally righteous group," the white Haoles founded the Reform Party in 1887;[48] native Hawaiians quickly dubbed it the "Missionary Party." For muscle, the Missionary Party established an all-white vigilante organization, the Honolulu Rifles.

On July 6, 1887, the Honolulu Rifles seized Iolani Palace and handed King Kalakaua a new constitution. His palace ringed by White soldiers with fixed bayonets, King Kalakaua signed the document that has been known ever since by many Hawaiians as the "Bayonet Constitution," which reduced him to a mere figurehead with little power.

The Bayonet Constitution rejiggered voting rights, with new property and income requirements. The result was a total exclusion of Asians as voters and the granting "to whites three-fourths of the vote... and one-fourth to the native."[49] Additionally, the State Department ruled that American citizens could take an oath to support the new Hawaiian Constitution, vote in local elections, and hold office without losing their American citizenship. Nowhere else in the world could American citizens pledge allegiance to and vote in another country while still retaining their U.S. citizenship. This put the real Hawaiians in an impossible situation. Their king was powerless and their government was controlled by white Haoles who—whenever it suited them—called themselves both Hawaiians and Americans.

BENJAMIN HARRISON WAS ELECTED president in the same year that the Missionary Party gained control of the Hawaiian government. A famous Indian slayer, Harrison ruled at the time Buffalo Bill and Ranchman Teddy were celebrating America's race wars. The first president to travel across the country entirely over the transcontinental railroad, Harrison believed that the Pacific beckoned as America's next step west.

Harrison appointed James Blaine, who for years had promoted the seizure of Hawaii, as his secretary of state. Blaine wrote Harrison, "I think there are only three places that are of value enough to be taken, that are not continental. One is Hawaii and the others are Cuba and Porto [*sic*] Rico. Cuba and Porto [*sic*] Rico are not now imminent and will not be for a generation. Hawaii may come up for decision at any unexpected hour and I hope we shall be prepared to decide it in the affirmative."[50]

Queen Lili'uokalani, the last ruler of the Hawaiian Kingdom, overthrown by the United States Marine Corps. (Stringer/Hulton Archive/Getty Images)

The American Aryan's golden hour in the Pacific arrived courtesy of the new monarch, Queen Lili'uokalani, who ascended to the throne in 1891 upon the death of King Kalakaua. Troubled by the usurpation of Hawaiian rights, she was determined to restore dignity to the Kingdom of Hawaii and power to her people. In the New York magazine *Judge,* a cartoon portrayed her as a demented Indian squaw, mouth agape, her lips fat, her feet rough and shoeless, around her neck a cannibal's bone necklace. A crooked crown on her head made Queen Lili'uokalani look stupid and sloppy, the Indian feathers sprouting from her hair another clue to her barbarity.

In early 1893, the queen, exercising her traditional rights as a Hawaiian monarch, decided to promulgate a new constitution that would abolish the humiliating Bayonet Constitution and restore power to the majority Hawaiians. On Saturday morning, January 14, 1893, Queen Lili'uokalani informed her cabinet of her plan. Word leaked immediately. The Missionary Party founder, Lorrin Thurston, quickly convened a meeting downtown of fellow party members to form a thirteen-member all-Haole "Committee of Safety." Thurston proposed the first order of business: annexation to the United States.

Over the next two days, Thurston and the Committee of Safety hatched their scheme with the U.S. minister to Hawaii, John Stevens, an old friend of Secretary of State Blaine. Missionary Party members complained to Stevens that they didn't have enough military force to topple the government and they feared arrest. Stevens promised them U.S. Marines then aboard the USS *Boston* anchored in Honolulu harbor. This was a historical first: an American minister accredited to a sovereign nation conspiring in its overthrow.

On Monday, two days after the queen had declared her intention regarding a new constitution, she posted a more modest official proclamation throughout Honolulu. It was a pledge from the queen that she would seek to change the constitution "only

John Stevens, U.S. minister to Hawaii. Stevens gave the order for the coup d'état in the Hawaiian Kingdom. Afterward he wrote the secretary of state: "The Hawaiian pear is now fully ripe, and this is the golden hour for the United States to pluck it." (Library of Congress)

by methods provided in the constitution itself."[51] But while Lili'uokalani had moderated, the colonizers had no intention of responding in kind. The Committee of Safety drafted an appeal to Stevens in which they noted the "general alarm and terror.... The public safety is menaced and lives and property are in peril.... We are unable to protect ourselves without aid, and therefore pray for the protection of the United States forces."[52] After signing this "general alarm and terror" document, the Committee of Safety adjourned for the day and its members ambled off through Honolulu's quiet streets for lunch.

Minister Stevens boarded the USS *Boston* at 3:00 p.m. and handed this written request to her captain:

UNITED STATES LEGATION
HONOLULU, JANUARY 16, 1893

Sir: In view of existing critical circumstances in Honolulu, indicating an inadequate legal force, I request you to land Marines and Sailors from the ship under your command for the protection of the United States Legation, and the United States Consulate and to secure the safety of American life and property.
Very truly yours,
John L. Stevens[53]

One hour later, 162 heavily armed United States Marines from the USS *Boston* marched through Honolulu's peaceful streets. The only large group of Hawaiians to be found were those enjoying the weekly Monday night Royal Hawaiian Band concert under the gazebo of the Hawaiian Hotel. The marines, making no effort to pretend that they had landed "to secure the safety of American life and property," surrounded the royal palace and forced out Queen Lili'uokalani. As the British minister to Hawaii, William Cornwall, observed, "If the troops were landed solely for the protection of American property, the placing of them so far away from the... property of Americans and so very close to the property of the Hawaiian Government was remarkable and suggestive."[54]

Sanford Dole. Son of missionaries and cousin of the founder of the Hawaiian Pineapple Company (now the Dole Pineapple Company), Sanford Dole served as president of the Hawaiian Republic after the American coup d'état of the Hawaiian Kingdom. (Hawaii State Archives)

The next day, representing the United States, Stevens recognized the Hawaiian provisional government. The new president of Hawaii was Sanford Dole, a son of missionaries, a white and blue-eyed Haole.

There were at long last no dark-skinned Hawaiians in the new Hawaiian government. Stevens raised the American flag in Honolulu and declared Hawaii an American protectorate. Then, in a letter to the secretary of state, he suggested, "The Hawaiian pear is now fully ripe, and this is the golden hour for the United States to pluck it."[55] Meanwhile, the new government began enforcing its regime by putting into practice a series of repressive policies to silence its critics.

President Dole dispatched five Missionary Party members to Washington to make a deal. President Harrison proclaimed, "The overthrow of the monarchy was not in any way promoted by this Government... and the change of government in the Hawaiian Islands... was entirely unexpected so far as the United States was concerned."[56] Added the new secretary of state, John Foster: "At the time the provisional government took possession of the Government buildings no troops or officers of the United States were present or took any part whatever in the proceedings."[57]

After seven meetings over a short ten days, Secretary of State Foster and the White "Hawaiians" signed the annexation treaty on February 14, 1893, less than a month after the U.S. Marines had captured Iolani Palace. The next day Harrison submitted the treaty to the Senate for ratification.

The president hoped the senators would approve Hawaii's annexation before the truth came out, but time was against him: Harrison had lost the election of 1892 and had less than a month before he would leave office.[58] Things started well. The Senate Foreign Relations Committee hastily approved the annexation treaty and sent it to the full Senate on February 17. But on that day a visitor appeared in Washington with a different story than what the president had told. He was Paul Neumann, Queen Lili'uokalani's personal attorney and envoy.

Neumann made the case that the queen had been unfairly dethroned and that Minister Stevens had improperly landed U.S. troops and had illegally proclaimed a United States protectorate over the islands. Neumann told senators and the press that native Hawaiians had not been consulted and would not favor a treaty. Suddenly senators went on record calling the American actions in Hawaii "an outrage" and "an act of war," and they "ridiculed annexation as a Hawaiian sugar planters' scheme to obtain American bounty."[59]

Neumann delivered a letter from Queen Lili'uokalani as head of government to president-elect

Grover Cleveland, requesting that the United States oust the usurpers and restore Hawaii's independence.

Cleveland smelled a rat. On March 8, Cleveland withdrew U.S. support for the Hawaiian annexation treaty. Two days later, he dispatched the former congressman James Blount of Georgia to Hawaii on a presidential investigation. Blount sailed immediately and lowered the American flag in Honolulu on April 1, which ended Hawaii's status as a U.S. protectorate.

Many Americans opposed annexing Hawaii—but not for reasons of sympathy. Some claimed that "the framers of the Constitution intended the Republic's territorial expansion to be restricted to contiguous land which would be settled by Americans of Anglo-Saxon lineage."[60] *Harper's Weekly* wrote, "History had shown that Anglo-Saxon democratic institutions could not survive in tropical colonies."[61]

On December 18, 1893, Cleveland sent a scathing report to Congress:

> There is as little basis for the pretense that forces were landed for the security of American life and property. When these armed men were landed, the city of Honolulu was in its customary orderly and peaceful condition. There was no symptom or disturbance in any quarter. Men, women, and children were about the streets as usual, and nothing varied the ordinary routine

or disturbed the ordinary tranquility, except the landing of the *Boston*'s marines, and their march through the town.[62]

...

The Provisional Government has not assumed a republic or other constitutional form, but has remained a mere executive council or oligarchy, set up without the assent of the people. Indeed, the representatives of that government assert that the people of Hawaii are unfit for popular government and frankly avow that they can be best ruled by arbitrary or despotic power.[63]

One month after President Cleveland's criticism, President Dole's provisional government celebrated its one-year anniversary. Missionary Party leaders realized that if Cleveland hadn't acted to restore the queen after twelve months, Hawaii was safely within their White hands.

A few days later, on February 7, 1894, the U.S. House of Representatives voted 177 to 78, with 96 abstentions, to condemn Minister Stevens. But nothing was done about the situation on the ground in Hawaii. And Dole was working hard to make sure that the Aryan would now dominate, consulting Teddy's law school mentor, the Columbia professor John Burgess, regarding a new constitution. In a March 31, 1894, letter to Burgess, Dole explained that Hawaii had "many natives...comparatively ignorant of the principles of government [and a] menace to good government." Burgess responded:

> If I understand your situation, it is as follows: You have a population of nearly 100,000 persons, of whom about 5,000 are Teutons, i.e., Americans, English, Germans, and Scandinavians, about 9,000 are Portuguese, about 30,000 are Chinese and Japanese, about 8,000 are native born of foreign parents, and the rest are natives.
>
> With this situation, I understand your problem to be the construction of a constitution which will place the government in the hands of the Teutons, and preserve it there.[64]

Dole thanked the professor: "Your letters showed a clear knowledge of our peculiar political circumstances."[65]

In fact, Hawaii would remain as Cleveland had described it: an oligarchy "set up without the assent of the people." But the president had been discreet about such imperial efforts—too discreet for some. Theodore Roosevelt was outraged that Cleveland had not proudly followed the sun to Hawaii. Indeed, it was this failure that sparked Roosevelt's interest in Pacific expansion. In 1896, Teddy fumed in the

Century Magazine: "We should annex Hawaii immediately. It was a crime against the United States, it
was a crime against white civilization, not to annex it
two years and a half ago. The delay did damage that
is perhaps irreparable; for it meant that at the critical
period of the islands' growth the influx of population
consisted, not of white Americans, but of low caste
laborers from the yellow races."[66]

FROM BOYHOOD TO MIDDLE age, William McKinley—a devout Methodist—had witnessed Christianity's conquest of the North American continent.
Once president, he concerned himself with the souls
of Pacific pagans. McKinley's Republican Party had
run on the platform that "the Hawaiian Islands should
be controlled by the United States and no foreign
power should be permitted to interfere with them."[67]
Once in office, McKinley resubmitted the Hawaiian annexation treaty to the U.S. Senate. Because the
United States had for so long dominated Hawaii, the
president said, "Annexation is not a change. It is a
consummation."[68]

Senator David Turpie of Indiana believed that
native Hawaiians should be heard, arguing, "There
is a native population in the islands of about 40,000.
They are not illiterate; they are not ignorant. A very
large majority can read and write both languages,

English and Hawaiian, and they take a very lively and intelligent interest in the affairs of their own country.... Any treaty which had been made without consulting [native Hawaiians] should be withdrawn and ought never to have been sanctioned."[69]

His was a minority viewpoint. And native Hawaiians were not to be heard.

A more powerful and persuasive voice was that of the assistant secretary of the Navy, Roosevelt. Teddy wrote that if the United States did not annex Hawaii, "it will show that we either have lost, or else wholly lack, the masterful instinct which alone can make a race great. I feel so deeply about it that I hardly dare express myself in full. The terrible part is to see that it is the men of education who take the lead in trying to make us prove traitors to our race."[70]

Export-minded U.S. businessmen imagined four hundred million customers in China, with Hawaii as an American coaling station and naval base. In January of 1898, McKinley—in a speech to the National Association of Manufacturers (NAM)—declared that using the U.S. military to pry open foreign markets was a legitimate function of the U.S. government. Senator William Frye of Maine urged the same room of NAM members to lobby Congress for a Central American canal and the annexation of Hawaii. Senator Cushman Davis of Minnesota proclaimed, "The nation which controls Hawaii will control that great gateway to commerce."[71] The Senate Foreign Relations Committee issued a majority report declaring that all of the traffic passing through a Central American canal would pass through Hawaii before continuing on to Asia.

The war with Spain provided a further excuse. Congressman De Alva Alexander of New York declared, "The annexation of the Hawaiian Islands, for the first time in our history, is presented to us as a war necessity." Added Representative Richmond Pearson of North Carolina, "I believe that this is a necessary step in the successful prosecution of the war with Spain." The historian Thomas Osborne writes in *Annexation Hawaii*, "Potential trade with China was the primary reason for the annexation of Hawaii. War with Spain was about timing."[72]

On July 6, 1898, Congress passed the Hawaii Annexation Resolution, and President McKinley signed it the next day. The *New York Sun* cheered: "The America of the twentieth century has taken its first and most significant step towards the grave responsibility and high rewards of manifest destiny."[73]

On July 8, a distressed former president Grover Cleveland wrote to his former attorney general: "Hawaii is ours. As I look back upon the first steps in this miserable business, and as I contemplate the means used to complete the outrage, I am ashamed of the whole affair."[74]

On August 12, 1898, in the "Hawaii Annexation Ceremony" in Honolulu, President Sanford Dole formally handed the former independent kingdom to the U.S. minister, Harold M. Sewall. The white Haoles applauded. Queen Lili'uokalani did not attend.

AFTER THE LUNCHEON, THE Taft party scampered off to world-renowned Waikiki Beach, the birthplace of surfing. Princess Alice donned a bathing costume—a high-necked, long-sleeved mohair dress with long black stockings and bathing shoes, her hair tucked under a tightly fitting cap. Alice recalled, "Mr. Taft thought that there was too much skin showing," and that he pleaded "with photographers not to take photographs of me in my bathing suit. It was considered just a little indelicate."[75]

Beachboys paddled Nick and Alice out into Waikiki Bay's famous waves in an outrigger canoe. A newspaper reported, "Cameras by the dozen snapped and clicked as she swept by. It was always with those on shore: 'There's Alice, see her now!' "[76] When she returned to the beach, a reporter heard her exclaim, "I never knew there could be so much enjoyment in a Hawaiian canoe, racing along with the billows, as I have found at Waikiki beach today. It was perfectly delightful, and I wish I could stay to enjoy more of it."[77]

Hawaii Annexation Ceremony, Honolulu, August 12, 1898. Americans cheered while native Hawaiians boycotted the ceremony. (Hawaii State Archives)

At 5:30 p.m., Taft ordered the *Manchuria* to pull out from Honolulu harbor even though Nick and Alice were not aboard. Remembered Alice: "We stayed on the beach at Waikiki until it was time to go back to the steamer. I did not want to leave. I missed

Alice Roosevelt and Congressman Nicholas Longworth,
Honolulu, 1905. (Library of Congress)

the boat at the wharf, as it had to sail at a definite time
because of the tides. So, in a launch with Nick...and
a few others, leis about our necks, regret in our hearts
at leaving, I pursued the *Manchuria* out into the open
Pacific."[78]

Chapter 6

HONORARY ARYANS

"The average Westerner ... was wont to regard Japan as barbarous while she indulged in the gentle arts of peace: he calls her civilized since she began to commit wholesale slaughter on the Manchurian battlefields."[1]

OKAKURA KAKUZO, 1906
FOUNDER OF THE TOKYO SCHOOL OF FINE ARTS,
JAPAN INSTITUTE OF FINE ARTS, AND THE FIRST HEAD
OF THE ASIAN DIVISION AT BOSTON'S MUSEUM OF
FINE ARTS

As the *Manchuria* steamed from Hawaii to Japan, the numerous reporters on board busily wrote articles for their hometown newspapers describing friendly breakfast conversations, a mock trial, fancy dance parties, and what Alice called "a sheet and pillow-case party."[2] But the story that seemed to delight readers most was when Alice spontaneously jumped into a pool with her clothes on. The reality was quite different: the plunge was a planned event, with an expectant crowd watching as workers laboriously poured water into an improvised canvas pool. Alice remembered: "Of course, I left shoes, watch, and such things that the water would hurt, in the care of onlookers."[3] But these antics as retold by grateful newsmen were exactly what the American public expected—and a useful distraction from the cruise's secret mission.

TAFT WAS CARRYING SECRET oral instructions that would alter America's course in Asia. Roosevelt had told his wife and a few trusted friends about his plan, but he kept it secret from his own State Department and Congress. The U.S. Constitution required Roosevelt to put agreements with foreign countries in writing and submit them to the Senate for review. Teddy considered such protocols a waste of time when Big Bill could button things up in Tokyo on the q.t. Only now can history understand it was these events in the summer of 1905 that would doom more than one hundred thousand American boys to die in the Pacific theater decades later. Operating as a two-man diplomatic tag team, Roosevelt and Taft would green-light what later generations would call World War II in the Pacific.

Before Taft's visit in the summer of 1905, relations between Japan and the United States could not have been warmer. After the deal, things changed. Knowing a lot about race theory but less about international diplomacy and almost nothing about Asia, Roosevelt in 1905 careened U.S.-Japanese relations onto the dark side road leading to 1941.

WHEN THE *MANCHURIA* DOCKED in Yokohama on Tuesday, July 25, 1905, it ignited the most boisterous welcome Japan had ever extended to foreigners. Tens of thousands of Japanese waving both countries' flags crowded the wharves, shouting, "banzai"—the traditional Japanese exclamation of good wishes meaning ten thousand years of good luck.

"American guests...banzai!"

"Alice and Taft...banzai!"

"Japan and America...banzai!"

At the Yokohama train station, rows of policemen held the cheering crowd back as the Americans boarded the emperor's personal train. The exact timing of their one-hour journey to Tokyo had been publicized and at each stop enormous smiling crowds banzaied the Americans. Entering Tokyo's Shimbashi train station, the dazzled Americans were buffeted by the banzai roar. The *Japan Weekly Mail* reported, "It is not within our experience that Tokyo ever previously offered such an ardent reception to any foreign visitors."[4] The *New York Times* wrote that Japan's welcome of the Taft party was "absolutely unprecedented in warmth and friendliness."[5] The American minister, Lloyd Griscom, helped Alice into his open carriage to take her to her quarters at the American legation. The horses were skittish as they pulled Alice through narrow streets lined with people waving Japanese and American flags and shouting, "Banzai!" Alice clutched Griscom's arm and shouted in his ear: "Lloyd, I love it! I love it!"[6]

JAPAN HAD JUST FOUGHT Russia over the past nineteen months in the Russo-Japanese War. They had whipped the Russian army in the largest land battle in history, then whipped the Russian navy in history's largest sea battle. The average Japanese was near delirious with pride over Japan's victories. Just fifty-two years earlier, Japan had been a closed, preindustrialized society. Now Japan had amazed the world by becoming the first non-White, non-Christian country to defeat a White Christian power.

In welcoming the Taft party, the Japanese were cheering their own accomplishments and hedging their bets. Although Roosevelt had declared the

United States neutral in the conflict, the Japanese were well aware of America's tilt. Surely this visit by an American Princess and the head of America's war machine was one more indication that Japan's stunning performance in the Russo-Japanese War meant great things. Japan had been shamed in the past by White Christian powers, but now after administering such one-sided beatings to the Russians, the Japanese expected that Alice's father would ensure a square deal for their country.

Only a few Japanese leaders, including Emperor Meiji, knew that the president had a secret plan for their country, a plan whereby Roosevelt would grant them a protectorate in Korea in exchange for Japan's assisting with the American penetration of Asia.

ONE TOKYO NEWSPAPER REPORTER observed, "This is truly the highpoint in the long history of Japanese-American relations."[7] In fact, for the first seventy years of America's existence—from 1783 to 1853—the United States had no relations with the nation known as Nippon. But as the United States took possession of its own Pacific territory, it began to seriously eye China. America's preeminent navy leader in the 1850s was Commodore Matthew Perry, who in the war with Mexico had commanded the largest U.S. invasion operation in history with a fleet that would not be equaled until Operation Torch—the U.S. invasion of North Africa in 1942. Commodore Perry followed the sun, proclaiming in a speech, "It requires no sage to predict events so strongly foreshadowed to us all: still 'Westward will the course of empire take its way.'...The people of America will, in some form or other, extend their dominion and their power, until they shall have brought within their mighty embrace the islands of the great Pacific, and placed the Saxon race upon the eastern shores of Asia."[8]

With Pacific ports now under Washington's control, Perry foresaw an American Aryan march to Asia. The Russian army had advanced into northern China overland and the British navy had bombarded its way into southern China. Now Perry dreamed of establishing a chain of stepping-stones for the U.S. Navy's approach to China.

The U.S. Navy used coal as fuel, and its ships required island coaling stations to complete long journeys. The Pacific—at eight times the size of the Atlantic—required big thinking. The distance from California to Hawaii is 2,100 miles, and American steamships could re-coal there. The real challenge was the distance from Hawaii to China—4,700 miles. If America could establish coaling stations in Japan to bridge the gap, the American Aryan could at long

Commodore Matthew Perry. After helping to conquer Mexico, Perry turned his attention to America's expansion to Asia. (Library of Congress)

last project its naval power in the region and compete with the British and Slavs for the riches of China.

Perry's strategy seems obvious today, but in his time, this was expensive, futuristic thinking and its implications were financially staggering. And there was one big challenge: Americans knew almost nothing about Japan.

White Christian missionaries had first arrived in Japan in 1543. The Japanese were open-minded

Commodore Perry's Strategy

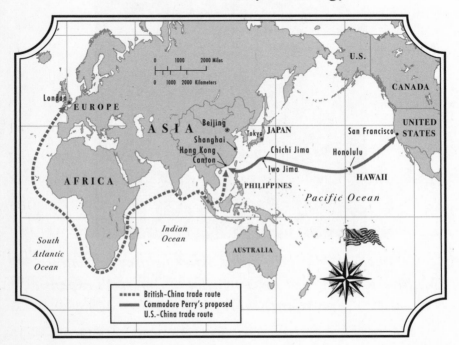

Commodore Perry's strategy to tap the China trade. In the 1850s the wide Pacific Ocean was a barrier to commerce between the United States and Asia. Commodore Perry envisioned Japanese coaling stations as U.S. stepping stones to the riches of China.

about other religions and welcomed the Christians. The Japanese animist belief system—Shintoism—coexisted peacefully with Buddhism, which had been imported from India via China. These were inclusionary belief systems—one could recite a Buddhist sutra at a Shinto shrine with no conflict. But the Christianity that came from the West was jealous and exclusionary, and the missionaries demanded that a choice be made. Japan's ruler, Shogun Ieyasu Tokugawa, became suspicious of a religion whose first commandment required loyalty to one non-Japanese God. And when he studied world conditions, Tokugawa realized that Christianity was a conquest religion in the service of state militaries. The Japanese scholar Seishisai Aizawa wrote in the 1820s, "The European powers endeavor to attack all nations in the world. The wicked doctrine of Jesus is an aid in this endeavor. Under the pretext of trade or whatever, they approach and become friendly with people in all areas, secretly probing to see which countries are strong and which are weak. If a nation's defenses are weak, they seize it by force. But if there are no weaknesses to pounce on, they take it over by leading the people's minds astray with the wicked doctrine of [Christianity]."[9]

In 1614, to prevent a Christian takeover of Japan, Tokugawa ordered a policy of *sakoku,* or "closed country"—the complete sealing off of the island chain. He banished all Western missionaries. Japanese converts had the choice of renouncing their new faith or being crucified. Laws forbade travel abroad by Japanese and foreigners' vessels from entering Japan. Only ships with squared-off sterns could be built, thus making them unseaworthy for long voyages. Death sentences awaited those who received foreign documents or gave foreigners information about Japan. Shogun Tokugawa even shut down profitable commerce with the West, trading only with the Dutch—and then very little—because the Hollanders agreed to trample upon crucifixes that had been laid before them by Japanese government interrogators. These Dutch merchants conducted their business from a small, prisonlike artificial island in Nagasaki Bay, an isolated spot where the Japanese could keep an eye on them.

The result was the *Taihei,* or "Great Peace"—more than two centuries of peaceful Tokugawa family rule and no wars. The country had no army or navy preying beyond its shores. Samurai rarely used their swords and instead became bureaucrats and teachers. And all of this occurred during the same period that White Christians in Europe and the Americas were constantly warring. These centuries of peace were a boon to the development of Japanese culture. With no expensive military, the Japanese government invested in its people. The arts by which we know Japan today—haiku poetry, the tea ceremony, wood-block prints, Kabuki theater—either originated or found their footing during this period. Japan became the most literate country in the world, with nearly every adult male in Japan's major cities able to read or write.

While *sakoku* protected Japan, it also created a power vacuum, and Britain, Russia, Spain, and the United States were free to contest for control of the Pacific.

THE AMERICAN GOVERNMENT KNEW Japan asked only to be left alone to live in peace, but the U.S. Navy repeatedly demanded that the Japanese "open" their closed country. "Between 1790 and 1853, the Japanese turned away at least twenty-seven visiting U.S. vessels."[10] As Japanese officials wrote to one U.S. Navy captain:

> Foreigners have come to us from various quarters, but have always been received in the same way. In all cases we have positively refused to trade and this has been the habit of our nation from time immemorial. In taking this course with regard to you, we only pursue our accustomed policy. We can make no distinction between different foreign nations—we treat them all alike; and you, as Americans, must

receive the same answer with the rest. It will be of no use to renew the attempt, as all applications of the kind, however numerous they may be, will be steadily rejected. We are aware that our customs are in this respect different from those of some other countries, but every nation has a right to manage its affairs in its own way.[11]

The Japanese phrasing "every nation has a right to manage its affairs in its own way" seemed naive to those who followed the sun. In an 1846 speech on the floor of the U.S. Senate, Senator Thomas Hart Benton noted that Asians were inferior to the American Aryan and, "like all the rest, must receive an impression from the superior race whenever they come in contact."[12]

As the American Aryan's desire to expand across the Pacific grew, Christian ministers observed that heathen Japan needed salvation and that Japan's seclusion policy was not God's way. The missionary Samuel Wells Williams wrote, "I have a full conviction that the seclusion policy of the nations of Eastern Asia is not according to God's plan of mercy to these peoples, and their government must change them through fear or force, that his people may be free."[13] In 1852, the secretary of the Navy, John Kennedy, wrote that Japan must recognize "its Christian obligation to join the family of Christendom."[14] Echoing similar arguments made earlier about Native American gold mines, the secretary of state, Daniel Webster, argued that Japan had "no right" to refuse the U.S. Navy's "reasonable" request to commandeer Japanese sovereign soil for its coaling stations because the coal at issue was "but a gift of Providence, deposited, by the Creator of all things, in the depths of the Japanese islands for the benefit of the human family."[15] The American Declaration of Independence established the right of an independent country to control its own destiny, and the State Department—in an 1851 memo to the Navy during the planning of the coming confrontation with Japan—maintained that every nation has "undoubtedly the right to determine for itself the extent to which it will hold intercourse with other nations."[16] So how could the U.S. government justify forcing itself on a sovereign nation? Writes Michael Rollin in his thesis *The Divine Invasion:*

> The easiest way out of this dilemma was to treat the Japanese in the same manner that the American Indians were treated: "as living outside of the law of nations, peoples undeserving of civilized treatment." Americans, by the 1840s and 1850s, simply did not conceive of a place for non-White or even non-Anglo peoples in the grand scheme of human and

The Western Spread of American Empire

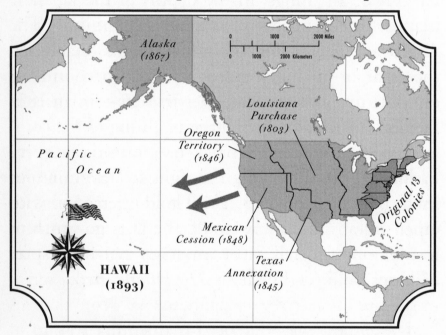

Manifest Destiny followed the sun west.

social evolution.... Having spread across North America with relative ease, there was little reason for American Anglo-Saxons to believe that this seemingly immutable historical and teleological trend would differ in the lands across the Pacific.[17]

On the American continent in the 1850s, many Indian chiefs were learning the lesson that their demise began the day an American Aryan arrived to negotiate a friendly treaty. Now President Millard Fillmore gave Commodore Perry a treaty of friendship for the heathens of Japan.

The cover story was that Perry was on a peaceful mission, but the plan was to use U.S. military power to shock the Japanese into capitulation. Perry sailed to Japan with the largest fleet of American warships to ever travel so far. Perry expected that his display of industrialized military might would strike terror in the pre-industrialized Japanese. He wrote that his arms "would do more to command their fears, and secure their friendship, than all that the diplomatic missions have accomplished in the last one hundred years."[18]

On July 8, 1853, Perry sailed unannounced into Tokyo Bay with a fleet of U.S. Navy warships bristling with civilizing cannons. As Perry had planned, the noisy, belching vessels shocked the Japanese, who had never seen such industrial machines, much less militarized ones. Temple bells pealed the alarm. The word spread quickly: Fleet-footed messengers ran through villages with incomprehensible news that the "Black Ships of the Evil Men" threatened and that one hundred thousand devils with white faces were about to overrun the country. Families fled their homes with their possessions on their backs. Out-of-practice samurai tried to scrape rust off their swords, but against civilizing American military power, Japan was defenseless.

Though they had no desire to get into negotiations, the Japanese were forced to allow Perry ashore when the commodore threatened violence. A Japanese observer wrote, "Perry said that he would enter into negotiations, but if his proposals were rejected, he was prepared to make war at once; that in the event of war he would have 50 ships in nearby waters and 50 more in California, and that if he sent word he could summon a command of one hundred warships within twenty days."[19] (Perry made his demands known with the aid of interpreters who used the Dutch language to bridge the gap between English and Japanese.) Perry further "warned them of what had happened to Mexico when it insulted and defied the United States."[20] To emphasize this point, Perry gave his Japanese counterparts two books—*War in Mexico* and *History of the War in Mexico*—that highlighted

Perry's role as the commander of the huge American amphibious assault of Mexico.

Soon America's first consul to Japan—Townsend Harris—arrived to negotiate the treaty of friendship. When Japanese leaders hemmed and hawed, Harris threatened that he would call on nearby British ships to bombard Japan. Convinced that the threat was real and immediate, the Japanese reluctantly signed the United States–Japan Treaty of Amity and Commerce on July 29, 1858.

Shame upon shame followed. On March 13, 1861, Russia invaded the island of Tsushima in the Sea of Japan between Japan and Korea. Several Japanese died in the fighting before the Russians withdrew, but Japan's rebuff of the intruders was seen by some as evidence of its increasing vulnerability. And in 1863 and 1864, the navies of both the United States and the United Kingdom shelled Japanese civilians in the port city Shimonoseki to discipline the Japanese for firing on their ships.

Furthermore, the shocked Japanese now encountered White Christians—banned for centuries—strutting their streets like little kings, immune from punishment thanks to unequal treaties that protected foreigners even when they committed violent crimes for which they would be punished back in their home countries.

In response to such conditions, Japanese patriots

arose from the southern island of Kyushu and fought their way into the royal capital of Kyoto. Early on the morning of January 3, 1868, these brave samurai stormed the royal compound and took control of the young emperor, then only fifteen years old. They renamed the boy "Meiji" ("enlightened rule") and called their revolution the "Meiji Restoration," though they didn't "restore" the emperor; instead they used his Oz-like image to exercise power.

The Japanese founding fathers were a remarkable group of men who would create the new Japan and guide her fortunes into the twentieth century, negotiating Japan's future with American presidents from Millard Fillmore to Theodore Roosevelt. Not surprisingly, Japan experienced the outside world primarily as a military threat. America had forced the country open at gunpoint. And a glance across the Japan Sea made it obvious there was much else to worry about. Once-proud China was being dismembered and sucked dry by Western merchants who used gunboats to foist opium upon the populace. Farther south, the Dutch had conquered Indonesia; the French ruled Vietnam, Laos, and Cambodia; while the acquisitive British held vast colonies in Hong Kong, Singapore, Malaysia, Burma, and India. To its north, Japan saw the marauding Russian Slav subjugate all within its path as it hacked its way to the Pacific coast.

No non-White country had ever maintained its

independence once a White military force had landed on its soil. China, India, and Egypt all had rich histories but were under the heel of White boots.

THE JAPANESE UNDERSTOOD THAT White Christians felt justified in subjugating Asians because they thought the Yellow man was racially inferior. So the Japanese set out to identify themselves as separate from other Asians, and more like White westerners. The Japanese military strategist Yukichi Fukuzawa wrote, "We cannot wait for neighboring countries to become enlightened and unite to make Asia strong. We must rather break out of formation and join the civilized countries of the West on the path of progress." Fukuzawa advocated a "Leave Asia" policy: the Japanese would present themselves as a separate race, disconnected from Asia just as their island chain was unattached to the Asian mainland. And the Japanese would emulate the West's military prowess. To the Japanese who had faced Commodore Perry's cannon, the most salient fact of White Christian power was that their imperialism was built upon industrialized militaries. Japan adopted a new national slogan: *Fukoku kyohei,* or "Rich country, strong military." To build a strong military and become a rich country, Japan did what no other non-White, non-Christian country had done: it threw open its doors to Western ways, modernized and militarized. Fukuzawa observed, "A hundred volumes of international law are no match for a few cannon. A handful of friendly treaties cannot compete with a little gunpowder. Cannons and gunpowder are machines that can make principles where there were none."[21]

Japan also took an important theological step toward the West: Japan had many Shinto and Buddhist gods, but none of them were conquest-minded. As the Pulitzer Prize winner John Dower writes in *Japan in War and Peace,* "Japan's new leaders soon concluded that they needed a counterpart to God and Christianity in the West."[22] With this in mind, the founding fathers reinvented their boy emperor in the Christian tradition: Meiji was made to be a god and "State Shinto" was born.

Another step was sartorial. Instead of shunning foreign ways as China and other Asian countries had, the Japanese doffed their Chinese-style robes and donned trousers and ties. And this was just the beginning. They strung telegraph wire, practiced with knives and forks, and opened Japan to Western teachers, missionaries, and governmental advisers. The founding fathers also dispatched the crème of Japan's youth to study abroad. When the first two Japanese students to attend Rutgers University were asked what they'd be studying, they answered "that it was to learn how to build 'big ships' and make 'big

"*The Progress of Civilization.*" *Civilized and uncivilized Japanese. Japan's "Leave Asia" strategy convinced Americans that Japan would spread Western values in Asia. (Beinecke Rare Book & Manuscript Library, Yale University)*

guns' to prevent the [Western] powers from taking possession of their country."[23]

Cannons, rifles, and warships now became part of the state budget. Japanese military men strutted in Western-style uniforms complete with handlebar mustaches, just like their English, American, and Russian counterparts. Emperor Meiji was depicted in paintings wearing a splendid Western-style military uniform, his chest bearing shiny medals.

While life in Japan's rice paddies continued its timeless routine, the English-speaking Japanese who interacted with U.S. diplomats, businessmen, educators, and media projected a Western-friendly front. One American marveled, "This is one of the most remarkable events in history. In a word, it has, as it were, unmoored Japan from the coast of Asia, and towed it across the Pacific, to place it alongside of the New World, to have the same course of life and progress."[24]

The Japanese strategy to emulate White Christian ways was so successful that they became "Honorary Aryans" in the American mind, often referred to as the "Yankees of the Far East." At the 1876 Philadelphia World's Fair, American Indians were presented as headed toward extinction, Blacks were thick-headed laborers, and the Chinese were a dying race. A Philadelphia newspaper wrote of the Chinese, "Cut off from the rest of the world by its great wall, and isolated behind her old feeling of distrust and apathy towards the peoples of Europe, the old empire of China has received but little benefit from western civilization and advancement."[25] The Yankee assessment of the Honorary Aryans was all sunshine: "Japan renders her verdict in favor of American machinery. The Japanese have already adopted the American costume in dress, and the progressive spirit pervading the Old World is inclining her people to adopt American ideas and American machinery."[26]

A DOMESTICALLY FOCUSED AMERICAN citizenry quickly lost interest in Perry's plan for expansion into Asia. But now the United States had a militarized, obedient ally on Asia's coast—and perhaps Japanese expansion could serve the American Aryan.

There were many impediments: The Japanese had lived in peace for centuries, and while there existed a samurai/warrior ethic, it had not been practiced on the battlefield for many years. The Japanese legal code was concerned with domestic order and there was no tradition of using international law to take over Others. For a generation after Perry, Japan seemed unable or disinclined to project its military force. Then an international incident occurred that the United States saw as Japan's opportunity.

In October of 1871, a ship from the island of Okinawa with sixty-nine people aboard had set sail for China. Okinawa was a tiny Pacific island kingdom located between Japan and China. To maintain its independence, Confucian Okinawa had traditionally paid homage to both China and Japan. And in Confucian style, neither China nor Japan threatened Okinawa or its people. On this trip, a fierce storm blew the Okinawans off course and smashed their boat on the southeastern coast of Taiwan. Sixty-six made it ashore safely, but natives from a local village massacred fifty-four of them. Twelve escaped and made it back to Okinawa safely.

Charles De Long, the U.S. minister to Japan, had often encouraged the Japanese government to follow the sun west. De Long suggested that Japan dispatch a military expedition to discipline the Taiwanese and lay the groundwork for the takeover of the island nation. Minister De Long assured the Japanese that the United States "was partial to its friends who desired to occupy such territory for the purposes of expansion."[27]

Such military moves under "international law" were old hat for American Aryans, but this was a new ball game for the Japanese and they hesitated. China had a substantial cultural influence over Taiwan and the Japanese feared their Big Brother's reaction. De Long assured the Japanese foreign minister that according to Western international law, Taiwan "would in the final analysis be subject to possession by the country successfully holding it."[28] Still, the Japanese did nothing.

Then, in the fall of 1872, an American arrived to teach the Japanese how to invade other countries. His name was Charles LeGendre, but everyone called him the "General," and he looked the part. In the Civil

Japan, Okinawa, Taiwan, China

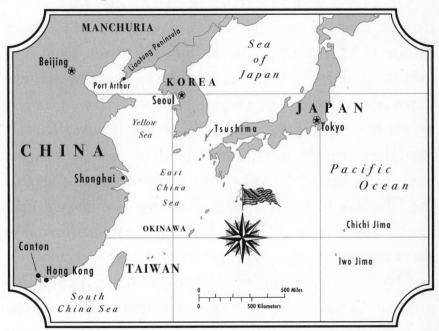

After Commodore Perry arrived in 1853,
Japan looked westward.

War he had twice walked through a hail of enemy bullets, which had torn away a section of his nose, a portion of his jaw, and one of his eyes. The *New York Times* described LeGendre as "an adventurer who fought for the fun of it, and who, though riddled with bullets as the result of this Civil War career, still longed for the clash of arms."[29]

General LeGendre had been on his way home from China, where he had served since 1866 as a minor U.S. diplomat. In Tokyo, Minister De Long told the general how he was encouraging the Japanese to invade Taiwan. LeGendre's ears perked up. During his service in China, he had lectured Chinese officials that they should invade and civilize the Taiwanese. LeGendre had gone as far as to submit legal briefs to the Chinese Foreign Office showing how they could justify the use of military force against Taiwan. He had even visited Taiwan and mapped its territory.

Over and over LeGendre had harangued the Chinese about how the U.S. government had acquired vast territory by civilizing uncivilized Indians and that China either had to follow international rules and civilize the Taiwanese or some other power would do it. The Chinese mandarins had shrugged and told the one-eyed "Foreign Devil" not to worry, that China was indeed sovereign over Taiwan, without using military force to prove it.

Now LeGendre sat before De Long in Tokyo

with legal rationales for the invasion of Taiwan and military plans of how to do it. De Long arranged a meeting between LeGendre and the Japanese foreign minister. The one-eyed general made a big impression. De Long reported to Washington that the Japanese were "surprised and delighted...to be brought in contact with one so well-informed on a subject so very interesting to them."[30]

The Japanese Foreign Ministry promptly offered LeGendre a job to help them civilize Taiwan, and the former U.S. Army general became "the first foreigner employed in a Japanese government post."[31] LeGendre resigned from his post as United States consul on December 12, 1872. LeGendre wrote a friend in the United States that he took the job after "it was proved to me that, in doing so, I was but aiding in the carrying out of certain views which our government looked upon with extreme favor."[32] In fact, assuming that he would be appointed governor of Taiwan if Japan acquired the island, he told his son that the opportunity was a way to "lay by quite a little fortune."[33]

General LeGendre had the ear of the founding fathers and consulted with Emperor Meiji a number of times. In terms of Japan's strategic big picture, he preached from America's founding document of international relations, the Monroe Doctrine. In 1823, President James Monroe had announced that from now on, only the United States could meddle in the Americas; the United States would view further European actions in the western hemisphere as aggression requiring U.S. military intervention. Now LeGendre suggested a Japanese Monroe Doctrine for Asia: "One must act courageously for the purpose of pushing forward the flag of the rising Sun in Asia and for the sake of the expansion of our empire. These actions are necessary in order to become the protector of the various nations in Asia against European expansion into our sphere. This policy resembles the one taken by the United States in the wake of the European filtration and encroachment into the American sphere of interest."[34]

Although Japan would later use similar words in the 1930s and 1940s in its wars against China and the United States, this was radical thinking at the time. No non-White, non-Christian country in the 1870s had a Monroe Doctrine–like sphere of influence. LeGendre suggested how Japan could sell the West on the idea: "Japan must keep her plan in the deepest secret, but must make adequate publicity to the people in the world that she is under-taking to bring the whole of Asia from its barbarous and primitive stage to the civilized stage."[35]

But how was Japan supposed to move Asia from barbarism to civilization? LeGendre recommended Anglo-Saxon methods: "Pacify and civilize them if possible, and if not...exterminate them or otherwise deal with them as the United States and England have dealt with the barbarians."[36]

LeGendre told his employers that by disciplining the Taiwanese over the murder of the Okinawans, Japan would be seen as the guardian of the Okinawan people and could thus claim both Okinawa and Taiwan: "Inasmuch as [the Taiwanese aborigines] have murdered Japanese subjects [Okinawans], and there is no known way of dealing with them as a community, Japan is perfectly justified in taking the matter into her own hands and occupying their territory."[37]

To deal with Taiwan and Okinawa, LeGendre first had to confront his old nemesis, China, which viewed those islands as part of its cultural realm. LeGendre had the Meiji government issue an imperial edict abolishing the kingdom of Okinawa. Okinawa became a Japanese fief, its king a Japanese peer, and its foreign relations a matter for the Japanese Foreign Office. Retroactively, the Japanese government claimed the Okinawa shipwreck victims as Japanese subjects so it would have a legal foundation on which to launch a punitive expedition against Taiwan.

On March 12, 1873, LeGendre boarded a Japanese warship in Yokohama harbor. LeGendre intended to take a Japanese diplomatic delegation to China, where the general would once again harangue his old adversaries about how somebody had better civilize Taiwan like the United States had civilized its Indians. As

Perry had arrived following the sun, now an American general would lead the Japanese westward.

THE CHINESE HAD LONG viewed Japan as a young upstart—it was only two thousand years old, compared to China's five-thousand-year history—seeing the Japanese as "Eastern dwarfs" who had imperfectly modeled superior Chinese ways. But times were changing. For centuries the Japanese had come peacefully to Beijing wearing Confucian garb. Now the Japanese came dressed in trousers and top hats, with a former U.S. Army general in tow. The Chinese took one look at the Western-dressed Japanese diplomats and sniffed that they had sold out to the White Christians. A Chinese viceroy saw the one-eyed Foreign Devil and snorted to the Japanese foreign minister, "We have made treaties before this one, and we did not find the need for foreigners to advise us; what reason is there for it now?"[38]

The Chinese objected to the Japanese's Western-oriented legalisms, saying that international law was a recent Western creation and that the affair should be settled on the basis of truth. But over the course of the months-long negotiations, LeGendre maintained that for a nation to claim Taiwan, that government must civilize the savages. He legalistically insisted that the Okinawans—

"Japanese natives"—had been harmed and that Japan had the right to punish the aboriginal Taiwanese. The Chinese responded that they had heard of Okinawans being injured, but no Japanese. In one negotiating session, the Chinese admitted that their political rule extended only to the "mature natives" of Taiwan and not the "wild natives." The Japanese would use this statement to justify their later attack on Taiwan.

Satisfied that they had outmaneuvered their Chinese hosts with Western diplomacy, the Japanese and one pleased American general sailed back to an ecstatic welcome in Tokyo. Twenty-one-year-old Emperor Meiji honored LeGendre with an imperial audience on March 9. The Japanese government created a "Bureau of Savage Affairs" and incorporated new Western words like *koronii* (colony) into the Japanese language. Japanese newspapers Otherized the Taiwanese aborigines, calling them cruel and inhuman, and spoke of Japan's responsibility to civilize the savages.

In early May of 1873, Japan invaded Taiwan with U.S. military advisers supporting the operation. Within two months, the Taiwanese submitted to Japanese military force.

AT THIS SAME TIME, Japan was also concerned about its neighbor to the west, Korea. Korea was a small kingdom enmeshed in a web of Confucian relationships with its neighbors. It had a father-son relationship with China summarized by the term *sadae*, "serving the great," and Korea dispatched regular missions to Beijing, where her representatives subserviently kowtowed to the Son of Heaven, the emperor. The Chinese government in turn bestowed honorary titles on the Korean king, extended a military umbrella, and allowed Korean merchants to conduct a limited but extremely profitable trade.

Korea's relationship with Japan was more along the lines of brother-brother, known as *kyorin*, "befriending the neighboring country." A comparably closed country, Korea had for centuries allowed Japanese traders access to just one port, just as Japan had done with the Dutch at Nagasaki.

After centuries of peace with its neighbor, Japan now gazed at Korea through American-style expansionist lenses. Because Korea had not danced to the White Western tune and had not modernized, industrialized, and militarized, the Japanese judged the Koreans as uncivilized.

But Korea was prey not only for Japan, but also for Russia to its north. The Russians had expanded to their Pacific coast in the 1600s and were edging into Manchuria in North China, next door to Korea.

Because Korea was so near to Japan, jutting

threateningly into the narrow Yellow Sea, Japanese alarmists styled Korea as "the dagger pointed at the heart of Japan." If Korea fell to a White Christian country like Russia, they argued, the Korean peninsula would become the springboard for the invasion of Japan.

The military theorist Fukuzawa provided a common-sense rationale for Japan's course with Korea: "A man who lives in a stone house is not safe from fire if his neighbor lives in a wooden one. The person with the more secure abode should try to persuade his neighbor to rebuild, of course, but if a crisis should be at hand, he is justified in arbitrarily invading his neighbor's land—not because he covets his neighbor's land or hates his neighbor, but simply to protect his own house from fire."[39] Thus the Japanese concluded that Korea must be made into a buffer between Russia and Japan.

IN 1873, EMULATING COMMODORE PERRY'S mission, Japanese diplomats sailed west in an American-made warship across the Yellow Sea to open uncivilized Korea to Western ways. They brought along an American-style treaty of friendship.

The shocked Koreans could hardly believe their eyes and ears. For centuries Japanese diplomats had come to Korea dressed similarly to the Koreans, in Chinese-style robes; now they came ashore in tight Western suits, wearing shiny, stiff top hats.

The two countries had enjoyed peace between them for hundreds of years, so the sudden need for a treaty of friendship made little sense to the Koreans. And when Japan described the terms, the Koreans wondered if the Japanese had lost their minds. From time immemorial the two small countries had recognized the Son of Heaven in Beijing as an emperor and agreed that lesser kings ruled Japan and Korea. Now the outrageously dressed Japanese explained that Meiji was godlike and that he was also an emperor. The Koreans were dumbfounded. How could there be two suns in the sky?

Japan's Perry-like attempt at opening Korea was an embarrassing flop. The Koreans shamed the Japanese, calling them traitors to the Confucian order. They refused to respond to a treaty based upon the "emperor versus king" nonsense, questioned the legitimacy of the new Meiji regime, and even ridiculed the Japanese for wearing Western woolen suits. When the Koreans accused them of going back upon Confucian tradition, it infuriated the Japanese, reminding them that by dealing with westerners they had betrayed their own history. As Hilary Conroy observes in *The Japanese Seizure of Korea*, "As with the man who curses his wife for reminding him of something of which he himself is ashamed, the wrath that consumed [Japan] over the Korean issue was fierce beyond all proportion to the question at hand."[40]

AMERICA HAD EXPECTED JAPAN to make Taiwan a "koronii" and "lead the natives to civilization," but cooler heads in the Japanese Foreign Ministry warned of war with China. Instead, Japan adroitly used the threat of colonization to extort an indemnity. The Chinese paid up and Japan withdrew from Taiwan at the end of 1874. In 1875, the Chinese government pacified the wild natives of Taiwan, and in later negotiations the Chinese recognized the "justice" of Japan's invasion. That acknowledged, the Meiji government ordered Okinawan leaders to stop their tributary relationship with China.

That same year, LeGendre retired from the Japanese Foreign Ministry, his mission accomplished. He had inspired the Honorary Aryans with the idea of a Japanese Monroe Doctrine for Asia, a vision that was championed by Japanese expansionists less than three generations later as the Greater East Asia Co-prosperity Sphere. He had shown them how—using international law and military force—Japan could gain by civilizing the uncivilized. Before he retired, the general with one eye wrote a final manifesto urging Japan to go west and expand into Korea.

*   *   *

KOREA HAD BEEN ABLE to shame Japan because big China was in its corner, so Japanese diplomats went to Beijing to argue that China should allow Korea to sign the proposed treaty of friendship. China saw little harm in the agreement—despite the conflict over Taiwan, the Chinese still saw the Japanese as a minor power—so Beijing allowed Korea to sign the treaty with Japan on February 26, 1876.

China viewed the treaty as a mere trade agreement, but Japan saw it as a fundamental reordering of the China-Korea relationship. This was because the Japanese had used a Western legal trick and created two versions of the agreement. All previous communications among China, Korea, and Japan had been written in the Chinese language, but this time Japan drew up an English as well as a Chinese version. As the Harvard professor Akira Iriye explains, "As an Eastern state, Japan was cognizant of the extreme ambiguity of the terms expressing traditional relations in the Far East. An example of this is cha-ju chi-bang (tzuchu chih-Pang in Chinese), which literally means 'a self-governing area or state,' and could also be used to mean 'an independent state.'" The Honorary Aryans, trained in American ways, were able to realistically exploit the convenient weakness: their English translation consistently used Japanese-friendly definitions.

As a result, Iriye notes, "neither the Koreans nor the Chinese perceived any serious break in traditional Sino-Korean relations. China in fact considered it an affirmation of the long-established practice."[41]

Over the next several years it became increasingly clear that Japan's behavior was more aggressive than the Chinese had expected. The Chinese government—still believing it called the shots in Korea—acted quickly to minimize Japan's influence. China had a long tradition of "using barbarians against barbarians" in its international affairs and now encouraged Korea to sign treaties with other countries. In 1880, the Chinese submitted a written report to King Gojong of Korea entitled "A Policy for Korea." The report proclaimed Korea's biggest national security threats to be the Japanese from the west and the Russians from the east. China recommended that Little Brother Korea modernize internally and choose America as the first White Western country with whom to make a treaty because "the United States [was] a powerful industrial and anti-imperialist power, was a moral state, founded upon Christianity, which usually supports weaker nations against strong oppressors."[42] Korea beheld the United States as a country that stood for liberty, and unlike Russia, it was far distant and had shown no inclination to encroach upon Asia.

Believing the United States had only benevolent motives, in 1882 thirty-year-old King Gojong happily accepted the U.S.-Korea Treaty, in which the first article declared that there "shall be perpetual peace and friendship" between Korea and the United States. If a third power acted unjustly or oppressively with either country, the United States and Korea promised to exert their "good offices, on being informed of the case, to bring about an amicable arrangement, thus showing their friendly feelings."[43]

Koreans knew as little about White Western legal concepts as the Americans knew about Confucian ideology. Korean leaders interpreted the "good offices" clause to mean that the United States would be Korea's new "Elder Brother," protecting Korea from Western predators. To them, the good offices clause was much more than a legal phrase; it meant that Elder Brother America had a moral commitment to their country. Thus, King Gojong thought his country's independence was assured when the first U.S. minister to Korea—Lucius Foote—arrived in Seoul in 1883. In their first meeting, Foote told Gojong that the United States was interested in "the comfort and happiness" of the Korean people and that "in this progressive age" there was a moral power "more potent than standing armies."[44]

IN 1883, HORACE ALLEN graduated from Miami Medical School in Cincinnati, Ohio. A good

King (later Emperor) Gojong and his son Sunjong in 1890. King Gojong said, "We have the promise of America; she will be our friend whatever happens." Theodore Roosevelt said, "I should like to see Japan have Korea."

Presbyterian boy, Allen asked the Board of Foreign Missions to send him overseas to proselyte for Christ. In the summer of 1884, he went to Seoul as the chief physician to the United States legation to the Empire of Korea.

On September 20, 1884, a royal prince—Min Yong Ik—was stabbed in an assassination attempt. Allen used Western medical techniques unknown in Seoul to save Prince Min's life. King Gojong was impressed and gratefully put Allen on the royal payroll. Allen became the embodiment of Elder Brother America: a benevolent White Christian come to help Younger Brother. Upon Allen's advice, Gojong turned his back on Korea's traditional policy of anti-Christianity and allowed Allen to bring American missionaries to build Korean hospitals, schools, and churches and Yankee businessmen to construct Korea's first electric works, waterworks, and trolley and railway systems.

Gojong did not travel the world; he stayed in Seoul, surrounded by friendly American advisers, who assured him that Elder Brother America was on his side. As a result, he did not know what Americans said about him behind his back. U.S. magazines such as *Outlook* and *North American Review* contrasted the Japanese "with what they routinely described as the degenerate Koreans."[45] Koreans, the elite chattering classes declared, were one of the races on the decline, like their Mongolian cousin, the American Indian. And since so many tribes had fallen as the Aryan westered, what was one more?

To their chagrin, the Japanese had quickly lost their imagined monopoly over Korea, and the reassertion of Chinese influence in Korea raised tensions between China and Japan. In a series of political proxy wars, Japan encouraged progressive politicians in Seoul who wished to reform along Japanese lines while China supported conservative politicians who wanted to maintain the Confucian status quo. The Korean progressives and conservatives battled sporadically until finally Japan declared war on China on August 1, 1894.

America supported the Honorary Aryans. The *New York Times* wrote, "The war is often called a conflict between Eastern and Western civilization. It would be more accurate to call it a conflict between civilization and barbarism."[46] The *New York Tribune* declared, "The present war may decide many things, including whether or not Korea is henceforth to exist as an independent nation. But one of its most important results will be to decide this question, which was its own cause, whether Korea is to march forward or to be carried forward with Japan on the high road of civilization or whether she is to remain with China in the stagnant slough of semi-barbarism."[47] Caustic, critical newspaper articles about uncivilized

China and wood-block prints depicting the Chinese as dim-witted Asians were suddenly the rage in Japan. Battlefield depictions featured tall, handsome, Western-looking Japanese soldiers in heroic poses, while the Chinese had jutting cheekbones and slanted eyes and wore pigtails.

The world expected China to make short work of the Eastern dwarfs, but Japan stung its larger rival with the power of its Westernized military, and China quickly sued for peace. The jubilant Japanese forwarded their terms to Beijing: a juicy cash indemnity and the cession of Taiwan and the Liaodong Peninsula, an enormously valuable and strategic piece of real estate that jutted into the China Seas and controlled access to both Beijing and Manchuria.

In the resulting Treaty of Shimonoseki, China was forced to cede both territories, pay a large indemnity, accept that Korea was truly independent, and accord the Japanese the same unequal diplomatic and commercial privileges enjoyed by White Christians in China. (The British had long been the dominant Western power in China, but after 1875 others had vied for spheres of influence and predatory trade privileges. The Western nations with special privileges in China included Great Britain, France, Russia, the United States, Germany, Portugal, Denmark, Holland, Spain, Belgium, and Italy.)

To the jubilant Japanese men in the street, the

resounding triumph over China swept away the humiliation of Perry's Black Ships and proved Japanese greatness. The political commentator Tokutomi Sohō boasted that with the triumph over China, the West would now recognize that "civilization is not a monopoly of the white man."[48] An American newspaper observed:

Ever since the Chicago Exposition [of 1892–1893] foreigners have gradually acquired some knowledge of Japanese culture, but it was limited to the fact that Japan produces beautiful pottery, tea and silk. Since the outbreak of the Sino-Japanese War last year, however, an attitude of respect for Japan may be felt everywhere, and there is talk of nothing but Japan this and Japan that.... Most amusing is the craze for Japanese women's clothes. Many American women wear them to parties, although they are most unbecoming, and the praise they lavish on the Japanese victories sounds exactly as if they were boasting about their own country.[49]

Chapter 7

PLAYING ROOSEVELT'S GAME

"I was thoroughly well pleased with the Japanese victory, for Japan is playing our game."[1]
—President Theodore Roosevelt after the surprise Japanese attack on Russian forces on February 8, 1904

Via the bloody art of conquest, Japan had become the first and only non-White, non-Christian member of the imperial power club. But for the White Christians, that was a problem, and Japan's elevation was soon proved temporary.

The Chinese—employing their "barbarian vs. barbarian" strategy—had shared Japan's demands with the ministers of Russia, France, and Germany, three Johnny-come-lately imperialists who thirsted for a larger slice of the Chinese melon. China's bet was that the greed of these White Christians would somehow restrain the Eastern dwarfs. On April 23, 1895, the ministers of Russia, France, and Germany called on the Japanese Foreign Ministry to announce that they opposed Japan's ownership of the Liaodong Peninsula. The Russian note read:

> The Government of His Majesty the Emperor of all the Russians, in examining the conditions of peace which Japan has imposed on China, finds that the possession of the peninsula of Liaodong, claimed by Japan, would be a constant menace to the capital of China, would at the same time render illusory the independence of Korea, and would henceforth be a perpetual obstacle to the permanent peace of the Far East. Consequently the Government of His Majesty the Emperor would give a new proof of their sincere friendliness for the Government of His Majesty the Emperor of Japan by advising them to renounce the definitive possession of the peninsula of Liaodong.[2]

Russia had long coveted the warm water harbor city of Port Arthur, located on the southern tip of the Liaodong peninsula. A Russian official warned that if the Japanese took control of the region, "Russia would need hundreds of thousands of troops and a considerable increase of her fleet for defense of her possessions and the Siberian Railway."[3]

Unable to militarily resist the three European nations, Japan yielded the Liaodong peninsula. The Japanese founding fathers—now middle-aged men—could hardly believe it. Japan had played the White Christian game fair and square—it had picked a fight with an uncivilized country, proven its battlefield superiority, and received concessions that were her due. And now here was this "triple intervention."

The Japanese public believed that the triple intervention was visited upon Japan because of the color of their skin. Japanese newspapers coined the term "Shame of Liaodong." Shame soon gave way to fury when Russia cynically grabbed the Liaodong peninsula for herself. None of the other powers complained when a White Christian country took the very same territory recently denied Japan.

THEODORE ROOSEVELT SUMMED UP his approach to foreign relations with the West African proverb "Speak softly and carry a big stick." Roosevelt first spoke of the "Big Stick" on September 2, 1901, at the Minnesota State Fair. The burning foreign policy issue of the day was whether to continue the brutal American war in the Philippines. For decades, Roosevelt had defended race cleansing because of the salutary result: American civilization had followed the sun. Now as vice president, he rose to declare that an American Big Stick would now civilize the world.

"We are a nation of pioneers," Roosevelt proclaimed. "Our history has been one of expansion [which] is not a matter of regret, but of pride. . . . We were right in wresting from barbarism and adding to civilization the territory out of which we have made these beautiful states. Barbarism has . . . no place in a civilized world. It is our duty toward the people living in barbarism to see that they are freed from their chains, and we can free them only by destroying barbarism itself." Roosevelt declared that the original American pioneers who conquered the Indians had exhibited "the essential manliness of the American character" and called American military invasions of foreign countries "the higher duty of promoting the civilization of mankind." He called for expansion beyond America's shores: "You, the sons of the pioneers, if you are true to your ancestry, must make your lives as worthy as they made theirs. . . . Speak softly and carry a big stick—you will go far."[4]

WHEN HE BECAME PRESIDENT, Roosevelt embraced the Monroe Doctrine as justification to wield the Big Stick, dispatching the U.S. Navy to quell a "revolution" in Colombia, an action that allowed him to tear

Panama away from that country. Then he extracted canal rights from Panama "in perpetuity." Roosevelt later admitted that he "took the Canal and let Congress debate."[5] He boasted that if "any South American country misbehaves," it should be "spanked,"[6] and once wrote, "I am so angry with that infernal little Cuban republic that I would like to wipe its people off the face of the earth."[7] Big Stick, indeed.

Teddy's most prominent enunciation of his Big Stick philosophy was the Roosevelt Corollary to the Monroe Doctrine. President Monroe's goal had essentially been defensive; now Roosevelt took the offense, asserting that the U.S. military was an "international police"[8] and that he had the right to order invasions to enforce American foreign policy. The world could trust such a policy, he argued, because the goal of U.S. foreign policy was "the peace of justice."[9] Roosevelt posed as reluctant to deploy his international police force but warned barbarian countries that if they "violated the rights of the United States," or if he observed "a general loosing of the ties of civilized society," the United States could exercise its "international police power."[10] Roosevelt informed Congress that American police powers extended to the Caribbean, Central America, and South America, as well as to North Asia (Korea and Manchuria) and to enforcing the Open Door policy in China.

Roosevelt believed he could advance U.S. interests

in North Asia through his own sense of the ebb and flow of civilizations.[11] To Teddy, North Asia was a waste space that would eventually be civilized by either the Anglo-Saxon or the Slav, the two main branches of the Aryan race. The follow-the-sun crowd saw the Slav, though of Aryan descent, as inferior to the Anglo-Saxon. Declared Professor Franklin Giddings of Columbia University, "The great question of the twentieth century is whether the Anglo-Saxon or the Slav is to impress his civilization to the world."[12]

By the time Roosevelt became president, China—a nation of four hundred million people—was a shrunken country squeezed between the Anglo-Saxon and Slav empires.

Roosevelt, who had grown up during the peak anti-Chinese years in American history, referred to Chinese people as "Chinks." He believed that the Chinese had lost the barbarian values and therefore China was the Darwinian prey of virile White Christians. Chinese men were viewed as particularly ludicrous—they tied their hair in sissy pigtails and wore dresses. Roosevelt believed that China's future would be determined by outside countries that were now slicing the Chinese melon.

Anglo-Saxon ascendancy in North Asia had traditionally been guaranteed by the British navy, but the construction of the Trans-Siberian Railway had allowed Russia to flood Manchuria with troops.

Meanwhile, Anglo-Saxon armies were far away in the Philippines and India. To counter the Slav's land power, the Anglo-Saxons would enlist the land armies of the Honorary Aryans.

Roosevelt loathed the Slav: "No human beings," he declared, "black, yellow, or white could be quite as untruthful, as insincere, as arrogant—in short, as untrustworthy in every way—as the Russians."[13] Teddy's sun-following friend, Senator Albert Beveridge, traveled to Manchuria via the Trans-Siberian Railway. Roughly the size of France and Germany combined, the region was rich with timber, minerals, and fertile soil. In a subsequent article in the *Saturday Evening Post,* Beveridge presented Manchuria as the American Aryan's next Wild West—if only the Slav could be pushed out of the way. Beveridge recalled that a Russian officer had gloated, "You may be stronger now, richer now, than we are—but we shall be stronger tomorrow than you....The future abides with the Slav!"[14] Such comments played right into the fears of Roosevelt and his allies. "There is but one agency which might dislodge the Russians from Manchuria," Beveridge wrote, "the sword-like bayonets of the soldiers of Japan, the war-ships of Japan, the siege guns of Japan, the embattled frenzy of a nation stirred to its profoundest depths by the conviction that the Czar had deprived the Mikado of the greatest victory and the richest prize in all the history

China and Foreign Territories

In Roosevelt's time, China was being squeezed by predatory countries that were "slicing the Chinese melon."

The Russo-Japanese War (1904–1905)

*Japanese leaders feared Russian control of Manchuria.
If Russia moved into Korea, Japanese expansion into Asia
would be blocked and Russia would dominate China
and North Asia.*

of the Island Empire."[15] The triple intervention had dashed Japan's expansionary hopes; now the United States would revive them.

As early as 1900, Vice President Roosevelt had written to a friend: "I should like to see Japan have Korea. She will be a check upon Russia, and she deserves it for what she has done."[16] The American motivation in North Asia was economic, but the Japanese focus was strategic: if the Russians expanded from Manchuria to Korea, Japan would be effectively surrounded. So American and Japanese interests meshed in opposition to the Slav. To Roosevelt, the Japanese were the champions of Anglo-Saxon civilization in North Asia and an antidote to the degraded "Chinks" and the slovenly Slavs. Roosevelt was convinced—courtesy of the founding fathers' "Leave Asia" strategy—that the Japanese were different from other Asians, that they were "a wonderful and civilized people...entitled to stand on an absolute equality with all the other peoples of the civilized world." Roosevelt dismissed fear of a Yellow Peril* by likening the Japanese to the Teuton of two thousand years earlier when "the white-skinned, blue-eyed...barbarian of the North" was a "White Terror" to the Greeks and Romans.[17] The Teuton rose to become civilized, just like the

---

* "Yellow Peril" was the term for westerners' fear that hordes of angry Asians would overrun them and destroy Western civilization.

Japanese were doing now. Early in his administration, the president practiced jujitsu grips used by the Japanese army, gaining insight into their barbarian virtues. Teddy considered himself to be on the cutting edge, witnessing a race phenomenon: the rise of the Japanese from barbaric to civilized. They could never be Aryan, but they could serve as a respectable partner, at least for now.

ROOSEVELT VIEWED JAPAN'S TAKEOVER of Korea as a progressive social experiment. For the first time in history, an Asian nation was making a serious attempt—complete with international lawyers and a huge military-industrial complex—to assume The White Man's Burden. And Roosevelt was eager to help, believing that Japanese conquest would benefit millions of Asians.

At the turn of the century, Britain was suffering a number of imperial crises. Rebellions in Burma, Siam, Afghanistan, Tibet, Egypt, the Sudan, the Ottoman Empire, Venezuela, Samoa, and South Africa all required British military action. By 1901, Lord Henry Lansdowne, the new foreign secretary, had developed a new strategy based on ententes and alliances. This was especially important in North Asia, where Britain had no land forces to counter the Russians.

Japanese leaders supported the Anglo-American Open Door policy* but their embrace of Anglo-Saxon ideals was born of strategic necessity. Britain's and the United States' motivation was the Open Door in China, and Japan's was to expand into Korea. Joint opposition to Russia was a means to an end.

SOON AFTER ROOSEVELT ASCENDED to the presidency, Tokyo shocked the world when it announced that Japan had signed a treaty with the mightiest White power of all—Great Britain. The terms of the 1902 Anglo-Japanese Treaty upheld the Anglo-Saxon Open Door policy, recognized Japan's "special interests" in Korea, and placed Britain on Japan's side in a potential conflict with the Slav. If any nation became allied with Russia during a war with Japan, the treaty stated, Britain would enter the war on Japan's side. Russia could thus no longer count on help from Germany or France if hostilities broke out. This meant that the next time Japan set foot on the Asian continent, it would not suffer another "Shame of Liaodong." One New York newspaper described the treaty as "a shaft aimed at Russia."[18]

---

*The idea that the other western countries colonizing parts of China would allow free trade to England and the United States within their spheres.

In contrast to Great Britain, the other Anglo-Saxon power was an isolationist country that shunned imperial power treaties, with a constitution that required its Senate to shine its examining light on all agreements. But in the White House sat a young president who planned to use his "little Jap" allies to enlighten Asia and wedge the Open Door even wider.

On April 23, 1903, Secretary of State John Hay wrote to President Roosevelt, "We could never get a treaty through the Senate the object of which was to check Russian aggression."[19] Hay said two days later that the American public was only dimly aware of America's interests in North Asia: "I am sure you will think it out of the question that we should adopt any scheme of concerted action with England and Japan which would seem hostile to Russia. Public opinion in this country would not support such a course, nor do I think it would be to our permanent advantage."[20] Big Stick Teddy responded in frustration, "The bad feature of the situation from our standpoint is that as yet it seems that we cannot fight to keep Manchuria open. I hate being in the position of seeming to bluster without backing it up."[21]

Czar Nicholas II of Russia believed it was his destiny to control North Asia and he dismissed the Japanese as *makaki,* or "little Jap monkeys." Hoping to forestall any bloodshed, Japan suggested an exchange: if Japan could have Korea, Russia could have Manchuria. In response, Nicholas ignored the little monkeys and moved thirty thousand more troops east. A Japanese newspaper complained, "A peaceful solution of the Manchurian question through indecisive diplomatic measures and humiliating conditions is meaningless. This is not what our nation wants."[22] On January 21, 1904, the American minister to Japan, Lloyd Griscom, warned from Tokyo: "The Japanese nation is now worked up to a high pitch of excitement.... Nothing but the most complete backdown by the Russian government will satisfy the public feeling."[23]

Roosevelt was so eager to see the Japanese initiate their mission of civilization that one month before the war broke, he boasted that he "would not hesitate to give Japan something more than moral support against Russia."[24] But Big Stick Teddy knew that he'd have to get permission from Congress to use military force in North Asia, something they almost certainly wouldn't authorize. Roosevelt could only watch from afar as his Japanese allies prepared to advance the cause of civilization.

On February 1, 1904, William Howard Taft became secretary of war, after Elihu Root resigned and returned to his remunerative Manhattan law practice. Roosevelt's wife, Edith, complained that Taft was "too much of a yes-man," but as Roosevelt became more secretive in his dealings, he disliked consulting experts who might disagree.[25] The whole idea was that Big Bill would be an "assistant president" who would always agree with his boss.

Roosevelt was already effectively serving as his own secretary of state as elderly John Hay declined in health. Now, having gathered the powers of the State and War departments into his own young hands, Roosevelt would shape America's reaction to history's largest armed conflict prior to World War I.

ON FEBRUARY 4, 1904, the prime minister of Japan, Taro Katsura, assembled his somber cabinet before Emperor Meiji and the founding fathers. Katsura reported that Japan had tried to work things out with Russia regarding Korea but that the Russians wouldn't negotiate seriously.

The founding fathers were not optimistic. Japan was much weaker than the Russian Bear, with only one hundred eighty thousand army troops compared to Russia's 1.1 million men. The Russians had nine battleships and five armored cruisers in the Pacific, compared to the Japanese navy's six battleships and six armored cruisers. The army figured it had an even chance against the Russians while the navy believed it might destroy the Russian fleet at the cost of half of the Japanese fleet. No one would assure Meiji of victory. But they reasoned that even if a war with Russia ended in a draw, it would still vault Japan into the White Christian power club. The Japanese ambassador to the United States, Takahira Kogoro, had already let Tokyo know that Roosevelt felt that Japan's plans constituted a wise course, which would meet the sympathy of the civilized world.

When Commodore Matthew Perry had kicked open Japan's closed doors, it caused a chain reaction now in play like balls on a pool table. Japan had been advised by General LeGendre in the 1870s to "act courageously for the purpose of pushing forward the flag of the rising Sun in Asia and for the sake of the expansion of our empire... [and] to become the protector of the various nations in Asia.... This policy resembles the one taken by the United States."[26]

Now was the time. On February 6, 1904, Japan broke relations with Russia. Roosevelt wrote privately, "The sympathies of the United States are entirely on Japan's side, but we will maintain the strictest neutrality."[27]

IN SEOUL, THE NOW Emperor Gojong (desiring to keep up with the imperial Joneses, he had recently declared Korea an "empire") watched Japan's moves with trepidation. Britain was allied with Japan, but in Washington sat Elder Brother Roosevelt. Roosevelt's minister in Seoul was Horace Allen, Emperor Gojong's favorite Elder Brother, and Allen led Gojong to believe "that the United States would indeed exercise good offices in accord with the treaty of 1882 should the occasion arise."[28]

The historical record is silent on whether the Americans ever warned the emperor what the Roosevelt Corollary meant for Korea. Roosevelt had written that "impotent" countries were legitimate prey for the civilized nations. In the dark, the Koreans had no idea what was about to happen. As war clouds gathered, a court official in Seoul assured a Western reporter: "We have the promise of America. She will be our friend whatever happens."[29]

To project their military power onto the Asian continent, the Japanese navy would first have to capture ports where they could land army troops. The best two harbor cities were Port Arthur, the Russian fortress on the tip of the Liaodong Peninsula, and Incheon, Korea, with a port that harbored warships from a number of countries, including Russia.

On February 8, 1904—with no declaration of war—Japanese torpedo boats surprised Russian ships at Port Arthur and Incheon. The Russians denounced the Japanese move as a shameful violation of international law, but Americans were delighted. Oscar Straus, later Teddy's secretary of commerce and labor, wrote the president, "Japan is certainly battling on the side of civilization—may Wisdom and Victory be on her side."[30] Elihu Root gushed to Teddy, "Was not the way the Japs began the fight bully?"[31] Roosevelt wrote his son, "I was thoroughly well pleased with the Japanese victory, for Japan is playing our game."[32]

Roosevelt's ideas about civilization and barbarism blinded him to the obvious: Japan's advances on the Liaodong and Korean peninsulas were the opening moves in Japan's expansion into all of Asia. The president believed that his Honorary Aryans would play America's game as loyal promoters of Anglo-Saxon ideals in Asia. He never imagined that the surprise-attack tactics he praised in 1904 would later bedevil another President Roosevelt. (As he planned the 1941 attack on Pearl Harbor, the Japanese navy admiral Isoroku Yamamoto would write, "We have much to learn from the Russo-Japanese War.... Favorable opportunities were gained by opening the war with a sudden attack on the main enemy fleet.")[33]

At Port Arthur, Japanese and Russian troops set in for a long siege. At Incheon, the Japanese navy quickly bested the surprised Russians, and Japanese army troops marched on to Seoul. Korean leaders were forced at gunpoint to accept an "alliance" with Japan.

The Japanese legation in Washington subsequently informed the Roosevelt administration that Korea was merely "allied" with Japan. In fact, Japan now

The Russo-Japanese Land War

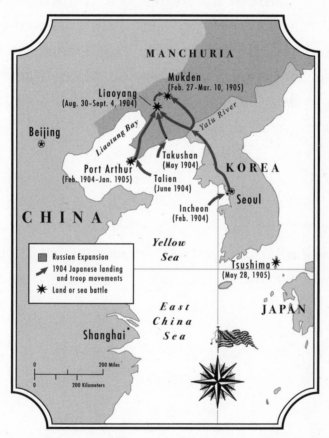

The Russo-Japanese War was fought on neither Russian nor Japanese territory, but rather was a contest to determine which country would dominate Korea and China.

had the right to station troops anywhere in Korea, controlled Korean officials, and even had veto power over Korea's relations with other nations.

As the Russo-Japanese War erupted, Roosevelt took action to ensure that Japan would not suffer another "Shame of Liaodong." He immediately notified Germany and France that if they assisted Russia, "I should promptly side with Japan and proceed to whatever length was necessary on her behalf."[34]

Chapter 8

THE JAPANESE MONROE DOCTRINE FOR ASIA

"Japan is the only nation in Asia that understands the principles and methods of Western civilization. She has proved that she can assimilate Western civilization, yet not break up her own heritage. All the Asiatic nations are now faced with the urgent necessity of adjusting themselves to the present age. Japan should be their natural leader in that process, and their protector during the transition stage, much as the United States assumed the leadership of the American continent many years ago, and by means of the Monroe Doctrine, preserved the Latin American nations from European interference, while they were maturing their independence."[1]
—PRESIDENT THEODORE ROOSEVELT TO BARON KENTARO KANEKO, JULY 8, 1905

The founding fathers of Japan had long monitored the Western media and had successfully crafted a positive image of Japan as different from other Asian countries. Now in 1904 the Japanese Foreign Ministry converted their embassies into public-relations bureaus, blitzing Western capitals with stories of how dashing Japanese warriors were, how the Japanese Red Cross respected Russian prisoners, and how Japan was battling for world civilization and the maintenance of the Anglo-American Open Door.

Japan had already cemented a treaty with one Anglo-Saxon country—Britain—and now Tokyo sought the other. The founding fathers searched their ranks for a Japanese man who had been educated in the United States, who spoke American English, and who knew the American political, social, and financial scenes. Above all, Tokyo's wise men sought someone who could roll the Rough Rider in the White House.

Baron Kentaro Kaneko was the man chosen to woo America. Kaneko was a disciple of the leading founding father, Hirobumi Ito. After the Meiji Restoration, Kaneko was one of the first Japanese students sent abroad. He studied law under the famous lawyer Oliver Wendell Holmes Jr. at Harvard, during the same time Roosevelt was an undergraduate there, and was awarded a law degree in 1878.

Baron Kaneko was exactly the type of guy to appeal to the patrician president: he was well born, a titled aristocrat, a Harvard lawyer, a mannered gentleman in tie and tails, a paramount representative of an aggressively militarized society, and a suave speaker who had mastered the language of civilization. The *New York Times* reported from Tokyo that Kaneko had been appointed by the founding fathers as a special envoy "to explain Japan's position to America."[2]

Teddy was quickly enamored with the new emissary. Some of his affection resulted not from an honest assessment of Kaneko—the Tokyo-based American minister, Lloyd Griscom, had warned Teddy that Kaneko was a lightweight.[3] But Kaneko had been born into a samurai family, the caste atop Japanese society, the exalted warriors of yore who had nurtured Japan's barbarian virtues. During the Tokugawa "Great Peace," the samurai had become the leaders of Japan in government, business, and academia. Thus, to Teddy, Kaneko was much like himself: a highborn inheritor of barbarian virtues, a Harvard man, literate and articulate, civilized and ready to charge the hill.

KANEKO TOOK THE COUNTRY by storm. In San Francisco his appearance garnered column after column of newspaper ink. In Chicago, he lectured at the Harvard Club and Northwestern University. In New

York, he explained to fifteen Manhattan newsmen that Japan was fighting Russia in the cause of Anglo-Saxon civilization. On April 2, the Supreme Court justice Oliver Wendell Holmes Jr. threw a glittering dinner party at his Washington home for his former protégé. At George Washington University, Kaneko spoke of the similarities between the constitutions of the United States and Japan, a lecture reprinted in the *Century Magazine.* Back in Manhattan, he gave a speech to Wall Street's barons at the University Club and at a private dinner at the home of Roosevelt's friend Oscar Straus.[4] At Harvard, President Charles William Eliot introduced the baron as a renaissance man astride Occidental and Oriental cultures: "Kentaro Kaneko, Harvard bachelor of laws, formerly chief secretary of the Imperial House of Peers in Japan, Minister of agriculture and commerce, life member of the House of Peers, the type of those scholars of two hemispheres through whom West would welcome East to share in the inheritance of Hebrew religion, Greek art, Roman law, and nineteenth century science."[5]

Baron Kaneko told a new generation of Harvard sun-followers that the Japanese "are yellow in skin, but in heart and mind we are as white as Europeans and Americans.... Our hearts beat just as much as Christian hearts—the civilized heart is the same the world over." In closing, he warned that if Japan doesn't defeat Russia, "the open-door policy is lost and the Anglo-American civilization will never take root."[6] The *Boston Herald* printed Kaneko's speech and it was then reprinted into six thousand small booklets.[7]

Baron Kaneko's most important assignment was to influence Theodore Roosevelt. Teddy most likely would have been bewildered by most Japanese, who ate rice with chopsticks, sat on the floor, and soaked nude in hot tubs. But Baron Kaneko was the very picture of an Americanized Honorary Aryan, and he would soon sweep Roosevelt off his feet.

The subsequent Roosevelt-Kaneko talks—kept secret and lasting for nineteen months—would prove disastrous for the United States. Roosevelt was far out of his league, with almost no understanding of Asia. In the Japanese founding fathers, Roosevelt was dealing with the world's most successful non-White, non-Christian revolutionaries. And—at the height of his Big Stick period—he sought no advice nor risked disagreement by explaining himself to his State Department or Congress.[8]

Kaneko knew that Americans such as Theodore Roosevelt and William Howard Taft believed that Aryans had journeyed west out of Central Asia. Kaneko crafted a complimentary myth about those ancients who went east at the same time, who would now join hands with the Aryans of the West. In Kaneko's telling, the Himalaya mountains were the fountain head of the two great waves of human energy [which created] all our enlightened modern civilization. From the western slopes there began...that Aryan march which established its dominion over the whole of Europe and flowered into Occidental civilization. From the mountain's eastern sides there flowed that slower but no less profound tide which we know as orientalism....After the visit of Commodore Perry, in 1853, we turned to the West for culture and science, and thus the laws, the philosophy, the religion and art of Occidental civilization were engrafted upon our institutions. The Japanese mind is earnestly engaged in moulding into one the two forms of culture, the Oriental and the Occidental, its ambition being to harmonize them, even as Rome harmonized the militarism of the northern tribes with the culture of the southern races of Europe.[9]

Kaneko explained that just as England, off the coast of Europe, had become the highest receptacle of Anglo-Saxonism, Japan, off Asia's coast, was the highest repository of orientalism. "Japan's geographical situation," he added, "has placed it between...both eastern and western civilizations, and [Japan] is rapidly absorbing and completely assimilating them."[10]

Kaneko portrayed Japan as battling the Slav in "an inevitable conflict...between Anglo-American civilization, as it has been inspired in the Japanese by England and America, on the one hand, and Muscovite despotism on the other."[11] He further explained that the Russo-Japanese War was one of Russian "continental militarism" against Anglo-Saxon "maritime commercialism." Russia, he said, would take China for itself, "whereas, England, the United States and Japan are...always striving for the open door policy."[12] And he warned that Japan's defeat of Russia was the last chance to civilize Asia: "If Japan be defeated now... the spirit and the principles of Anglo-American civilization will be obliterated from a vast portion of the eastern world. And it may be that centuries will pass before ever again humanity, and the universal brotherhood of Christianity, will dawn over the horizon of the continent of Asia."[13]

The Roosevelt-Kaneko talks began on March 26, 1904, when Ambassador Takahira brought Kaneko to the State Department to pay respects to Secretary Hay. Kaneko spoke so enthusiastically about America's obvious tilt toward Japan that Hay later fretted in his diary, "I had to remind him that we were neutral."[14]

Takahira and Kaneko then went to the White House. More than thirty visitors were waiting to see the president, but when Roosevelt saw Kaneko's calling card, he bypassed the others to pump Kaneko's hand. As Raymond Esthus writes in *Theodore Roosevelt and Japan,* Roosevelt "took the Baron into his confidence completely."[15] Roosevelt spoke in decidedly unneutral terms about Japan's mission of civilization in Asia. Roosevelt asked Kaneko for reading material on Japan. The baron whipped out articles he had authored and recommended the book *Bushido* by Inazo Nitobe, which likened samurai values to Europe's chivalric code. The founding fathers must have been elated when they read Ambassador Takahira's summary of the first Roosevelt-Kaneko talk, in which Takahira reported that the president expressed confidence that Japan would win the war and establish herself as Asia's great civilizing force.[16]

EMPEROR GOJONG—HIS COUNTRY now held hostage by the Japanese—met with Minister Allen and requested America's protection. Allen cabled Washington about the meeting: "He falls back in his extremity upon his old friendship with America.... The Emperor confidently expects that America will do something for him at the close of this war, or when opportunity offers, to retain for him as much of his independence as is possible.... I am obliged to assure His Majesty that the condition of Korea is borne in mind by the United States Government, who will use their good offices when occasion occurs."[17] The American minister's statement of obligation was false, as Gojong would soon learn.

Then most of Gojong's palace was burned down, probably by the Japanese. The emperor retreated to a detached palace library, which was next to America's legation building. Gojong requested political asylum from the United States. Allen told him that if the emperor scaled the legation walls, he would put him out.

Despite the setback, Gojong was not without hope. True, his neutral country had been occupied by a foreign power, but he had reason to believe that once the war ended, Japan would withdraw and Korean independence would resume. After all, he had signed that important treaty that promised Korea a square deal. But as Gojong scrambled, Roosevelt informed Secretary Taft, "I heartily agree with the Japanese terms of peace, insofar as they include Japan having the control of Korea."[18]

THE BATTLE OF YALU River, ending on May 1, 1904, was the first major land clash of the Russo-Japanese War, with Japanese troops crossing the river and routing the Russians. With the victory, the Japanese army was now prepared to invade Manchuria from the north as well as from Port Arthur in the south. Far away in his palace, a White Christian czar imagined it impossible for "little Jap monkeys" to best his army, but in fact Japan now had the Russians in a headlock.

ON JUNE 6, 1904, Roosevelt again welcomed Baron Kaneko and Ambassador Takahira to the White House, this time for a private luncheon. Roosevelt knew he was speaking through these two interlocutors to the founding fathers in Tokyo, yet he kept these discussions secret, informing neither the State Department nor Congress.

Roosevelt's guests immediately addressed the critical subject always at the forefront of the president's thinking: race. They pointed out that it had been the thirteenth-century Mongolians who had terrorized Europe and that this Yellow Peril had also threatened Japan. The diplomats reiterated that Japan was different from the rest of Asia, with its own two-thousand-year civilization, and they "did not see why they should be classed as barbarians."[19]

Roosevelt agreed and complimented the two by saying he thought the Japanese people were more racially similar to Americans than were the Russians. By way of analogy, the president explained that riff-raff races such as the Turks and Russians—"European peoples who speak an Aryan tongue"—were not very civilized; instead they were "impossible members of our international society...[while] Japan would simply take her place from now on among the great civilized nations."[20]

Then Roosevelt gave his little Jap guests a lesson in race history, saying that in the AD tenth century, his Teutonic ancestors had been considered the White Terror, "and that as we had outgrown the position of being a race threat, I thought that in a similar fashion such a civilization as [the Japanese] had developed entitled them to laugh at the accusation of being part of the Yellow Terror."[21] He informed Kaneko and Takahira that Japan should have "a paramount interest in what surrounds the Yellow Sea, just as the United States has a paramount interest in what surrounds the Caribbean."[22] Though Roosevelt had just made a momentous pronouncement, his Japanese guests missed its implications. Big Stick Teddy was suggesting that because the Japanese had assimilated Anglo-Saxon values and would support the Open Door policy, they should have a Monroe Doctrine–like protectorate on the Asian continent. Teddy did not make the analogy clear at this meeting—as he later would—and neither Takahira nor Kaneko referred to it in their cables back to Tokyo.

Roosevelt now brought up the possibility that Japan might covet the Philippines, stating bluntly that if Japan attacked America's Pacific colony, "we would be quite competent to defend ourselves."[23] The two guests earnestly assured Roosevelt that "tall talk of Japan's even thinking of the Philippines was nonsense."[24] Roosevelt later recalled that he was confident that the Japanese would not expand beyond what he had bequeathed, because when he mentioned to Takahira and Kaneko the challenge of civilizing China, "they grinned and said that they were quite aware of the difficulty they were going to have even in Korea and were satisfied with that job."[25]

Over the next year and a half, Roosevelt would repeat his Japanese Monroe Doctrine concept with the intent that Takahira and Kaneko would communicate his desire to the founding fathers and Emperor Meiji. Because Teddy relayed these ideas only orally, with no U.S. officials overhearing the exchanges that were said to Asian people who spoke and wrote a difficult language that few in the West could decipher, the president had excellent plausible deniability.

After their lunch in the White House, Ambassador Takahira quickly telegraphed Roosevelt's views to Tokyo, where they were warmly received. Roosevelt had committed nothing in writing, so he had placed the interpretation of the conversation completely in the hands of an employee of the Japanese government, who portrayed the president as a Japan cheerleader, telling Tokyo that Roosevelt would shape

American public opinion and take the diplomatic actions necessary to suit the desires of the Japanese government.[26]

Perhaps a junior-level State Department diplomat or a young staffer on the Senate Foreign Relations Committee would have known better, but Rough Rider Teddy had no fear. The Japs, he was certain, would be Honorary Aryans, content with the territory Roosevelt granted them, committed to the Open Door. Teddy never imagined that Russian power would soon collapse in revolution and that the powerful Japs and weakened Slavs would become friends after this war and unite—against American interests in North Asia.

Japan's foreign minister, Jutaro Komura, was so grateful for the American tilt toward Japan that he suggested that Emperor Meiji formally thank Roosevelt. However, Ambassador Takahira intervened to keep Teddy's commitment secret,[27] cautioning Tokyo to put nothing in writing. Takahira did orally pass on Tokyo's appreciation to Secretary Hay and asked Hay to convey this sentiment to Roosevelt "if [Hay] found it proper."[28] Two weeks later, a confident Roosevelt wrote Hay, "The Japs have played our game because they have played the game of civilized mankind.... We may be of genuine service... in preventing interference to rob her of the fruits of her victory."[29]

*   *   *

AMERICANS COULD JUDGE THE high level of Japanese civilization for themselves at the 1904 World's Fair in St. Louis. While the United States displayed its Indian reservation and Philippines reservation, Britain brought African "Kaffirs" to do maintenance work and to live in an open village where they could be gawked at. In emulation of its Anglo-American allies, Japan brought along its colonized Others: eight good specimens of Ainu people, the aborigines the Japanese had long ago chased into the northern wastes of Hokkaido island. As an official World's Fair publication stated: "Japanese civilization presents a striking contrast to the Ainu who are simple barbarians. Their stupidity... has never been... explained and they are ethnically listed with the races who are incapable of civilization and education."[30]

Nearby was the Japanese merchant marine exhibit. Millions of American visitors saw its immense topographical map of North Asia, featuring Korea and Manchuria. The name of the map was "The Japanese Empire."[31]

AMERICAN MEDIA COVERAGE OF the Russo-Japanese War was heavily pro-Japanese. The American infatuation with Japan increased as Jap soldiers gave chase to the Slavs. Popular magazine articles with titles such as "How Russia Brought On the War" and "Why We Favour Japan in the Present War" informed readers that the war was "a general revolt of all the civilized peoples of the earth against the perfidy and insincerity of Russia" and that "Russia stands for reaction and Japan for progress."[32] A British politician visiting Washington told Baron Kaneko, "Since coming to America I have traveled to every part of the country and met with people of every walk of life, and have been astonished by the great sympathy felt for your country. They support your country with an enthusiasm that one does not easily see even in my country, England, which is an ally of yours, and the antipathy they have for Russia was truly quite unexpected."[33] From the U.S. legation in Seoul, Minister Allen watched as Japanese troops took over Korea. He cabled Washington: "Japan is the rightful and natural overlord."[34]

In the White House, Roosevelt lectured his cabinet on jujitsu holds and quoted the book *Bushido*. He wrote Secretary Hay, "What nonsense it is to speak of the Chinese and Japanese as of the same race!"[35] Still, he had occasional doubts; after all, no matter their mimickry, these Honorary Aryans were not White. In December of 1904, Roosevelt called Takahira into the White House and warned him that despite its victories Japan should not get a big head regarding the White race. Privately the president occasionally worried whether Japan viewed Americans "simply as white devils inferior to themselves"[36] and about "Japanese hostility to the white race in general and especially to Americans."[37] As he watched the Japanese army lay siege to Russian fortifications at Port Arthur, Roosevelt fretted that he wanted Japan to succeed, "but not too overwhelmingly."[38]

JAPAN HAD HOPED TO capture Port Arthur quickly, but its troops encountered well-prepared Russian defenses and the bloody siege stretched on for months. In a preview of World War I, hundreds and thousands of young men perished in trenches as shrapnel rained down on them or died charging uselessly into the bullets of machine guns.

But the Japanese kept coming and the Russians eventually surrendered Port Arthur on New Year's Day, 1905.

By that January, it appeared to Roosevelt that his predictions were coming true. Russia's surrender of its seemingly impregnable Port Arthur fortress to the Japanese demonstrated that Slav civilization was sinking while Japan's was rising. Then "Bloody Sunday" exploded in St. Petersburg as two hundred thousand protestors assailed the Winter Palace demanding victory over Japan or an end to the war. This was one of the first in a string of events later called the Russian Revolution, and Roosevelt saw it as further proof that the Slav was a declining race. With Roosevelt's knowledge and approval, Japan began negotiating an updated treaty with England, in which seven months later England would trade India for Korea.

The arrangement was yet another round of imperial board gaming. Great Britain had supported Japan's modernization efforts, and both were concerned with Russian expansion in Asia—British leaders worried that the Russians might move deeply into China. In 1902, Japan and Great Britain proclaimed an official Anglo-Japanese Alliance. This agreement might have been signed earlier if not for disagreements between the two parties regarding each other's imperial ambitions. The alliance was built around two concepts: a declaration of neutrality if either signatory went to war; and a promise of support if either signatory went to war with more than one power. But the Japanese had no interest in supporting British claims to India, and Great Britain had no desire to be brought into defending Japanese interests in Korea. So a trade was arranged: both would stay out of each other's way. Neither signatory would be obligated to come to the other's defense in those seized territories.

The British saw the agreement as a velvety warning to Russia—no, the alliance did not mandate joining in the Russo-Japanese War, but the existing thicket of agreements between the powers meant that France could not easily come to Russia's aid without resulting in a war with Great Britain. And it was no small thing to come up against the most powerful empire in the world, even if only in a court of diplomatic opinion. Yet if the British understood the alliance as more flute than drum, the Japanese saw things very differently. The greatest of the White Christian powers had just agreed that they would not do anything about a Japanese occupation of Korea.

Roosevelt—through private intermediaries that included his wife—signaled London and Tokyo that he supported the swap and wished he could trade the Philippines for Korea and make it a triple alliance. But Roosevelt had to ask his allies to spare him the exposure of "open evident agreement." This, too, would be secret. Writing King Edward VII of England, Teddy said, "I absolutely agree with you as to the importance...to all the free peoples of the civilized world, of a constantly growing friendship and understanding between the English-speaking peoples....All I can do to foster it will be done....With affairs in the orient...our interests are identical with yours."[39]

Still hopeful, Emperor Gojong dispatched twenty-nine-year-old Syngman Rhee to Washington to urge America to honor its treaty obligations. In February 1905, Rhee met with Secretary of State Hay. Later Rhee remembered that Hay had blandly assured him that the United States would fulfill the "good offices" provision of the U.S.-Korea Treaty.[40]

BY NOW, THE FOUNDING fathers in Tokyo knew Roosevelt's thinking like the back of their aged hands. The foreign minister, Jutaro Komura—a fellow Harvard grad—sent Roosevelt a copy of Japan's plan for a postwar world that just happened to mesh with Teddy's thinking: after beating the Slavs, Japan would retain Port Arthur and Korea while supporting the Open Door. As Raymond Esthus concludes in *Theodore Roosevelt and Japan:* "Thus by February, 1905, Roosevelt and Japan were in complete agreement on peace terms."[41]

As Japanese soldiers marched north from Port Arthur to attack the Manchurian city of Mukden (today's Shenyang), Roosevelt fretted. He certainly leaned strongly toward the Japanese, but his ultimate priorities were the United States and his dream of Anglo-Saxon expansion. Making certain of some sort of balance of power in North Asia seemed wise. Observing the Japanese advance, he advised Czar Nicholas to make peace. Teddy wanted his line of friction to be south of Mukden, and he feared a Russian loss would unmoderate the plan. The czar ignored the meddlesome young president and the "little Jap monkeys."

*　　*　　*

ONE FEBRUARY DAY, ROOSEVELT staged a match between his American wrestling instructor and his Japanese jujitsu teacher. The assembled generals, summoned to the White House for the occasion, observed the "yellow man" triumph. Back in Asia, the Japanese were putting the moves on the Russians. Their diplomatic offensive was no less robust. That same month, Baron Kaneko handed Roosevelt a written statement he had solicited from several Yale professors while visiting New Haven, which informed the president, "Japan has fairly earned the right to paramount influence in Korea, by reason of her sacrifices, to prevent the Russianization of Korea."[42] This opinion was echoed by Roosevelt's most trusted adviser on North Asia, William Rockhill, the U.S. minister to China. Rockhill had proclaimed, "The annexation of Korea to Japan seems to be absolutely indicated as the one great and final step westward of the extension of the Japanese empire.... I cannot see any possibility of this government using its influence to bolster up the empire of Korea in its independence. I fancy that the Japanese will settle this question when the present war is finished."[43]

Roosevelt didn't wait until the war was finished. The same month, Teddy secretly told the founding fathers that he approved of Japan having a Monroe Doctrine–like protectorate in Asia. To further the triple alliance on the Atlantic side, Roosevelt used his wife, Edith, and the Brit who had been best man at their London wedding, Cecil Spring-Rice: from Teddy's mouth to Edith's ear, then into a folksy coded letter to "Springy," who finally delivered the message to Whitehall. Sealing deals with London and Tokyo, Roosevelt felt himself at the center of international affairs, navigating the ship of civilization into twentieth-century Asia. And it was all so deliciously secret.

If Congress had been aware of the president's alliances, perhaps a senator would have challenged Roosevelt to think through the consequences of the United States' carving out a chunk of Asia for Japan to nibble on. Perhaps a congressman might have inspired Roosevelt to imagine a Japan that later would chafe at Teddy's leash.

ROOSEVELT TOOK HIS SECOND oath of office from the chief justice, Melville Fuller, in a March 1905 ceremony before thousands in front of the East Portico, the grand balustrade entrance to the Capitol building. With his hand on the Bible, Roosevelt swore to uphold American values. A statue to Roosevelt's immediate left represented some unwritten American values. Seventy-one years earlier, Congress had commissioned sculptor Horatio Greenough to create a statue that would "represent the conflict between the Anglo-Saxon and Indian races."[44] Greenough testified before Congress that the statue recalled "the peril of the American wilderness, the ferocity of our Indians, the superiority of the white man, and why and how civilization crowded the Indian from his soil."[45] Greenough called his monumental work *The Rescue.*

Greenough's masterpiece features a terrified, cowering White mother shielding her baby from danger with her body. Barbarism, in the form of a savage Indian clad in a loincloth, hovers over her, hatchet in hand, ready to strike. Towering behind the Indian is a heroic White man who is restraining the savage by the wrist, restoring safety and civilization.

(The first president to be inaugurated next to *The Rescue* was Franklin Pierce in 1853, and the final one would be Dwight Eisenhower in 1953. By 1958, Congress deemed *The Rescue* an embarrassment and the statue is now hidden in the government's memory vaults.)

Roosevelt, newly reelected, was determined to continue America's civilizing mission. Later on his inauguration day, seated in his reviewing stand on Pennsylvania Avenue, he saw native troops from the

The Rescue *statue. For one hundred years—from 1853 to 1953—American presidents took their oaths of office standing next to* The Rescue. *(Library of Congress)*

Philippines and Puerto Rico march by and joked that they were "rejoicing in their shackles."[46]

IN MARCH OF 1905, the Japanese army ground down Russian forces in the largest land battle in the history before World War I. The month-long battle for the Manchurian city of Mukden involved nearly one million combatants and resulted in almost two hundred thousand casualties. Wave after wave of Japanese soldiers charged into Russian bullets. Americans would later deride Japan's suicidal tactics in World War II, but in 1905 Rough Rider Teddy praised their willingness to die: "The Japanese are the most dashing fighters in the world."[47] Enthused, he intensified his jujitsu practice, wrestling three times a week with two Japanese wrestlers, and studied Inazo Nitobe's book, *Bushido,* "one of his favorite books."[48] Roosevelt secretly told ambassadors from a number of countries—including Russia—that Russia should throw in the towel before Japan beat the country again.[49]

To express his admiration for Tokyo regarding their monumental victory at Mukden, Roosevelt invited his secret interlocutor, Baron Kaneko, to lunch. Observers remembered that when the president saw Kaneko in the White House waiting room, the president's "face shone with joy over the unprecedented victory."[50]

On April 2, 1905, Baron Kaneko took the stage at fabled Carnegie Hall to explain to a paying audience of New Yorkers that Japan was civilized because it had adopted Western morality in its international relations:

In the struggle for the survival of the fittest, when the West and the East have met, might has prevailed over right. The nations believing in the right have been crushed and trampled on for fifty years, as in the English opium war and when we had acquired Port Arthur and the peninsula of Liaodong in the war with China. In that instance Russia, with Germany and France, snatched away the spoils of victory, and might made us yield without a murmur. We knew as long as ten years ago that war was coming and prepared for it. We had to become mighty to preserve the right.[51]

Perhaps inspired by the great Japanese victory, Roosevelt decided to get a refill of barbarian virtues for himself. In April, the president left for a month-long vacation, including a bear hunt in Colorado's snowy Rocky Mountains. Bears had been good for the Roosevelt image: in 1902, he had declined to shoot a roped one in Mississippi, and the retelling of that story had inspired the "Teddy bear" craze.

Roosevelt's Colorado bear hunt turned out to be a brilliant public-relations stroke. He received more newspaper coverage than if he had stayed in Washington, and Roosevelt projected just the right image to the American Aryan electorate: a manly president with rifle in hand taming the wilderness. Front-page stories chronicled Roosevelt's sleeping under the stars, how the Rough Rider handled a horse, and whether the president killed one or two large mammals that day.

Roosevelt came down with malaria in Colorado, but this fact was kept secret, just like his secret tennis playing, his secret asthma attacks, and his secret diplomacy. And Americans were not aware that the president's bear hunt sent a secret message to Tokyo, an inside joke between Teddy and Japan's founding fathers. When Roosevelt had told Kaneko he was about to go bear hunting, Kaneko recalled that the bear was a symbol for Russia and said to the president, "The Russian fleet is about to enter the Pacific, and there is certain to be a great naval battle with our fleet in the near future. If you should kill a bear, this will be an augury of victory for the Japanese fleet. I pray that you will have great success." Replied Roosevelt, "I fully intend to."[52] And Roosevelt informed none of the American press that one of the bears he had shot was to be skinned and presented to Emperor Meiji.

The bear that Roosevelt bagged for Meiji must have brought good luck, for on May 28, 1905, the Japanese navy demolished the Russian navy in the largest sea battle in world history. It took place near the Japanese island of Tsushima in the Japan Sea and is today called the Battle of Tsushima. The Japanese—who two generations earlier had no military-industrial complex—sunk all of Russia's warships while losing none of their own. Roosevelt, a lifelong student of naval history, gushed to Kaneko, "This is the greatest phenomenon the world has ever seen.... I grew so excited that I myself became almost like a Japanese, and I could not attend to official duties."[53]

On the Sunday after the Battle of Tsushima, Reverend Robert MacArthur—for thirty-five years the pastor of New York City's Calvary Baptist Church and one of America's best-known clergymen—preached a sermon entitled "Japan's Victory—Christianity's Opportunity":

> The Great Master said, 'By their fruits ye shall know them.' Apply that standard, and you will find that the nominally heathen Japan is more Christian than 'Holy Russia.'
>
> The victory of the Japanese is a distinct triumph for Christianity. The new civilization of Japan is largely the result of Christian teaching. A very great proportion of Japan's leading men to-day, especially those who fight her battles on land and sea, with such skill and valor, profess the Christian faith.[54]

After Roosevelt calmed down from almost being Japanese, he began to suffer from some qualms. Japan's navy had just proven itself world-class, a fact that must have worried him; after all, Teddy still wanted a significant and unthreatened American presence in Asia. Before he turned in on the evening that news of the Japanese triumph had reached the White House, he wrote a letter to Secretary Taft. When his party reached the Philippines, Roosevelt instructed, the secretary should take the senators and congressmen on a tour of the U.S. Navy's Pacific headquarters at Subig Bay.[55] In time, Congress would enthusiastically embrace Roosevelt's vision of the bay, a former Spanish naval station captured in 1899, as America's naval outpost in Asia, pouring many millions of taxpayer funds into building a U.S. Navy citadel there.

THE NEWS THAT THE Japanese navy had so completely dominated the Russians electrified Japan. The founding fathers rejoiced, but they did not tell the public that its military brass had notified Tokyo that in victory the military had expended itself and had little strength remaining. Out of a productive male populace of ten million, a staggering two million boys and men were in the military and one million had endured the rigors of the front. And the war was bleeding Japan financially, costing a staggering one million U.S. dollars a day. And while hit hard, Russia could still tap the enormous resources of its large army. The Japanese government allowed the people to believe that Japan was strong in victory and Russia weak in defeat, when it wasn't true. Japan had won battles in Manchuria and had won them handily, but only the impossible task of marching to St. Petersburg could defeat Russia. Japan simply did not have the strength to demand an indemnity from Russia, and the Japanese government hesitated to tell its jubilant population the hard truth.

The founding fathers worried that if they revealed their hand, Russia would sense weakness and Japan's bargaining position would be reduced before the negotiations began. At odds with its own public, the founding fathers now turned to Theodore Roosevelt.

On May 31, Ambassador Takahira brought Roosevelt a secret telegram from the foreign minister, Komura, requesting that his fellow Harvard graduate invite Russia and Japan to open direct negotiations.[56] Roosevelt was to keep it secret from the world that Japan had requested the president's help and instead tell the Russians that negotiations were his idea.

Roosevelt, a lame-duck president beleaguered by his dealings with Congress, jumped at the chance. With no Senate looking over his shoulder, the president would friction the powers in North Asia. And Roosevelt had the international stage to himself because his secretary of state lingered on his deathbed and his secretary of war was about to embark upon a three-month cruise in the Pacific.

It never occurred to Roosevelt that China should participate in a peace conference that would parcel out Chinese territory. As Howard Beale writes in

Theodore Roosevelt and the Rise of America to World Power, "Blinded by his concept of the Chinese as a backward people, he utterly failed to comprehend or take into account the rise of an independent and assertive China to a role of major importance in the twentieth century."[57]

Roosevelt acted immediately on Komura's request and told the Russian ambassador the white lie that the idea of a peace parley was his. If the czar agreed to the concept, Roosevelt said, he would then approach the Japanese. Given Teddy's obvious tilt, it's doubtful the Russian diplomat was taken in, especially when Roosevelt said he had a hunch that Japan would agree to his plan.

As Roosevelt fronted for them in Washington, the founding fathers met in Tokyo to work out their peace demands. These included Korea and parts of Manchuria, but the demand for an indemnity was listed as "not absolutely necessary."[58]

On June 5, 1905, the czar agreed to the concept of discussing peace with Japan, but "without intermediaries." Roosevelt would not sit at the negotiating table. That same day, Teddy welcomed to the White House a group of victorious Japanese navy admirals, who regaled the president with stories of their stunning victories at sea.

Roosevelt so enjoyed his day with the Japanese military men that he didn't want it to end. He asked

Ambassador Takahira to stay with him until 10:00 p.m., and then, after the ambassador left, a still-energized Roosevelt was unable to sleep and so took up his pen. In a series of letters, Roosevelt marveled that the Battle of Tsushima was "a rout and a slaughter," that the Japanese fleet was left "practically uninjured," while the Russian fleet "was demolished."[59] Roosevelt called the Slavs "hopeless creatures...helplessly unable,"[60] but still hoped the Russians would balance the Japs as the Anglo-Saxon walked through the Open Door. Roosevelt was captivated by his secret diplomacy, as he wrote to his son Kermit:

> I have of course concealed from everyone—literally everyone—the fact that I acted in the first place on Japan's suggestion. . . . I have kept the secret very successfully, and my dealings with the Japanese in particular have been known to no one.
>
> Remember that you are to let no one know that in this matter of the peace negotiations I have acted at the request of Japan and that each step has been taken with Japan's foreknowledge, and not merely with her approval but with her expressed desire.[61]

Gazing out from Washington, Roosevelt looked west and wrote: "I believe that our future history will be more determined by our position on the Pacific facing China than by our position on the Atlantic facing Europe."[62] To make sure that future Americans could walk through a wide Open Door in North Asia, Roosevelt would balance the powers just so: "It is best that [Russia] be left face to face with Japan so that each may have a moderative action on the other."[63]

Roosevelt imagined the Japanese as eternal opponents of the Slav, not entertaining the possibility that Japan and Russia would kiss and make up after the war. And since Roosevelt kept his analysis secret from everyone except his Japanese allies and yes-men like Taft, there was no one to grab the reins before Roosevelt drove America's future in Asia into a ditch.

ROOSEVELT LEFT WASHINGTON AND arrived at Sagamore Hill, his compound on the Long Island Sound, on Thursday, June 29. He would spend his summers there. Roosevelt complained that he had "been growing nearly mad in the effort to get Russia and Japan together," but he was excited that a large trophy room had been added to his already sprawling mansion by the sea. There, Roosevelt could sit among his stuffed conquests. The trophy room's sleek wood paneling was from America's largest colony, the Philippines.

Though Roosevelt had tried to draw London into his secret diplomacy, the much more experienced hands at the British Foreign Office were unenthusiastic. The foreign secretary, Lord Lansdowne, thought it better not to encourage Roosevelt and his frictioning. Lansdowne had written his ambassador in Russia, "Is there any case of a war of this kind in which the losing side has not had to pay for its folly or ill luck?"[64] The British ambassador in Washington had warned Lansdowne that Roosevelt was managing the negotiations, "not altogether I venture to think in a very adroit manner."[65] In frustration, Roosevelt wrote his ambassador in London, "President desires you to find out whether the English Government really does wish peace or not."[66]

The secretary of state, John Hay, passed away on July 1, but it had no effect on Roosevelt's secret diplomacy. Reflected Roosevelt in a letter to Taft, "For two years [Hay] had done little or nothing in the State Dept. What I didn't do myself wasn't done at all."[67] Roosevelt selected Elihu Root to replace Hay but did not share his Asian strategy with the new secretary of state. Root later wrote about Roosevelt's diplomatic secrets that summer: "He held them in his hands and kept them in his hands."[68]

On July 2, Roosevelt announced the news that Russian and Japanese envoys would meet at Portsmouth, New Hampshire, on August 5. They would negotiate between themselves without Roosevelt. Unofficially, Teddy would coach the Honorary Aryans from the sidelines. That same month, Roosevelt would complain that "the Senate is a very poor body to have as part of the treaty-making power" because of constitutional "defects which cannot be changed." Teddy was determined to institute "a wise foreign policy on his own."[69]

A few days later, Roosevelt invited Baron Kaneko to be his houseguest at Sagamore Hill. Roosevelt and Kaneko both understood that the purpose of the visit was for Teddy to give his private thoughts to Kaneko, who would then convey them to the founding fathers and Emperor Meiji.

The baron arrived at the village of Oyster Bay by train on the afternoon of July 7. A waiting Roosevelt carriage took him to Sagamore Hill, where Teddy warmly welcomed Kaneko. The baron and Roosevelt ate dinner together, then chatted in the president's study and retired after 10:00 p.m. Years later, Kaneko remembered how Roosevelt put him to sleep:

The President...lit two candles, one of which he gave me, while he carried the other himself, and showed me to my bedroom upstairs. Thinking that the bed cover was too thin and that I would be cold in the night—he explained that a cold north-east wind usually came from the bay after midnight—he went downstairs and returned with a blanket on his shoulder.[70]

The next morning Roosevelt and Kaneko break-fasted together and then went out onto the porch alone. The baron later wrote that what he heard Roosevelt say that July morning overlooking the Long Island Sound "made such an ineffaceable impression upon my mind as can never be forgotten as long as I live."[71] Kaneko paraphrased Roosevelt's words from memory:

Japan is the only nation in Asia that under-stands the principles and methods of Western civilization. She has proved that she can assimi-late Western civilization, yet not break up her own heritage. All the Asiatic nations are now faced with the urgent necessity of adjusting themselves to the present age. Japan should be their natural leader in that process, and their protector during the transition stage, much as the United States assumed the leadership of the American continent many years ago, and by means of the Monroe Doctrine, preserved the Latin American nations from European interference, while they were maturing their independence. If President Monroe had never enunciated the doctrine, which bears his name, the growth of the independent South America republics would have been interfered with by influences foreign to this continent. The future policy of Japan towards Asiatic countries should be similar to that of the United States towards their neighbours on the American continent. A 'Japanese Monroe Doctrine' in Asia will remove the temptation to European encroachment, and Japan will be recognized as the leader of the Asiatic nations, and her power will form the shield behind which they can reorganize their national systems.[72]

Roosevelt couldn't back up his vision with any signed pledge notes because what he was doing was against the Constitution he had sworn to uphold. So instead Roosevelt blustered to Kaneko that if Tokyo proclaimed a Japanese Monroe Doctrine for Asia after the Portsmouth peace negotiations were concluded, "I will support her with all my power, either during my Presidency or after its expiration."[73]

This was the first time Kaneko had heard anyone enunciate the concept of a "Japanese Monroe Doctrine." Three days later Roosevelt's historic idea was rendered into Japanese diplomatic code and pulsed through the long cable deep below the Pacific.[74]

Japan's founding fathers cannot be faulted if they believed that Roosevelt was powerful enough to control American policy even as he kept Congress in the dark. Throughout the summer, Teddy continued to signal that he could sway the U.S. government and people his way. On Saturday, July 15, 1905, Ambassador Takahira visited Roosevelt at Oyster Bay to complain of the anti-Japanese prejudice that had erupted in San Francisco. After this meeting, Roosevelt wrote this astounding sentence for transmittal to the founding fathers: "While I am president, there will be no discrimination."[75] Thus, Roosevelt, relaxing in his Long Island mansion, sparing no time from his vacation to consult anyone at the State Department, furthered the impression that a president could control U.S. states like he could corral rebels in the Philippines. Later, when Roosevelt delivered neither on his promises nor his boasts, Tokyo could only wonder why.

America's love affair with Baron Kaneko never faded, even after more than a year of his constant propagandizing. On July 23, citizens of Seattle applauded as the suave Harvard-tongued lawyer assured them, "Not only Japan and China, but the entire civilized world, will gain immeasurably by our conflict with Russia."[76] Recognizing the Aryan male's chivalrous feelings for foreign females (a key motivation for the invasion of Cuba), Kaneko wrote an article entitled "Japanese New Women," which the *New York Times* honored with six-column prominence. Kaneko played to America's benevolent intentions when he wrote, "One of the results of the Russo-Japanese war will

be that a new era will arise for the women of Japan."
Like a famous celebrity known to all Americans, the
editors of the *Times* identified the author as simply
"Baron Kaneko."[77]

On Wednesday, July 26, 1905, Roosevelt welcomed Ambassador Takahira to his seaside mansion
to iron out some last-minute details for the deal. On
that same day, Alice dined with Emperor Meiji in
his moated palace in the center of Tokyo. To influence Teddy, Meiji showed Alice his private gardens,
an honor never before accorded a White Christian.

At a dinner the next night, Alice tapped the minister Griscom on the shoulder:

"Do you see that old, bald-headed man scratching
his ear over there?"

"Do you mean Nick Longworth?"

"Yes. Can you imagine any young girl marrying a
fellow like that?"

"Why, Alice, you couldn't find anybody nicer."

"I know, I know. But this is a question of
marriage."[78]

The following evening, Prime Minister Katsura
threw a gala banquet at the Imperial Hotel. In his
speech, Katsura saluted Roosevelt as "a true exponent
of the best principles of civilization." Speaking next,
Taft cited "the fifty-year-old friendship of America
and Japan, a friendship which had never been dimmed
by a cloud nor ever ceased to grow, which would be

*Secretary William Howard Taft and Alice Roosevelt
in Tokyo, July 1905. One Tokyo newspaper reporter
observed, "This is truly the highpoint in the long history
of Japanese-American relations." (Collection of the
New-York Historical Society)*

stronger and more durable than ever in the future."[79] Taft also said of Japan, "during the past 50 years she made an advance unparalleled in the history of nations, an advance which had placed her in the very foremost rank of the world's leading Powers."[80]

Emperor Meiji. He oversaw Japan's tilt toward the West and away from Asia. President Roosevelt sent him the skin of a Colorado bear. (Stringer/Hulton Archive/ Getty Images)

The banquet was a public expression of mutual goodwill; the secret deal between the nations would be done the next morning behind closed doors. For generations, British imperialists had sat in their private London clubs or the back rooms of Parliament charting new boundaries on maps, lines that cut through nations, tribes, and families. The United States had redrawn the map of the North American continent with unmarked graves as they spread westward. Now

The Taft party observing a sumo match, July 1905. While the American public saw photos like this, Taft was secretly negotiating agreements with Japan not discovered until years later. (Collection of the New-York Historical Society)

two new Pacific powers would play the civilizer's board game.

On Thursday, July 27, Roosevelt met publicly with Baron Kaneko, Minister Komura, and Ambassador

Takahira aboard his presidential yacht, the *Mayflower*. In Tokyo, the morning after the Imperial Hotel banquet, Secretary Taft and Prime Minister Katsura met secretly in a simple, unadorned room in Shiba Palace. Besides Taft and Katsura, the only other person present was the interpreter, the foreign affairs vice minister, Shutemi Chinda. No transcript was made of the conversation and the palace has since burned down.

Katsura knew that in speaking to Taft he was communicating with Roosevelt, and from Baron Kaneko's many notes, the prime minister was well aware of how Roosevelt's mind worked.* So race was the topic of conversation as Katsura assured Taft that "the insinuation of a 'Yellow Peril' was only a malicious and clumsy slander circulated to damage Japan." Taft asked for a promise that Japan would keep its hands off the Philippines. Katsura responded that "Japan had no aggressive designs whatever on the Philippines."

Katsura told Taft that "the only means for accomplishing" peace in North Asia "was the drafting of an understanding among Japan, the United States and Great Britain which would uphold the Open Door principle." The prime minister understood that "a formal alliance was out of the question"—meaning that

---

*The following conversation between Taft and the prime minister of Japan is remarkably similar—in order of topics and content—to the Roosevelt–Kaneko–Takahira lunch discussion in the White House on June 6, 1904.

Tokyo knew that the U.S. Senate would not approve what Roosevelt was now granting Japan—but because "such an understanding would benefit all the powers…could not an understanding or alliance—in practice if not in name—be arrived at?"

At this point, former judge Taft had to know that he was in hot constitutional water, and he replied legalistically that of course it was "impossible for the President of the United States to enter even an informal understanding without the consent of the Senate." But then Taft quickly added, "Without any agreement at all…just as confidently as if a treaty had been signed…appropriate action by the United States could be counted upon" to support Japan's sphere of influence in Asia because "the people of the United States were so fully in accord with the policy of Japan and Great Britain."

This remarkable American commitment to Japan's expansion "as if a treaty had been signed" would remain secret for almost two decades and has been obscured by time. Here was the triple alliance for which Japan had struggled since the Shame of Liaodong. And now that the prime minister had promised to support the Anglo-Saxon Open Door, Katsura submitted the bill.

Katsura told Taft that "Korea was the direct cause of the war with Russia," an outrageous overstatement that Taft judged "wholly reasonable." Katsura said that

to prevent further "international complications...
Japan felt compelled to take some definite steps to
end the possibility of Korea lapsing into her former
condition."[81]

It wasn't until nineteen years later—after Roosevelt's death—that a researcher came across Taft's top
secret summary to Roosevelt of his meeting with Katsura. For protection, Taft had composed his memo
with no direct quotes. Upon reading the summary,
Teddy quickly cabled Taft, "Your conversation with
Count Katsura absolutely correct in every respect.
Wish you would state to Katsura that I confirm every
word you have said."[82] The Japanese Foreign Ministry
rendered the Taft-Katsura agreement into diplomatic
code and sent it through a deep Pacific cable to the
foreign minister, Komura, now in America.

The Taft-Katsura secret treaty sentenced Koreans
to Japanese subjugation for forty-five tortuous years.
Teddy would later dissemble regarding his role, and
his many apologists have downplayed its significance;
one historian advanced the curious argument that the
agreement wasn't important because Roosevelt didn't
mention it in his autobiography. But Teddy consistently whitewashed unpleasantries from his past, even
the existence of his first wife. The president of the
United States had skirted the Constitution and negotiated a side deal with the Japanese at the same time
he was posing as an honest broker between Japan and

Russia at the Portsmouth peace talks. And he would lacquer his accomplishment with multiple coats of obscurity.

Proof that Taft was aware that he had pulled a fast one can be found in the words the secretary used in his departure speech at Tokyo's Shimbashi station. (Alice remembered, "I have never seen a denser and more enthusiastic crowd than that which packed the open spaces around the station."[83]) Bidding good-bye to his Tokyo hosts, Taft curiously devoted his speech to the Japanese "ability to keep a secret." He said, "For example, Lady Oyama here [wife of a heroic general] speaks very good English and from our conversation I realize she knows of many things from her husband. However she will never talk about a military secret. If this was an American lady she would speak everything she knows and everything that she think she knows. Secrets have to be kept strictly especially in military matters."[84]

Prime Minister Katsura now announced the new triple alliance via an interview with the *New York Times,* in which he said:

Our Far Eastern policy [will be] the introduction of all the blessings of modern civilization into the East Asiatic countries. [Japan's] policy in the Far East will be in exact accord with that of England and the United States. [Japan would soon force] upon Korea and China the same benefits of modern development that have been in the past forced upon us.... We intend to begin a campaign of education in [Korea and China] such as we ourselves have experienced [and to develop] Asiatic commercial interests that will benefit us all. China and Korea are both atrociously mis-governed.... These conditions we will endeavor to correct at the earliest possible date—by persuasion and education, if possible; by force, if necessary. And in this, as in all things, we expect to act in exact concurrence with the ideas and desires of England and the United States.[85]

Simple as that and conveniently translated into English by the *New York Times:* at the behest of London and Washington, the Japanese military would expand into Korea and China to civilize Asia. Later generations would call it World War II.

The Japanese public knew nothing of Roosevelt's giveaway of Korea to Japan. They were focused only upon the indemnity they expected Roosevelt to wring from the Russians. On July 31, Kaneko warned Roosevelt in a letter, "My own opinion is that the payment of the actual cost of the war by Russia is absolutely necessary... because the public sentiment in Japan is strongly demanding a far larger amount of indemnity."[86]

Roosevelt gave little thought to the Japanese public's strong yearning for the dignity a White Christian cash indemnity would bring Japan. But as Alice wended her way south from Tokyo to Nagasaki, millions of Japanese banzaied her, delirious with the expectation that her father would help Japan finally secure a square deal.

The Taft party slipped into Nagasaki harbor on Monday, July 31. On Tuesday morning, August 1, crowds gawked at Alice purchasing some cigars, a business-card case, and a tortoiseshell-handled knife. Lunch was at the American consulate, and afterward the city of Nagasaki threw a huge send-off party in Suwa Park for the honored guests, who would next depart for the Philippines.

The mayor of Nagasaki addressed the happy crowd and toasted the Americans with champagne, thought to be much more Western and civilized than traditional Japanese sake. Then Taft, a mountain of a man, the Lord of the Philippines and the American God of War, rose to speak. Taft concluded his speech with a happy war chant in Japanese and English that brought the cheering crowd to their feet:

Japanese emperor . . . banzai!
Japanese navy . . . banzai!
Japanese army . . . banzai!

Japanese emperor . . . banzai!
Japanese navy . . . banzai!
Japanese army . . . banzai![87]

Chapter 9

THE IMPERIAL CRUISE

---

*"I did not come to give you your
independence.... You will have your
independence when you are ready for it, which
will not be in this generation—no, nor in the
next, nor perhaps for a hundred years or more."[1]*
—The secretary of war, William Howard Taft,
Iloilo, Philippines, August 1905

As the *Manchuria* steamed from Nagasaki to Manila
in August of 1905, dawn's first rays revealed the
rotund figure of the secretary of war, William Howard
Taft, on his daily four-mile walk around the big ship's
circumference. Early-bird strollers received the trademark Taft treatment: the famous smile, the twinkling
eyes, and the hearty guffaw. But beneath the friendly
facade, Big Bill had a lot to worry about.

Wife Nellie nagged from afar. She could have been by his side, supporting her prominent husband. But instead of the tropics and boring chitchat, Nellie had chosen the cool weather and royal conversationalists in Windsor, England. From her vacation perch, Nellie complained that if Bill hadn't been away at the time of John Hay's death, Roosevelt would have named him secretary of state.

Then there was Alice. She was just twenty-one years old and, in Taft's opinion, sometimes too naughty. He wrote Nellie, "She and Nick indulge in conversations on subjects that are ordinarily tabooed between men and women much older than they are and indeed are usually confined to husband and wife."[2] Once he'd seen Alice reach for her gold vanity case and assumed she was searching for a hairpin. Instead, the Princess picked up a strategically placed cigarette and put it between her teeth. Taft told Alice he'd give up drinking if she'd give up smoking. He never had to keep his side of the bargain.

Taft knew Nick Longworth well and didn't like what he knew. The Tafts and the Longworths were both leading families of Cincinnati, and Nick was Taft's congressional representative. Before the trip, Big Bill had warned Nick's mother that if her son went with Alice, they would surely return an engaged couple. Mrs. Longworth had dismissed the notion, saying that Nick was a confirmed old bachelor, not realizing the Princess was attracted to such men. As Alice later wrote, "I really didn't have many friends of my own age when I was young. The ones of my own age...were frightfully nice and proper and respectable but they were not terribly interesting. I always liked older men. A father complex coming out, presumably."[3]

One day Big Bill cornered her: "Alice, I think I ought to know if you are engaged to Nick." She responded, "More or less, Mr. Secretary. More or less."[4]

There was more on his mind than Alice's shadow engagement. Taft was returning to a troubled Philippines. Back in 1898, the promise had been bright: Americans had benevolent intentions, and the Filipinos were to behave like Pacific Negroes by submitting to the White Christian's globe-girdling destiny. In 1898, President McKinley had assumed that civilizing the Philippines would be accomplished quickly with few troops. By 1905, however, Taft and Roosevelt both realized that the Philippines was a black hole for the U.S. taxpayer and would never generate a significant strategic or financial advantage. This was a puzzle, since it seemed obvious that the higher races would eventually triumph—so went the Aryan myth, and so went Taft. Walking in circles around the *Manchuria,* wondering what to do next, Big Bill could not imagine that Asians would ever stem the westering tide.

Alice Roosevelt and Secretary Taft aboard the
Manchuria, *summer of 1905. (Collection of the*
New-York Historical Society)

As early as 1905, William Howard Taft had the inside track on the 1908 Republican presidential nomination, based mostly upon his reputation as a nation builder. But the only thing he had built in the Philippines was a pile of ruined dreams.

For six years Filipino patriots picked off U.S. soldiers in the countryside as the American colonial government in Manila issued rosy reports. In 1900: "A great majority of the people long for peace and are entirely willing to accept the establishment of a government under the supremacy of the United States." In 1901: "The collapse of the insurrection came in May." In 1902: "The insurrection as an organized attempt to subvert the authority of the United States in these islands is entirely at an end." In 1904: "The great mass of the people, however, were domestic and peaceable."[5]

When Big Bill left the Philippines in 1903, Roosevelt appointed Luke Wright to be his successor as governor. Wright was a crusty fifty-nine-year-old former Confederate soldier, who overtly favored a military solution rather than a civil one for Pacific Negroes. He did not jolly the Filipinos as did Taft. Furthermore, he enraged Taft's collaborator buddies when he cut off U.S. funds for the Federal Party and raised taxes to pay for the top-heavy, expensive American colonial bureaucracy. The house of cards that Taft had left behind slipped toward collapse.

Just a few months before Taft returned on this 1905 trip, an Englishwoman named Mrs. Campbell Dauncey, who lived in Iloilo in the Philippines, wrote to her family in England:

> The Americans give out and write in their papers that the Philippine Islands are completely pacified, and that the Filipinos love Americans and their rule. This, doubtless with good motives, is complete and utter humbug, for the country is honeycombed with insurrection and plots; the fighting has never ceased; and the natives loathe the Americans and their theories, saying so openly in their native press, and showing their dislike in every possible fashion. Their one idea is to be rid of the U.S.A. to have their government in their own hands.[6]

The *Manchuria* dropped anchor in Manila Bay at 10:30 a.m. on Friday, August 4.

A reporter for the *Manila Times* noted, "It was the same William H. Taft who left here about two years ago that stood on the upper deck of the Manchuria.... Perhaps a trifle heavier than when he left here, there is no less warmth in his handshake. 'I am certainly pleased to be back in Manila again,' said the secretary, as his eyes swept over the low outline of the city as seen from the bay. 'It seems like coming home again.'"[7]

The visiting Americans would spend twenty-seven days in the Philippines—the first nine in Manila, thirteen sailing around the islands, five days back in Manila, and then on to Hong Kong. On Saturday, August 5, Secretary Taft kicked off the visit in classic colonial style: he took everyone to the racetrack. Wrote the *Manila Times:*

MISS ROOSEVELT AT THE RACES

All eyes seemed to hunt out the one figure, to forget the political and economic significance of the visitors to these island possessions, and to realize only that before them, there in the grandstand, chatting animatedly with old and new friends, totally unconscious of the fact that she was the center of interest, stood the daughter of the president of the United States. Jaunty, yet possessing a queenly grace which showed in every gesture, vivaciousness itself, she was the life of the party, as she'd been at prior stops, a brilliant distraction.[8]

On Monday evening, August 7, Governor Wright threw the largest party in the history of the American occupation. The Malacañang Palace was ablaze with electric lights as American military men in gold braided uniforms twirled their jewel-covered ladies across the gleaming dance floor. Filipino newspapers commented with disapproval on the lavishness considering "the poverty stricken condition of the country" and noted that beleaguered Filipinos in the reception line "raised their hats in salutation to the Secretary of War without emitting a single shout of welcome."[9] Ever since Admiral Dewey had arrived, proud Filipinos had heard themselves described as niggers and gugus. The humiliation had been furthered as new Americans had arrived in Manila with "the St. Louis exposition idea of the Philippines."[10] One Filipino gentleman, observing the line of his countrymen outside the Malacañang Palace, mourned, "Instead of being a triumphal entrance, this looks like a funeral procession."[11]

In the following days, Taft announced that he found "tranquility throughout the islands, except in one or two provinces." While he acknowledged that "it is true that business prosperity does not now exist," he blamed the Philippines' sorry economic condition on acts of God: rinderpest, cholera, famine, locusts, and drought.[12] Taft made no mention of the American concentration camps as breeding grounds for cholera, of American atrocity warfare's causing the famine, or of the bloated American colonial government's holding back progress. Instead, Taft promised a plan to revitalize the Philippines: Americans would build railroads to uplift the nation, which didn't impress residents of this archipelago consisting of seven thousand islands. Meanwhile, mutilated corpses—American and Filipino—were carried daily into Manila by barge and wagon.[13] The Manila Chamber of Commerce informed Taft that "the country is in a state of financial collapse."[14] Yet benevolent Big Bill, blinders on, assured all that everything would be well—someday.

Taft's big night in Manila was Friday evening, August 11, at a banquet held in his honor at the Hotel Metropole. In his address, Taft described the Filipinos as "sacred wards of the United States" and reassured the American colonials that a benevolent President Roosevelt was committed to "elevating them as a whole to a self-governing people." Taft cautioned that this Americanization would take generations: "Nine tenths of the people of the Philippine Islands are today utterly incapable of exercising intelligently self-government." As usual, Big Bill bubbled benevolence. "I am greatly distressed," he said, "to learn that in some of the provinces of this archipelago hunger stalks." He advised a solution: "All these [problems] are easily overcome by the industry which is manifest in Java and Japan. The foundation of a great nation like Japan is in the industry, thrift, and intelligence of the people."[15]

Princess Alice's big night followed on Saturday, August 12, with a lavish ball thrown in her honor. The *Washington Post* wrote, "The eyes of the world are on her representing as she does not only the Chief Executive of our nation, but the typical American girl."[16] Alice, wearing a traditional Filipino gown that three seamstresses had labored over for three months, sweltered as she shook hands with twenty-four hundred guests. Reported the *Manila Times*:

> The impression made by Miss Roosevelt has been one of girlish simplicity. Her smile and greeting has been uniformly cordial and her attire appropriate. Even possessing eight trunks and a maid, with the necessity of a fresh frock for every occasion, with the knowledge of being the cynosure of all eyes every moment of the day and night most women would find the situation difficult, yet this young woman is as self-possessed as a princess and uses her tiny hand glass and powder puff with an unconcern which is the marvel of all observers.[17]

The next day, the Taft party boarded the U.S. Army ship *Logan* for a thirteen-day sail around the Philippines. The English-language press informed readers that the Taft party would encounter "bashful tree-top dwellers, dog-eaters, blood-thirsty head hunters and other strange tribes," as well as "simple natives" and their "wild island chiefs." One newspaper was sure that "Miss Roosevelt will every now and then come across the not especially appetizing spectacle of a couple of natives carrying on a pole between them a nice fat dog prepared for some village banquet."[18]

THEIR FIRST STOP WAS Iloilo, the third largest city in the Philippines. Iloilo had for hundreds of years been a picturesque place. Then in March of 1899, the U.S. Navy arrived and demanded that Iloilo submit to American rule. Residents responded that they preferred President Aguinaldo. The U.S. Navy then shelled the town, killing civilians. Fleeing residents set Iloilo on fire to prevent the Americans from capturing anything valuable. As the Taft party came ashore that Tuesday, August 15, many residents still remembered the "terrible drunkenness and looting" exhibited by the U.S. military just six years earlier.

Three events were scheduled for the Americans' one-day visit: a morning welcoming ceremony with speeches and a parade, a ladies' luncheon, and an evening banquet. Mrs. Campbell Dauncey, the English-woman who lived in Iloilo, arrived at the pre-parade reception held in the Gobierno (government building).

Alice Roosevelt in the Philippines. Notice the Filipinos in the background, with whom she does not interact. (National Archives)

She noticed Alice: "A young girl with a fluff of fair hair tied behind with a big bow of black ribbon, a very pale complexion, and heavily-lidded blue eyes. She had on a coat and skirt of stiff white pique, which did not do justice to her pretty figure, and a plain straw hat with blue ribbons on it tilted over her forehead."[19] The secretary of war was even more noticeable:

> Mr. Taft, who is a very tall, fair man of enormous build, towered over the heads of everyone about him. I don't think I ever saw anyone so vast....He has a large clever face, which creases up into an amiable smile for which he is famous, and which has helped him enormously in life. In curious contrast are his eyes, which are small, and placed rather close together, and very shrewd in expression. When he is serious, it is a stern, rather hard face, and not very prepossessing, but when he smiles the Taft smile, it is altered in the most extraordinary manner, and he really looks charming.[20]

Glancing around the reception room, Dauncey was surprised that "the Americans were all at one end and the Filipinos at the other....I thought it a great pity that it did not occur to Mr. Taft, Miss Roosevelt or the Governor, or anyone like that to go and stand amongst the Filipinos and give a real and tangible demonstration of the theories they were here to express....A little thing like that would convey more truth about equality than miles of bombastic print or hours of windy rhetoric."[21]

Soon the crowd moved out to the balcony to

observe the parade. Dauncey noted floats "prettily done up with banana plants, one had sugar canes growing in it, there were ploughs and rows of men carrying spades and hoes and things." But then a group of stone-faced protestors filed by, holding aloft large colorful three-sided lanterns bearing pleas written in English and Spanish. One lantern asked the American colonial rulers for "A Square Deal," another declared "We Are At Your Mercy," and yet another was a plea "To Govern Ourselves Our Own Way." At the sight of these demands, "Mr. Taft stared very solemnly and steadily, standing upright in front of the balcony with Miss Roosevelt beside him, his arms folded across his chest."[22]

Big Bill's dark scowl transformed into the radiant Taft smile when the young students from Iloilo's American school filed by. Here were the little Pacific Negroes that Yankee teachers were training to abandon their parents' ways in favor of things American. Taft raised his hands over his head to applaud, signaling the other Americans, who followed his lead and clapped enthusiastically. An attendee glanced at the Filipinos nearby: the parents of the students stood unsmiling and still.[23]

After the parade, the crowd went back inside the government building. Remembered Dauncey, "Mr. Taft took the chair assigned to him, into which he wedged himself with infinite trouble; but the chair at once broke into pieces. Everyone laughed very much, Mr. Taft most heartily of all, saying in a good-natured, jolly way: 'Here! Someone give me a chair I can sit down on. I'm tired of standing.' They brought him another chair, and he took his place, and the speechifying began."[24] One after another, the people of Iloilo arose and addressed their desire for freedom and self-government. Then Secretary Taft arose and laid it on the line: "I did not come to give you your independence, but to study your welfare. You will have your independence when you are ready for it, which will not be in this generation—no, nor in the next, nor perhaps for a hundred years or more."[25]

Recalled Dauncey, "You can have no idea of the effect these words had upon the audience. We were simply staggered."[26] Then, as if to add salt to the wound, Taft and the Americans exited for a luncheon hosted by an American lady. No Filipinos had been invited.

The climax of the day was a big banquet at the Santa Cecilia Club. Princess Alice did not attend, declaring that she was too tired. There were many other empty chairs that evening, because most of the invited residents of Iloilo did not show up. Perhaps they boycotted the dinner because they didn't want to endure another American lecture on their deficiencies. Maybe they were insulted because earlier that day not one of their lady folk had been deemed worthy to sup tea with the White women. Or perhaps, like Alice, they were simply too tired.

Throughout dinner, anyone could stand up and speak his mind. The editor of the Iloilo newspaper "made a most fiery and eloquent speech. . . . He declared that the Philippine Islands had been discovered as long as America, and that the Filipinos had the same spirit as that which had caused the Americans to revolt from England." Recalls Dauncey, "He got fearfully excited, and called God to witness that his people were only asking for their rights in wishing to have this foreign burden removed; he and they demanded, insisted on, their Independence!" At the end of this speech, the few Filipinos in the room—mostly waiters, the orchestra, and a few stragglers who had wandered in off the street—"applauded frantically." When the interpreter rendered the editor's speech into English, the Americans sat in "utter silence." The evening ended with another Taft speech telling the Filipinos they would have to wait generations for their independence. The Americans applauded enthusiastically. The Filipinos were silent. After dinner, one drunk American picked a fight with a Filipino waiter.[27]

So it went throughout the Americans' tour. The Taft party visited areas deemed safe by the U.S. military, met with preapproved locals, dismissed Filipino calls for independence, and ignored American culpability for the country's sad state.

Secretary Taft and Alice Roosevelt in Malolos, Philippines, August 1905. (National Archives)

On Tuesday, August 22, at a banquet in Cebu, the Philippines' second-largest city, one audience member described the "pitiful" conditions there and requested American aid. Taft swatted his request away by lecturing the Filipinos that they had to pull themselves up by their own bootstraps:

The problem that the United States has entered upon in these Islands is to prepare a whole people for self government, and that problem

349

includes not only the teaching of that people how to read, write and figure in arithmetic, but also to teach that people that if they would have prosperity they must labor and to teach them how to labor. You cannot have bricks without straw. You cannot raise crops without labor, and until the people understand the necessity of labor, this cannot be a great people. I am revealing no secret of the Congressional delegation when I say that the one fact that they will carry away from here, more deeply impressed on their minds than any other, is the necessity for changing this people from an idle people to a laboring people....No one can be blind to the fact that the effort of these calamities might have been much reduced and made much less had the people been more industrious.[28]

The *Manila Times* summarized Big Bill's Cebu speech:

MUST LEARN THE DIGNITY OF LABOR

Taft Makes Vigorous Yet Kindly Speech to Entreaters in Cebu Who Plea to Be Helped Put Industry Before Self-Government[29]

Unmentioned by the press was the fact that for the past six years the U.S. military had burnt down homes in and around Cebu and destroyed crops and farm animals in an effort to flush out Filipino freedom fighters. American troops had decapitated the local leadership by assassinating four of Cebu's mayors and had terrorized the populace by waterboarding prisoners, raping women, and torturing priests and even the chief of police. A U.S. soldier had written home from Cebu, "We can burn them out and kill them one by one and thus quiet them down for a time, but it is my belief that we can expect permanent peace only when the last Filipino plants his little brown feet on the golden shore."[30]

AT 8:30 A.M. ON SATURDAY, August 26, the *Logan* dropped anchor in Manila Bay. The *Manila Times* called it a "triumphal tour of the southern islands of the Philippine archipelago."

Over the next week in Manila, the Congressional delegation met with Filipino leaders who argued that they had the political capacity to govern themselves. The *Manila Times* reported that the listening Americans laughed out loud at the idea.

On Thursday morning, August 31, the Taft party waved good-bye to the American colonials and their

Filipino collaborators as they steamed out of Manila
Bay on their way to Hong Kong. One American official with long experience among the Filipinos wrote,
"The real epic pathos of the whole thing was that
Mr. Taft was actually sincere. He believed that the
majority of the Philippine people were for him and
his policies."[31] A former American colonial official
later quoted a senator on the cruise, "When we left
the islands I do not believe there was a single member
of our party who was not sorry we own them, except
Secretary Taft himself."[32]

There had been a final send-off banquet in the
Grand Ballroom of the Hotel de Francis the evening before. The honored guest speaker had been
the chairman of the Committee on Naval Affairs,
the Illinois representative George Foss. Congressman
Foss certainly followed the sun; a Harvard graduate,
he had studied political science at Columbia University under Professor John Burgess and was a heart-
land Republican. The audience of American colonial
officials leapt to their feet in applause as Congressman Foss concluded his speech:

> I believe that it has been a providential guid-
> ance which has brought the Americans to these
> islands.... The question then arose: What shall
> we do with the Philippines? Give them back to
> Spain? No. Turn them over to the Filipinos?

No. The Filipinos had no experience which would warrant their governing themselves. They were not prepared. A solemn duty rested upon the American people to lift them to the clear, bright sky of American liberty and American independence. You, gentlemen, are here to do as your forefathers did in New England.[33]

Chapter 10

ROOSEVELT'S OPEN AND CLOSED DOORS

"We do not understand why your people in China preach the doctrine of Love, while in America you treat Chinese worse than any other nation, nay even the negroes!"[1]
—PETITION TO PRESIDENT THEODORE ROOSEVELT FROM STUDENTS OF THE ANGLO-CHINESE COLLEGE IN FUZHOU, CHINA, 1903

On September 3, 1905, the secretary of war, William Howard Taft, steamed west from British Hong Kong to the Chinese city of Canton. For this segment of the cruise he was not following the sun. Instead, Big Bill was traveling secretly at night, aboard the U.S. Navy gunboat *Laliao* that glided quietly through the Pearl River Delta, entering China on

The Pearl River Delta

The Chinese of the Pearl River Delta had the most experience with American Foreign Devils— in both China and the United States.

a warship under the cover of darkness because U.S. consular and military officials had warned him that he risked personal harm. Anti-American posters were plastered on city walls up and down China's coast, and furious attendees at packed mass meetings shook their fists as they listened to emotional anti-Yankee speeches. Nevertheless, after much debate, Taft had decided he would face local wrath and deliver a tough message from President Roosevelt in the Chinese city most aflame with anti-Americanism.

From ancient times, the emperor—the Son of Heaven—had reigned from Beijing. Uninterested in dealing with lowlife traders, he had designated the southern port city of Canton as a backdoor service entrance for those "Foreign Devils" hoping to do business in China. The emperor had assigned Cantonese merchants the odious job of dealing with these barbarians and thus Canton became the international commercial outlet for the Middle Kingdom.

As a result, for centuries Foreign Devils had come to Canton from Arabia, Persia, Africa, Egypt, Rome, France, England, Germany, Holland, Spain, Japan, the Philippines, Vietnam, Thailand, Cambodia, India, and the United States. During that time, the Cantonese had endured, and in a number of ways benefited from, these intrusions. That changed three years into the Roosevelt administration. To protest

Teddy's treatment of them as uncivilized beings, the Chinese had united to boycott all things American.

UNCIVILIZED THE CHINESE WERE certainly not. For most of human history, China was the most populated, wealthiest, and most sophisticated country on earth. *The Travels of Marco Polo,* published in 1295, told astonishing tales of enormous banquet rooms with five thousand seats, walls studded with precious stones, and consumers using paper money to purchase mass-printed books from well-stocked bookstores. (Marco Polo was so amazed by Chinese paper money that he devoted a chapter to it.) In Europe, monks hand-copied books while thousands of best-selling tomes rolled off China's modern printing presses. China's iron manufacturing industry produced one hundred twenty-five thousand tons a year—an amount not equaled by Europe until the twentieth century. Chinese wore soft, luxurious silk versus the Europeans' rough-hewn tunics, and at home the Chinese lived in a stylish comfort of which Europeans could only dream.

The Chinese invented movable type four hundred years before Johannes Gutenberg was born. China built a suspension bridge two thousand years before one appeared in the West. It took the civilized Aryans seventeen hundred more years than it did the

Chinese to figure out how to make porcelain. Cast iron, the crank handle, deep drilling for natural gas, the belt drive, the fishing reel, chess, matches, brandy, gunpowder, playing cards, the spinning wheel, the umbrella, and countless other innovations—such were the products of China's inventive genius.

Europeans would eventually borrow such Chinese innovations as the plow and experience an agricultural revolution. Similarly, literacy spread as the Europeans exploited paper and printing, both Chinese inventions. The British public would become addicted to drinking tea from China mixed with adrenaline-pumping sugar from its Caribbean colonies. This was the heady stimulant that would eventually transform the English from agricultural laborers to alert, regimented cogs in Britain's new factories. But when the English asked the Chinese to accept their manufactured goods as payment for tea instead of expensive silver, the Son of Heaven wrote dismissively to King George III in 1793, "We possess all things. I set no value on objects strange or ingenious, and have no use for your country's manufactures."[2]

The Chinese insistence upon silver as payment for tea was a serious economic threat to the British Empire and a huge windfall for the Chinese. As the historian Carl Trocki writes in *Opium, Empire and the Global Political Economy*:

The 1700s were boom times for the Middle Kingdom as English silver flooded into China. China's population over that period tripled from about one hundred million to over three hundred million. The constant importation of Asian products into the European markets caused a permanent drain of gold and silver from Europe towards Asia. Only a small trickle of precious metals must have re-entered Europe.... The greater part of gold and silver remained in Asia never to return to Europe.[3]

To the British Empire's financial rescue came a very clever colonial official, Warren Hastings, the governor-general of Bengal in northern India. Bengal had long produced opium, for centuries used across Asia as a medicinal and social drug. Portuguese sailors in Asian waters had observed a profitable Bengal-to-China opium trade conducted by Arab merchants. The Portuguese muscled in on this trade, also bringing to the Chinese market tobacco from their Brazilian colony. Tobacco mixed with Indian opium proved to be a pleasing combination to the Chinese, and opium smoking soon became popular. Realizing the harm to his people, the Son of Heaven banned opium's sale and use in China.

Nevertheless, his edict meant little to those Foreign Devils hoping to profit and restore a more favorable (to

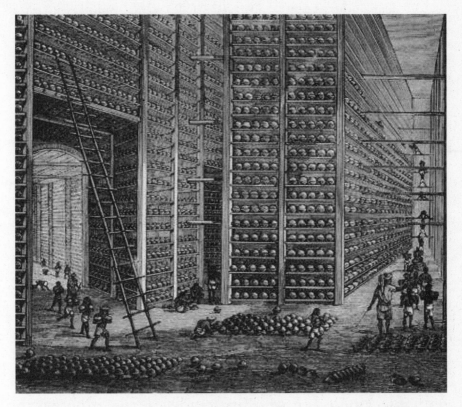

Patna opium factory. Opium grown in British India and sold in China was the most profitable commodity trade of the nineteenth century and accounted for 15 to 20 percent of the British Empire's revenue. (Drawing by Lt. Colonel Walter B. Sherwill, London Weekly Magazine, *June 24, 1882)*

them) trade balance. England controlled a vast swath of prime opium-growing country, stretching five hundred miles across Bengal, and the British Empire invested enormous sums in state-of-the-art opium farming and production systems. More than two thousand British opium agents oversaw the efforts of one million registered Indian opium farmers. Opium sap was dried into balls, each weighing 3.5 pounds, then placed on floor-to-ceiling factory shelves, where Indian boys would rotate each ball a quarter turn once every six days as it dried. Each opium ball was then stamped with the coveted trademark brand Patna or Benares.

White Christian opium smugglers could not legally sell the banned drug on Chinese soil, so they installed floating wooden warehouses in the Pearl River Delta, where they sold their booty to Chinese criminals who rowed out under the cover of darkness.

Before long, opium accounted for 15 to 20 percent of the British Empire's revenue, as the Bengal-to-China opium business became the "world's most valuable single commodity trade of the nineteenth century."[4] Western banks, shipping companies, and insurance companies sprouted to serve this enormously profitable trade. As Carl Trocki notes, "The entire commercial infrastructure of European trade in Asia was built around opium."[5] It was Christians who smuggled the poisonous drug into China, so the Chinese called it "Jesus opium."

This Christian drug running was nearly fatal to the Middle Kingdom. Between 1814 and 1850, the Jesus-opium trade sucked out 11 percent of China's money supply.[6] China lost more silver in thirty years than had flowed into the country in the 125 years leading up to the opium trade. As the Chinese money supply contracted, silver became unnaturally scarce, peasants had trouble paying their taxes, counterfeiting rose, waves of inflation and deflation whipsawed the economy, and unrest grew.

The Jesus-opium trade also tore at the moral fabric of Chinese society. Since the sale of the banned drug was illegal, the Christian smugglers' Chinese business partners were criminal lowlifes who now got rich and gathered power.

The Son of Heaven finally put his foot down and dispatched a royal representative to Canton in 1839 to stop the Foreign Devil drug trade. Buckingham Palace shook at the news. Queen Victoria was just twenty years old at this point, on the British throne less than two years, but when the Chinese leader threatened to cut her largest single source of income, she understood the dire financial consequences. Opium production and smuggling not only paid for imports from China that England could not afford in silver, but the drug trade also provided the easy money that most sustained her empire. Victoria dispatched her industrialized navy to enforce Britain's ability to push an illegal drug. What followed were the two Opium Wars—one from 1839 to 1842, the other from 1856 to 1860. What Victoria spent on these military operations against China was paltry compared to her take of profits from the illegal Jesus-opium trade.

Victoria also grabbed Hong Kong as part of the spoils in the first of her two Opium Wars. Sir John Francis Davis, governor of Hong Kong from 1844 to 1848, admitted: "Almost every person ... not connected with government is employed in the opium trade."[7] The British Empire grew fat on Chinese silver drained from the formerly richest country in the world. The sums were so enormous that Queen Victoria stands as history's largest drug dealer.

As SECRETARY TAFT CUT through the night on his way from Hong Kong to Canton that September evening, he was passing the homes of the Pearl River Delta families who had more experience dealing with American Foreign Devils than people in any other part of China. Starting with the California Gold Rush, it was primarily the families of the Pearl River Delta that had sent their sons to the United States in search of opportunity.

These Cantonese had brought with them their ancient habits of hard work, cooperation, self-denial, and thrift. Compared to the White workers, the Chinese mined more gold more efficiently, saved more of their earnings, drank and caroused less, behaved better, and almost never caused trouble. An American minister, Augustus Loomis, testified to the Chinese workers' diligence, steadiness, and clean living: "They are ready to begin work the moment they hear the signal, and labor steadily and honestly until admonished that the working hours are ended. Not having acquired a taste for whiskey, they have few fights, and no 'blue Mondays.' You do not see them intoxicated, rolling in the gutters like swine."[8]

White workers claimed that the Chinese competed unfairly because the Mongolians could live cheaper on their diet of rice and rats. But in truth, while the Whites ate a bland diet—"boiled beef and potatoes, beans, bread and butter, and coffee"—the Cantonese "ate healthy, well-cooked, and tasty food...an astonishing variety—oysters, cuttlefish, finned fish, abalone meat, Oriental fruits, and scores of vegetables, including bamboo sprouts, sea-weed, and mushrooms. Each of these foods came dried, purchased from one of the Chinese merchants in San Francisco."[9] The Chinese drank tea from boiled water. "The Americans drank from the streams and lakes, and many of them got diarrhea, dysentery, and other illnesses."[10]

Some admired the Chinese miners' superior work and living habits. The White miners did not. Unable to compete on a level playing field, the Whites soon employed state laws to hold the Chinese back, as Stephen Ambrose explains in *Nothing Like It in the World*:

Chinese Immigration

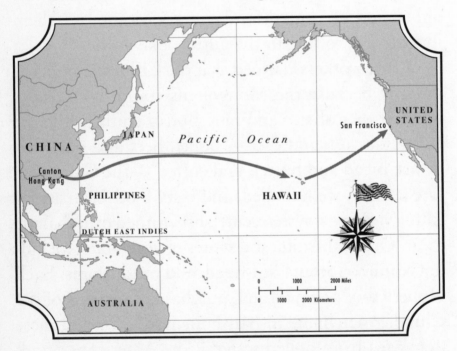

The Chinese emigrated from one large Pacific bay to another.

"A Picture for Employers." Puck, *August 21, 1878. Chinese laborers smoked opium and ate rats while the manly White laborer came home to wife and family.*

California law discriminated against them in every way possible, and the state did all it could to degrade them and deny them a decent livelihood. They were not allowed to work on the 'Mother Lode.' To work the 'tailing,' they had to pay a 'miner's tax,' a $4-per-head so-called permission tax, plus a $2 water tax. In addition, the Chinese had to pay a personal tax, a hospital tax, a $2 school tax, and a property tax. But they could not go to public school, they were denied citizenship, they could not vote, nor could they testify in court. Nevertheless, they paid; more than $2 million in taxes. If Chinese dared to venture into a new mining area, the whites would set on them, beat them, rob them, sometimes kill them. Thus the saying, 'Not a Chinaman's chance.'[11]

Nevertheless, the Chinese workers continued to outperform the White laborers. George Hearst, later a U.S. senator from California, who observed Chinese miners for ten years in four different states, proclaimed worriedly, "They can do more work than our people and live on less. They could drive our laborers to the wall."[12]

In 1863, President Abraham Lincoln called for the construction of a transcontinental railroad. Two teams of White workers—one proceeding west from the Mississippi River and one working east from the Pacific Ocean—began work on the giant undertaking. Those proceeding west over the Great Plains made progress, but those proceeding east from the Pacific coast hit the solid granite of California's Sierra Nevada mountains. The White workers laid down their picks in defeat. The Chinese, from the country that had built the Great Wall, filled the gap and succeeded where the Aryan had tried and failed. Governor Leland Stanford of California wrote President Andrew Johnson, "Without the Chinese it would have been impossible to complete the western portion of this great National highway."[13]

The U.S.-China Treaty of 1868 finally offered a formal welcome: "The United States of America and the Emperor of China cordially recognize the inherent and inalienable right of man to change his home and allegiance, and also the mutual advantage of the free migration and emigration of their citizens and subjects respectively, from one country to the other, for the purposes of curiosity, of trade, or as permanent residents."[14] By then, the railroad was edging closer and closer to completion, a national goal impossible without the Chinese.

Most American textbooks feature the May 10, 1869, photograph depicting the east and west construction teams meeting at Promontory Summit, Utah, to drive the golden spike that completed the transcontinental railroad. Although there were many Chinese on the scene—some who had that very morning laid the last ties—when history's flashbulbs were about to pop, the Aryans self-consciously pushed aside the yellow men who had succeeded where the Whites had failed.

With the transcontinental railroad completed, the workers who had built it were dismissed and they dispersed across the West. The pop culture image of the American West is based more on the films of director John Ford and Monument Valley than fact.

This Hollywood version features John Wayne walking through a White town. What's missing is the Chinese hotel that John Wayne would have slept in, the Chinese restaurant where he would have dined, the Chinese laundry where he would have done his wash, and the Chinese general store where he would have purchased his provisions. Notes the historian Stephen Ambrose, "In nearly every Western railroad town there used to be a Chinatown."[15]

With their better work and living habits, the Chinese produced services and sold goods of higher quality at a lower price, driving out their humiliated White competitors. And to those who viewed the world through the prism of Aryan superiority and following the sun, the threat went well beyond the economic. If 10 percent of the Chinese in China came to the United States, China would still have 360 million people. But if 40 million Chinese crossed the Pacific, they would become America's majority race.[16] And those Chinese might breed with White women, causing Aryan westering to halt.

Luckily for civilization, the Aryan instincts came to the fore. The media consistently presented the Chinese as opium-besotted, rodent-eating, filthy creatures, whose lifestyle and lack of morals threatened the White race. In 1877, the Order of Caucasians for the Extermination of the Chinaman declared its goal: "to drive the Chinaman out of California...by every manner and means within the thin gauze of the law."[17] Anti-Chinese labor unions such as the Knights of Labor and the Workingman's Party spread their slogan across the land: "The Chinese Must Go."

Senator James Blaine of Maine warned that those "who eat beef and bread and drink beer...will have to drop his knife and fork and take up Chopsticks [if] those who live on rice"[18] are allowed to stay in America. "Either the Anglo-Saxon race will possess the Pacific slope or the Mongolians will possess it."[19] In 1877, the United States Congress established a Joint Special Congressional Committee to Investigate Chinese Immigration. The White Christian male legislators concluded:

> There is not sufficient brain capacity in the Chinese to furnish motive power for self-government. The Mongolian race seems to have no desire for progress and to have no conception of representative and free institutions. There is no Aryan or European race which is not far superior to the Chinese as a class.[20]

California's second constitution, ratified in 1879, prohibited companies from employing "directly or indirectly, in any capacity, any Chinese or Mongolian"; prohibited the employ of Chinese "on any state, county, municipal, or other public work, except in punishment for crime"; and mandated that the legislature "delegate all necessary power to the incorporated cities and towns of this state for the removal of Chinese without the limits of such cities and towns, or for their locations within prescribed portions of those limits, and it shall also provide the necessary legislation to prohibit the introduction into this state of Chinese after the adoption of this Constitution."[21]

From America's inception in 1783 to 1882, a period of ninety-nine years, there had been no concept of illegal immigrants in the United States. That changed with the Chinese Exclusion Act of 1882. For the first time in U.S. history, an immigration gate was erected with the specific goal of blocking non-Whites. Senator George Hoar of Massachusetts described the Chinese Exclusion Act as "nothing less than the legalization of racial discrimination."[22] But because of the dire race threat presented by the yellow men, most Americans had no problem with the new legislation. Twenty-four years old and just out of Harvard, Theodore Roosevelt proclaimed in 1882, "No greater calamity could now befall the United States than to have the Pacific slope fill up with a Mongolian population."[23]

ROCK SPRINGS, WYOMING, WAS a mining town that produced almost half the coal that fueled the

"The Nigger Must Go" and "The Chinese Must Go."
Harper's Weekly, *September 13, 1879. The caption reads:*
"The Poor Barbarians Can't Understand Our Civilized
Republican Form of Government."
(Courtesy of HarpWeek, LLC)

transcontinental railroad. Approximately six hundred Chinese and three hundred Whites lived in the dust-blown settlement. On the evening of September 1, 1885, the Rock Springs chapter of the Knights of Labor held a "Chinese Must Go!" meeting. The next day, the race cleansing began. "White men fall in" was the call to arms.

Armed White miners surrounded Chinatown. The local Chinese laundryman was in his washhouse when a bullet shattered his skull. White wives and daughters laughed and clapped as their men shot fleeing Chinese and then searched their pockets. White women who had earlier taught English classes to the Chinese now looted their students' homes. Chinese who escaped into the countryside were picked off by waiting Knights of Labor snipers.

The first Wyoming state official to arrive in Rock Springs described the scene: "Not a living Chinaman—man, woman or child—was left in the town...and not a single house, shanty, or structure of any kind, that had ever been inhabited by a Chinaman was left unburned. The smell of burning human flesh was sickening and almost unendurable, and was plainly discernible for more than a mile along the railroad both east and west."[24] In the court trials that followed, there were no convictions.

Rock Springs was just the beginning. All across the West, the American Aryan raged against the Chinese.

The Rock Springs Massacre. Rock Springs, Wyoming. Theodore Roosevelt wrote, "No greater calamity could now befall the United States than to have the Pacific slope fill up with a Mongolian population." Harper's Weekly, *September 26, 1885. (Library of Congress)*

From California, north to Alaska, west to Colorado, and south to New Mexico, posters told the Chinese to get out and those who hesitated would face the barrel of a White man's rifle. In Fresno, a mob killed Chinese workers in their beds. In Tacoma, the mayor led hundreds of armed Aryans in rousting the Chinese from their homes and pushing them onto waiting trains. In Seattle, the chief of police led a mob who marched the local Chinese at gunpoint up the gangplank of a waiting ship.

Theodore Roosevelt deemed the Chinese a "race-foe" and called upon the United States to maintain "race-selfishness" to exclude "the dangerous alien who would be ruinous to the white race."[25] When he became president, Roosevelt inherited two competing U.S. approaches regarding China. In America, voters demanded Chinese exclusion. In China, U.S. businessmen demanded "The Open Door."

The United States had come late to the slicing of the Chinese melon. It wasn't until 1898 that the nation had acquired the Pacific links—Hawaii, Guam, and Manila—required to tap China's riches. President McKinley's challenge at that time had been how to insert U.S. business interests into the powers' ongoing scramble for the Middle Kingdom. For his China policy, he chose the kindly slogan "The Open Door." The Open Door called on the Western powers to benevolently avoid partioning China to the point that it could not function as a national entity, allowing all to compete within one another's allotted sections.

The Open Door was a huge hit among humanitarian Americans who saw the Chinese as "wards" in need of protection. But when foreign ministers in London, Rome, Berlin, Paris, Moscow, and Tokyo considered McKinley's request to open their China doors, not one bothered to respond. Nevertheless, in July of 1900, the secretary of state, John Hay, declared that the powers agreed with McKinley "in principle." McKinley did not bother sending a copy of his new Chinese policy to Beijing. Yellow men would not decide Asia's fate. Secretary of State Hay sniffed, "We have done the Chinks a great service, which they don't seem inclined to recognize."[26]

In fact, McKinley's policy had no practical effect on commercial competition in China. It did, however, humiliate the Chinese. Outraged at the attitude of these distant powers who felt that they had rights to dismember their country, Chinese patriots arose to oppose the Foreign Devils within their midst. Because these athletic young men often practiced martial arts, foreigners called them "Boxers." In June of 1900, the Boxers entered Beijing and laid seige to the embassies of the Foreign Devils, who held out for fifty-five days until twenty thousand troops from the Eight-Nation Alliance[27] came to their rescue. Now armed barbarians marched outside the Forbidden City.

While President Roosevelt would have been happy to nab almost every Chinaman in the United States and ship him back to where he came from, strong U.S. business interests were concerned that if this happened, the Chinese in China might stop doing business with the United States. To straddle the diametrically opposed positions, Teddy spoke in favor of allowing a minuscule number of "upper-class"

Chinese into the United States and blamed the Bureau of Immigration for any anti-Chinese abuses. But even when he did point a finger at the bureau, he could never find his Big Stick to discipline anyone.

Roosevelt's first bureau commissioner-general was Terence Powderly, the rabid former leader of the Knights of Labor, which had led the race war against the Chinese in the 1880s, including the Rock Springs massacre. Early in Roosevelt's accidental presidency, Powderly wrote an article in *Collier's Weekly* assuring voters that the new, young president had their race interests at heart: "American and Chinese civilizations are antagonistic; they cannot live and thrive and both survive on the same soil. One or the other must perish."[28] In his December 1901 Message to Congress, Roosevelt called for a closed door for Chinese in America but an open door for Americans in China. Roosevelt's stand was deplored by the *Jewish Exponent* of Philadelphia, which contended that the president was in effect telling the Chinese, "You must take our goods, the missionaries, and anything else we choose to send you . . . but you must not show your faces within our borders, for you are too far beneath us to be fit company for us."[29] But far more Americans agreed with Teddy than they did such editorials, and in April, Roosevelt signed into law the most draconian anti-Chinese piece of legislation in U.S. history, the Chinese Exclusion Act of 1902, which continued the odium of the original 1882 version and extended exclusion of Chinese laborers to Hawaii and the Philippines.[30]

Viceroy Kin was the governor of Shanghai province. His son studied in England and wanted to transit across the United States to return to China. He obtained a letter of introduction from Joseph Choate, the American ambassador to England. When Viceroy Kin's son arrived in Boston harbor in June of 1902, he was detained by federal officials for twenty-four hours, strip-searched, and photographed naked. This upper-class Chinese boy was then forced to post a bond not to open a laundry or become a manual laborer. Another Chinese student arriving in San Francisco with admission papers from Oberlin College was held in one of Teddy's immigration pens for one year. And on October 11, 1903, Roosevelt's immigration men swooped down upon Boston's Chinatown. Two hundred thirty-four Chinese were arrested and fifty were deported.[31] The next day a United States district judge declared the raid perfectly legal. Students from the Anglo-Chinese College in Fuzhou petitioned Roosevelt: "We do not understand why your people in China preach the doctrine of Love, while in America you treat Chinese worse than any other nation, nay even the negroes!"[32]

In January of 1904, Beijing notified Roosevelt that it would end the U.S-China Treaty—due for renewal in 1905—and called on him to renegotiate a fairer agreement. With the presidential election months away, Roosevelt righteously demanded that China maintain an open door and at the same time called for an indefinite extension of his Chinese Exclusion Act.

In an attempt to be shown as tolerant, Roosevelt invited Yu Kit Men, a Shanghai shipping magnate, to serve as one of China's representatives at the St. Louis World's Fair. Yu entered the United States in New York and boarded a train for St. Louis. The Shanghai businessman was asleep when he heard a knock on his stateroom door. Bureau of Immigration goons seized him, pulled him off the train, and jailed him near Buffalo. Running for president, Roosevelt did nothing and wrote meekly, "I have been for a long time uneasy about the way in which Chinese merchants and Chinese students have all kinds of obstacles thrown in their way when they come to this country."[33]

For years White Christians had treated China with disrespect. But with Theodore Roosevelt, the Chinese drew a line. In May 1904, Shanghai businessmen called for a boycott of American goods beginning August 1. A united, peaceful, yet effective response to a barbarian country was an unprecedented event in Chinese history, and the idea spread like wildfire throughout China and to the world's Chinatowns. In Havana, Chinese chipped in ten thousand dollars to get the anti-American word out. In Victoria, British Columbia, Chinese established a fund of six thousand dollars to compensate Chinese dockworkers who refused to unload American ships. Distraught U.S. merchants suddenly bombarded Roosevelt, and missionaries and educators demanded that something be done. But with his thick race lenses, Teddy could not see that the Chinese harbored patriotic feelings and that they would actually do something about it. Surely this sudden flame would quickly fizzle.

Roosevelt's inability to recognize third-world nationalism in Asia had already cost—and would cost—America much treasure and many lives. He had dismissed Aguinaldo and the result had been quagmire. Roosevelt simply could not accept that Asian primitives could cause much trouble—all of race history had made that clear. Such underestimation—indeed, lack of any attempt at estimation—would cost the United States dearly in the twentieth century. Aguinaldo had been the first. Others yet to come included Mao Tse-tung and Ho Chi Minh.

ON MARCH 17, 1905, one of the most significant weddings in American history took place in a house in New York City at 8 East 76th Street, between Madison and Fifth avenues. At 3:30 p.m., Alice Roosevelt—serving as a bridesmaid dressed in a white veil and holding a bouquet of pink roses—opened the ceremony as she proceeded down the wide stairs from the third floor to the second-floor salon. The bride—her cousin Eleanor Roosevelt—followed, and behind her was President Theodore Roosevelt, who would give his niece away to the bridegroom, his fifth cousin Franklin Delano Roosevelt.

Eleanor wore a pearl necklace and diamonds in her hair, gifts from Franklin's rich Delano relatives. Even though Franklin had never made much money himself, Teddy knew that he would be able to care for his new wife: FDR was heir to the huge Delano opium fortune.

Franklin's grandfather Warren Delano had for years skulked around the Pearl River Delta dealing drugs. Delano had run offices in Canton and Hong Kong. During business hours, Chinese criminals would pay him cash and receive an opium chit. At night, Scrambling Crabs—long, sleek, heavily armed crafts—rowed out into the Pearl River Delta to Delano's floating ware-houses, where they received their Jesus opium under the cover of darkness. The profits were enormous, and at his death Delano left his daughter Sara a fortune that she lavished on her only son.

The Delanos were not alone. Many of New England's great families made their fortunes dealing drugs in China. The Cabot family of Boston endowed Harvard with opium money, while Yale's famous

Skull and Bones society was funded by the biggest American opium dealers of them all—the Russell family. The most famous landmark on the Columbia University campus is the Low Memorial Library, which honors Abiel Low, a New York boy who made it big in the Pearl River Delta and bankrolled the first cable across the Atlantic. Princeton University's first big benefactor, John Green, sold opium in the Pearl River Delta with Warren Delano.

The list goes on and on: Boston's John Murray Forbes's opium profits financed the career of transcendentalist Ralph Waldo Emerson and bankrolled the Bell Telephone Company. Thomas Perkins founded America's first commercial railroad and funded the Boston Athenaeum. These wealthy and powerful drug-dealing families combined to create dynasties.

IN HIS SAVAGE-TO-CIVILIZED DOGMA about human evolution, Roosevelt imagined Chinese laborers as bucktoothed dummies, and he appealed to the better class of Chinese, who he assumed looked down on their own, just as aristocratic Teddy looked down on his American inferiors. In late June, the president held several conferences with K'ang Yu-wei, a respected Chinese community leader. Roosevelt tried to convince K'ang that besides Chinese laborers, America welcomed the Chinese. Roosevelt's pose did not fool

K'ang, who after the White House meetings said that "the whole nation of China [was] indignant," and he endorsed the boycott of American goods to "prevent the exclusion of any Chinaman from the United States."[34]

Back in China, enraged patriots swung into action. Newspapers featured the boycott as front-page news; refused advertisements for American goods; announced boycott meetings and reprinted anti-American speeches as breaking news; listed American trademarks and asked readers to refuse all goods marked "Made in the U.S.A.," "United States," or "America"; sponsored boycott essay contests; and even argued that their 1905 boycott was comparable to the colonists' boycott of British tea during the American struggle for independence.

Chinese homes and stores boasted huge colorful placards that read "Do Not Use American Goods," while students marched with flags inscribed "Boycott American Goods."[35] The Cantonese danced to a hit song titled "Boycotting the Cruel Treaty."[36] A Chinese publisher translated Harriett Beecher Stowe's *Uncle Tom's Cabin,* pointing out in the preface that White America's treatment of its Negroes had now been transferred to the Chinese. Thousands of fans were distributed in Canton portraying scenes of Chinese being abused by Americans. Gambling houses that had offered their customers free American cigarettes switched to a Chinese brand, and on August 16, the U.S. consul to Canton, Julius Lay, "wrote of the loss in sales of 10,000 cases of oil by Standard Oil and of the failure to sell any flour at a time when 500,000 bags would normally have been sold."[37]

Chester Holcombe, a former U.S. State Department diplomat in China, tried to signal Washington about "the intense racial pride of the Chinese."[38] Roosevelt must have been puzzled. Of what could the "Chinks" possibly be proud?

On June 28, the *New York Times* wrote:

CHINESE VERY BITTER AGAINST THIS COUNTRY

The question of Chinese exclusion from the United States continues chiefly to occupy the attention of the Chinese. The extent and depth of the feeling manifested astonish foreigners, and are regarded as an evidence of the growth of a national sentiment and public spirit which five years ago would have been inconceivable.[39]

Roosevelt sought to counter the boycott with the Big Stick. When Taft arrived in Hong Kong from Manila, he read a telegram from Roosevelt instructing him to be tough on the Chinese: "Make them realize that we intend to do what is right and that we cannot submit to what is now being done by them."[40] The implicit "wrong" Teddy presumed was a rumor that the government of China had ordered its army to enforce the boycott. In fact, the Chinese were for the first time intentionally employing nonviolent tactics. With a plank in his eye, Roosevelt focused the U.S.-China rift on a sliver that wasn't even there.

Canton was plastered with anti-American posters, one entitled "Turtles Carrying an American Beauty." The poster pictured turtles carrying Princess Alice on a palanquin. To the Chinese, a turtle was a low-life weakling with no integrity. Teddy's consul in Canton—Julius Lay—huffed to the viceroy of Guangdong and Guangxi provinces on August 30, 1905: "Today a poster in gold is posted in several places in the city with an illustration of a young girl being carried by four turtles meant to represent the daughter of our President. This disgraceful insult to the daughter of the President of the United States is only another evidence of what the boycott organization has been allowed to resort to, and for which the Chinese officials are alone responsible."[41] American newspapers did not inform their readers that Roosevelt's daughter had been portrayed in a demeaning manner; the *Washington Post* mentioned only "obnoxious placards" and the *New York Times* referred only to "insulting posters."[42]

When Alice examined the drawing, she chuckled. Nevertheless, Consul Lay and some American military officers advised Taft not to allow Alice to travel to Canton. But Burr McIntosh, the party's official photographer, recalled: "Miss Roosevelt wanted to see Canton and that settled it."[43]

TAFT RISKED ONLY A few jittery daylight hours in Canton. His party disembarked after dawn on September 3 at the U.S. consulate, located on the small island of Shaneen, in a river that flowed through Canton. Taft ordered Alice to remain in the fortress safety of America's island consulate. Taft then traveled under guard to the Manchu Club for a luncheon hosted by the viceroy of Guangdong. But when Taft arrived at the club, his Chinese host was not there. The *New York Times* reported, "The Viceroy was seriously ill in bed."[44] Claiming illness was a polite way for Chinese officials to snub irksome Foreign Devils.

Oblivious to the diplomatic rebuff, Taft delivered a rambling speech accusing the Chinese government of using intimidation to enforce the boycott and claiming that President Roosevelt would give the Chinese a square deal. The September 7 *Washington Post* reported:

TAFT IS BREAKING BOYCOTT
Instructed by the President to Disillusionize
Rabid Chinese
He Gives Assurances that the United States
Intends to Treat Immigrants Fairly.[45]

In fact, Big Bill's tough talk had little pacifying effect. Days after Taft's visit, Consul Lay cabled the State Department that "the agitation has taken a new lease of life and instead of subsiding is growing."[46] A Cantonese jeweler later refused to serve the American consul's wife, and Lay told Washington: "My chair coolies are hooted in the streets and I would not be surprised if my servants left me."[47] James J. Hill, a railroad titan trying to build track in China, later described the boycott as "the greatest commercial disaster America has ever suffered; [Europeans in China had] practically monopolized the trade."[48]

Taft got out of Canton under cover of darkness, returning to the safety of Hong Kong the evening of September 3. The party spent September 4 being entertained by the more welcoming British Anglo-Saxons. On September 5, the party split in two: Taft and about sixty people decided to return to San Francisco on the Pacific Mail steamer *Korea* via Shanghai, Nagasaki, Kobe, and Yokohama; Princess Alice and about twenty-eight people would go on to tour Beijing, Korea, and Japan.

ALICE BEGAN HER NORTHERN explorations in Beijing, where the court cared little about the boycott by China's southern merchants. On the throne was the elderly despot, Empress Cixi, who wasn't Chinese at all, but the last in a line of Manchu rulers. The empress housed Alice in her Summer Palace, a series of ornate structures, complete with an artificial lake, in the cool hills beyond the Forbidden City. At the welcoming dinner, Alice remembered, "I got quite drunk. I remember...thinking, 'Am I able to walk that line without swaying?' as I wove my way off to bed."[49]

The next morning a hungover Alice, "feeling slightly unsteady on my feet," made the obligatory three curtsies as she approached the empress, who sat "very erect and looking just like her picture."[50]

Alice was escorted to another room for a luncheon banquet with no interpreters, so neither side could understand the other. Next she was taken out into the palace gardens, and she later recalled Empress Cixi showering her with gifts. Alice gushed: "I absolutely loved all the loot I amassed."[51]

Further gifts and partying followed, enough to

Empress Cixi of China, 1905.

leave a bad impression with their American host, Consul William Rockhill, who wrote to James Rodgers, the American consul-general at Shanghai, "My experience with a section of the Taft party which came up here was identical with yours. I never saw such a pack of irresponsible men and women in my life.... Yesterday, at 11 A.M., I was glad to say goodbye to the last of them."[52]

ESTIMATES VARY, but some conclude that the 1905 boycott cut U.S. exports to China by more than half. Outraged by the Rough Rider in the White House, China had stood up to a White Christian country for the first time with a coordinated, peaceful response. One man in Shanghai foresaw a new era: "If we succeed in getting justice from America now, we may then boycott the nation that forces opium down our throats and the others that grab our provinces."[53] Indeed, the *New York Tribune* warned that "the greatest significance of the boycott is the possibility of future use of this method of coercion if the first attempt succeeds."[54] The paper had it right. The boycott united China's nationalists for the first time as they coordinated national communication, staged rallies, managed propaganda, and distributed millions of giveaways to rally their countrymen. Many of the leaders of the 1905 boycott would use their skills in further uprisings against domination by Foreign

Devils. Unable to imagine that the Chinese would behave as patriots and assuming that they'd always react as merchants, Roosevelt had fundamentally underestimated the Chinese character and had lit another long fuse.

Chapter 11

INCOGNITO IN JAPAN

*"I was told to say I was English if anyone asked
my nationality.... I have never seen such a
more complete change.... Americans were about
as unpopular as they had been popular before.
[There was] not a banzai to be heard."*[1]
—ALICE ROOSEVELT ON HER RETURN TO JAPAN,
SEPTEMBER 1905

Theodore Roosevelt was a master with the carefully staged photograph. He launched his Ranchman and Rough Rider personas from New York photo studios. Roosevelt always gave serious thought to how the visual record would reinforce his manly image. As Roosevelt wrote, "You never saw a photograph of me playing tennis. I'm careful about that. Photographs on horseback, yes. Tennis, no."[2]

As a result, the world didn't realize that as president, Roosevelt stocked his closets with costumes. One of his most cherished was his Rough Rider uniform, kept in fine trim by his personal Brooks Brothers tailor. One hot summer day, Roosevelt put it on for a meeting with two visitors, but forbade photographs.[3] He didn't want to be embarrassed if the public found out that the president still played soldier. Also, Roosevelt wanted what transpired that day to remain invisible to history.

On August 4, 1905, two emissaries of Gojong, the emperor of Younger Brother Korea, arrived at Roosevelt's Sagamore Hill retreat to beg Elder Brother to exercise his "good offices" to save Korea.[4] It was before them that Roosevelt dramatically appeared, dressed in full Rough Rider regalia, looking tough pacing back and forth across his new trophy room in front of the trembling Koreans. But in his response to their impassioned plea, Roosevelt struck a curiously powerless note. He explained that his hands were tied and that he could not consider Gojong's request until it was processed through official channels. Roosevelt and the Koreans knew Japan controlled Korea's "official channels."

The next day—August 5—Roosevelt wore a different costume for a meeting he dearly wanted captured on film. Roosevelt chose the grandest of settings, the 273-foot ship *Mayflower*. Built privately as a luxury yacht in 1896, the U.S. Navy had purchased the *Mayflower* in 1898 for the invasion of Cuba. In 1903, Roosevelt had deployed it to wrest Panama away from Venezuela. In 1904, Taft had traveled around the Caribbean on the *Mayflower* to survey the Caribbean nations newly under Roosevelt Corollary scrutiny. Now Roosevelt had commandeered the Big Stick ship as his enormous personal yacht.

The occasion was the commencement of the negotiations to resolve the Russo-Japanese War. Roosevelt posed the photo below the *Mayflower*'s deck, just outside the ship's seagoing banquet hall. He stood between the men, two Russians on his right and two Japanese on his left. Privately Roosevelt loathed the two Russians, Sergei Witte and Roman Rosen, and considered his Harvard buddy Jutaro Komura and Baron Kaneko's sidekick, Kogoro Takahira, civilized fellows. Posing as a worldly diplomat wrestling with war and peace—dressed in a brilliant white silk vest, white tie, black tails, black silk top hat, white cotton gloves, and monocle—Roosevelt placed himself dead center in the photo. But, like his tennis costumes, there was much left out of the frame.

After the photograph, Roosevelt led his guests to a smorgasbord lunch laid out on a round table with no chairs, so no one could choose sides. No negotiations took place then; the Russians and Japanese would negotiate between themselves. Indeed, after lunch the Russians and Japanese steamed north to Portsmouth. Roosevelt, meanwhile, played sailor, enjoying himself by descending below Long Island Sound in a U.S. Navy diving bell. By then Roosevelt had the photograph that would misrepresent the champion of war as a peacemaker.

A week earlier, Roosevelt had huddled on the *Mayflower* with Baron Kaneko, the foreign minister Komura, and Ambassador Takahira, while Secretary Taft had met with Prime Minister Katsura in Tokyo. These simultaneous meetings had affirmed the triple alliance.[5] A more accurate photo on August 5 would have been of Roosevelt, Emperor Meiji, and King Edward VII holding hands in a triple alliance circle, with the Russians looking on from afar.

BARON KANEKO REPEATEDLY WARNED Roosevelt that the Japanese public yearned for a cash payment from Russia. The Japanese army and navy had bested the Russians in every battle, and an indemnity would signal that Japan was the recognized victor. Concessions of territory would not be enough, because the Japanese army had already secured the lands through the sacrifice of hundreds of thousands of its soldiers. The millions upon millions of friendly banzais that had been given to Alice were in expectation that her father would secure a square deal for Japan. Roosevelt never understood that by so publicly aligning himself with Japan against Russia, he was encouraging the assumption across Japan that he was the man who would help expunge the "Shame of Liaodong."

Czar Nicholas II had no plans to cooperate with the Japanese with regard to any financial compensation, vowing "not a ruble" for the "little Jap monkeys," and thundered from St. Petersburg: "The Japanese desperately need money, and we will not give it to them."[6]

Roosevelt stepped into the middle of the dispute and sent two unsolicited and strongly worded letters of advice to the founding fathers. Lecturing Japan's wise men, the Rough Rider wrote that in the "interest of civilization and humanity," Tokyo should forgo an indemnity:

> Ethically, it seems to me that Japan owes a duty to the world at this crisis. The civilized world looks to her to make peace; the nations believe in her; let her show her leadership in matters ethical no less than in matters military. The appeal is made to her in the name of all that is lofty and noble; and to this appeal I hope she will not be deaf.[7]

Ethically? Lofty? Noble? Baron Kaneko had already informed an adoring Carnegie Hall audience that Japan had abandoned the "Right Is Right" ethics of the East and embraced the "Might Is Right" ethics of the West. The founding fathers saw nothing lofty or noble about the U.S. Army's mowing down civilians in the Philippines or the British navy's shelling Chinese cities. This was about war. Hundreds of thousands of Japanese sons had perished to expunge the "Shame of Liaodong." With these letters, once again a White Christian power was asking the non-White Japanese to forfeit their hard-won spoils of war.

On the same day Roosevelt dispatched his lecture to the founding fathers in Tokyo, he upbraided the Foreign Office in London: "Every true friend of Japan should tell it as I have already told it, that the opinion of the civilized world will not support it in continuing the war merely for the purpose of extorting money from Russia."[8] This was the third time Roosevelt had asked the big boys to play with him. In the margin of Roosevelt's plea, the foreign minister, Lord Henry Lansdowne, wrote: "This is a suggestion that we should press the Japanese to make further concessions. Were we to do so, our advice would not be taken and would be resented."[9] What was so clear to the experienced diplomats in London never occurred to the Rough Rider, lost in his dress-up fantasies that summer by the sea.

AFTER THE FINAL SESSION of the Portsmouth peace talks, the chief Russian negotiator rushed out and told the press: "The Japanese yielded on everything. We pay not a Kopek of indemnity.... It was a complete victory for us."[10]

For the second war in a row, Japan had won all the battles but afterward was shamed by White Christians.

An Osaka newspaper drew a picture of a weeping skeleton of a Japanese soldier holding the treaty. Underneath were the words "We are ashamed to report this."[11] The *Mainichi Shimbun* wrote: "The fruits of our arms have been lost by weak diplomacy. Japan victorious in the field has been defeated in the conference chamber."[12] In London, King Edward VII, the prime minister, Arthur Balfour, and Lord Lansdowne were surprised by the Japanese concession. The foreign affairs editor of the *Times* in London wrote to the British ambassador in Russia about Roosevelt: "I should like to know what kind of pressure he finally applied to Tokyo. I am told it amounted almost to a threat of the financial boycotting of Japan."[13]

Riots broke out in the cities that had so recently cheered Roosevelt's daughter. In Tokyo, furious mobs burned thirteen Christian churches, threw stones at passing Americans,[14] and destroyed thirty tramcars, and U.S. Marines bivouacked on the grounds of the U.S. legation to protect it from the howling mob.[15] Though he had not sat at the Portsmouth negotiating table, Roosevelt had made himself Japan's guy, and the

betrayed Japanese now booed the president they had
so recently applauded. In his memoir, Minister Lloyd
Griscom wrote, "President Roosevelt's picture, which
adorned many Japanese houses, was turned to the wall.
I had quite a number of anonymous letters saying the
mob would shortly again visit the Legation to express
appreciation for the part we had played in depriving
Japan of the fruits of victory."[16] Minister Griscom
wrote to Roosevelt in an understatement, "Your popu-
larity has suffered a distinct check."[17] Roosevelt blamed
Tokyo, as he wrote to his ambassador to Russia: "Why
in the world the Japanese statesmen, usually so astute,
permitted their people to think they had to get a large
indemnity, I cannot understand."[18]

Secretary Taft laid over in Yokohama on his way
home from China. The rioting had died out, but not
the anti-Roosevelt feelings. Taft cabled the U.S. minister, Rockhill, in Beijing: "Conditions in Japan...
will make it unwise for Miss Roosevelt to spend any
considerable time in Japan."[19]

After the riots, Baron Kaneko suggested that
Roosevelt repair the damage by keeping his prom-
ise to publicly endorse a Japanese Monroe Doctrine.
Roosevelt blanched and postponed, pledging that
he would do so once he departed the presidency.[20]
Kaneko left the president with only one of Teddy's
earlier promises fulfilled: Roosevelt gave Kaneko the
Colorado bearskin for Emperor Meiji.

Teddy's pose as a diplomat in a white vest caught on with the Anglo-Saxons. The *Times* of London reported: "Admiration for the President's splendid success is the first sentiment of Americans; the next is admiration for the magnificent generosity of the Japanese." American newspapers gushed: "Theodore Roosevelt stands unchallenged as the world's first citizen. He has sheathed the swords of a million men."[21] Roosevelt—a professional author—quickly forwarded to friends dramatic anecdotes portraying himself in the middle of the action. On September 2, he wrote to Alice that if he hadn't gotten Japan and Russia together, "they would not have made peace.[22]

IN SEOUL, EMPEROR GOJONG awaited Princess Alice. The year before, the frightened emperor had fled his burning palace as the Japanese had taken over, and now he resided in the much humbler royal library. Each day Japanese "advisers" brought Gojong papers to sign, and Japanese guards tucked him in at night. But Gojong considered himself a skilled survivor, fifty-seven years old in 1905 and allied with the United States since Chester Arthur had been president. He had hope.

And despite it all, Gojong perceived Roosevelt as a glowing moral force. Indeed, Elder Brother's summons had brought Russia and Japan together and ended history's largest war. Over the decades, Gojong had believed that America would come through, though he had worried when the American legation had suggested that the United States couldn't help in the wake of the Japanese takeover. Still, Gojong's heart beat expectantly; Elder Brother Roosevelt's daughter was on her way. Perhaps Alice's father would now come to the rescue.

Alice traveled from the east coast of China to the west coast of Korea through the Yellow Sea on a commercial passenger ship, passing the fortress of Port Arthur at the tip of the contested Liaodong Peninsula. They arrived at the Korean port of Incheon on September 19 and were met by the U.S. minister, Edwin Morgan (who had replaced Horace Allen), and his personal secretary, Willard Straight. The emperor's personal train took them to downtown Seoul, where the Korean Royal Band welcomed Alice with "The Star-Spangled Banner." Emperor Gojong pulled out all the stops to welcome Alice—complete with a sedan-chair trip down newly cleaned streets. She later remembered that she was unimpressed: "Somehow it was all slightly sad and pathetic.... The country was beginning to slip into Japanese hands and I must say that the Japanese army officers I saw looked exceptionally smart and competent."[23]

Alice stayed in the American legation building with Morgan, whom her father had sent to Seoul to pave the way for the Japanese takeover. Recalled Alice, "The legation was just next door to the Imperial Palace and one could see the little Emperor peeking through the curtains to see what was happening on our side of the fence."[24]

Gojong had never dined publicly with a foreigner but broke precedent with a grand luncheon to honor Roosevelt's daughter. Alice later remembered Gojong's desperation: "We went to lunch with him. It was all a little pathetic. He was a sad-looking man, wearing lots of lovely, fluttery little garments. Not grand at all. When we went in to lunch, he positively hung onto my arm. I didn't have his. He had mine."[25] Willard Straight wrote a friend, "These people are looking for straws and the Roosevelt trip [looks] like a life preserver to their jaundiced imaginations."[26]

The next day Gojong tried again to impress Roosevelt by allowing women from the royal family to dine with Alice, also a first. Willard Straight observed that Alice's party was "treated with more consideration than has ever been shown visiting royalty."[27]

The emperor controlled the luncheons but the Japanese controlled the emperor. Desperate, Gojong took Senator Francis Newlands of Nevada aside and begged him to ask Teddy to exercise his good offices and save Korea from Japan's tightening grip. Newlands sniffed that Gojong should submit a proper legal request through official channels, which Newlands

Emperor Gojong of Korea. He told the U.S. State Department, "We feel that America is to us as an Elder Brother."

knew Gojong could not do because of his Japanese minders.[28] Alice later recalled, "At a farewell audience, the Emperor and Crown Prince each gave me his photograph. They were two rather pathetic, stolid figures with very little imperial existence ahead of them."[29]

Before he departed Yokohama for San Francisco,

Taft revised his earlier opinion and cabled Rockhill that Alice could go to Japan under one condition: "Further investigation satisfies me that Miss Roosevelt's contemplated trip with her party incognito to Japan can be quite safely made."[30]

Incognito. Before Teddy's summer of secret diplomacy, the Roosevelt name had been cheered across Japan. Now Theodore Roosevelt's daughter had to hide her face. Alice later admitted, "I was told to say I was English if asked my nationality."[31]

Alice slipped furtively into the Japanese port of Shimonoseki on a passenger ship from Korea guarded by Japanese plainclothes police. There were no photographs or press coverage, and she was allowed out only when heavily guarded. "I have never seen such a more complete change," Alice recalled. "Americans were about as unpopular as they had been popular before. [There was] not a banzai to be heard."[32]

Nevertheless, Alice continued to generate convenient headlines for American consumption. According to newspaper editors, Alice's steamer, the *Siberia,* had made record time out of Yokohama. A world speed record was in the making.

Chapter 12

SELLOUT IN SEOUL

"We feel that America is to us as an
Elder Brother."[1]
—EMPEROR GOJONG OF KOREA, 1897

"I should like to see Japan have Korea."[2]
—THEODORE ROOSEVELT, 1900

America's princess had set a new Yokohama-
to-San Francisco record of thirteen days. Then
breathless coverage of her cross-country train trip
entertained readers. Engineers slept in relays as they
full-throttled their engines. Brass bands greeted Alice,
and children waving American flags bid her farewell.
Alice set a new transcontinental speed record.

When Alice returned to the White House, Edith was
shocked by her appearance. The twenty-one-year-old

girl had lost twenty pounds. Edith confided to Kermit, "Alice is looking very careworn and troubled about something. She will not say what is wrong."[3] Alice brooded alone about her marital future.

Back in Tokyo, the foreign minister, Komura, was being severely criticized for not having wrested an indemnity from Russia. By contrast, Komura regarded the Taft-Katsura agreement—made while he'd been in the United States—as a good bargain. In one quick meeting, Japan had received concrete U.S. support for the triple alliance "as if a treaty had been signed." Why not publicize this bargain to offset the indemnity criticism? In fact, historians suspect that the Foreign Ministry leaked the following sensational description of the secret Taft-Katsura agreement to the government-friendly newspaper, *Kokumin,* on November 4, 1905:

> The Anglo-Japanese Alliance is in fact a Japanese-Anglo-American alliance. We may be sure that when once England became our ally, America also became party to the agreement. Owing to peculiar national conditions America cannot make any open alliance, but we should bear in mind that America is our ally though bound by no formal treaty.... The majority of America, under the leadership of the world statesman President Roosevelt, will deal with

her Oriental problems in cooperation with Japan and Great Britain.[4]

Roosevelt must have felt as if he had been punched in the stomach. *The Anglo-Japanese Alliance is in fact a Japanese-Anglo-American alliance!* But luckily for Roosevelt, who could have been impeached for making a secret diplomatic partnership, Americans couldn't make sense of the *Kokumin* article, as only Roosevelt and Taft were aware how true that line was. (Roosevelt had kept even Minister Griscom in the dark.)

Like two naughty boys, Taft and the president got their stories straight before being asked questions. Roosevelt coached Taft, "I doubt if it calls for any reply at all. If it did, I think that a sufficient answer would be that we neither ask nor give any favor to anyone as a reward for not meddling with any American territory. We are entirely competent to prevent such meddling, and require no guarantee of assistance to preserve our territorial integrity."[5]

Roosevelt then complained to Ambassador Takahira, who in turn had Prime Minister Katsura send him a telegram dutifully denying that the *Kokumin* article was based on information supplied by the Japanese government, that there was no secret Japanese-Anglo-American alliance, and that Roosevelt's friendly attitude toward Japan's Korea problem was entirely spontaneous.[6] Roosevelt provided a further distraction for the reading public: that same month, *Scribner's Magazine* published the Rough Rider's latest tale of daring and conquest, "Wolf Hunt in Oklahoma."

AFTER SENATOR NEWLANDS BRUSHED him off, Emperor Gojong sent appeals to London, Paris, and Moscow, all of which were intercepted by Japanese agents. Desperate, Gojong again reached out to Elder Brother Roosevelt. The Korean leader still naively believed that if Roosevelt knew the truth—that Japan held a knife to Korea's throat—he would stay the Japanese hand.

Gojong charged an American friend named Homer Hulbert with the dangerous and secret mission of reaching out to Roosevelt. Tailed by Japanese agents, Hulbert took a ship to San Francisco, then a train to Washington, and finally on November 15, 1905, made it to the State Department. But no high official in the Roosevelt administration would see him. Teddy was stalling for time, waiting for the other shoe to drop.

As Hulbert had journeyed from Seoul to Washington, Korea's new dictator traveled from Tokyo to Seoul. He was Hirobumi Ito, the senior founding father and Baron Kaneko's sponsor. On the evening of November 17, two days after Hulbert's arrival in Washington, Ito corralled Gojong's ministers and told them they would now "agree" to a new treaty. The treaty began, "The government of Japan, through the Department of Foreign Affairs at Tokyo, will hereafter have control and direction of the external relations and affairs at Korea, and diplomatic and consular representatives of Japan will have the charge of the subjects and interests of Korea in foreign countries."[7] The Korean ministers saw gleaming Japanese bayonets through the windows, while witnesses outside the room remembered hearing anguished shouting and wailing from those assembled within. In telegrams to Washington, Minister Edwin Morgan described how the Korean cabinet ministers had been coerced into signing and how Gojong had appealed to him for help.

But it was too late—Korea was no more. A two-thousand-year-old country was now folded into a department within the Japanese Foreign Ministry in Tokyo—the same ministry from which an employee named General LeGendre had written follow-the-sun notes to Emperor Meiji.

Back in Washington, Roosevelt now considered Homer Hulbert's plea from Emperor Gojong. Korea's existence was in the balance. Roosevelt wrote to Secretary of State Root:

I have carefully read through the letter.... It is the wish of the Emperor that the existence of the letter should be kept secret and nothing said to anyone about it.... These facts render it impossible for us to treat the letter as an official communication, for there is no way in which we could officially act without violating what Mr. Hulbert says is the Emperor's wish. Moreover, since the letter was written we have been officially notified that the Korean Government has made the very arrangement with Japan which in the letter the Emperor says he does not desire to make. All things considered, I do not see that any practical action on the letter is open to us.[8]

Roosevelt had secretly promised his Japanese friends an "alliance in practice as if a treaty had been signed." There was, of course, no chance that Roosevelt would bring the United States openly into the alliance. At the end of January, however, he had informed British leaders through their ambassador to the United States, Sir Mortimer Durand, that he considered the interests of the two countries identical in the Far East and that he wished Britain and the United States to stand together. But he had cautioned that in order to avoid exciting criticism, they should do so by their actions rather than by an "open evident agreement."⁹ Now he ordered the closing of the U.S. legation in Seoul as a signal to London and Tokyo.¹⁰

Americans remember the exact date of Pearl Harbor, but not the day Theodore Roosevelt gave Japan the keys to the kingdom. The date was November 28, 1905, when Roosevelt turned over the U.S. legation building in Seoul. Now the Honorary Aryans had a grand base from which to begin civilizing Asia.

Theodore Roosevelt stands as the first world leader to endorse with promises and actions Japan's advancement onto the Asian continent. Like America's earlier expansion, this westward movement would leave millions dead. But in 1905, Roosevelt had it all worked out: the Japs would respect the Anglo-American Open Door, and the Slavs would friction the Japs' ambitions.

The Roosevelt Room in the White House is just across the hall from the Oval Office. Along one wall is a portrait of Rough Rider Teddy on a horse. Along another wall is Roosevelt's Nobel Peace Prize. The Nobel committee never knew that the Rough Rider had green-lighted Japan onto the Asian continent.

Roosevelt later defended himself against charges that he betrayed Emperor Gojong by not acting on the "good offices" clause of the 1882 U.S.-Korea Treaty: "The treaty rested on the false assumption that Korea could govern herself well.... [Korea was] utterly impotent either for self-government or self-defense."¹¹

Willard Straight observed Americans fleeing Seoul "like the stampede of rats from a sinking ship."[12] But to Roosevelt, it was a rising ship, a great progressive experiment whereby one Asian country would civilize another. An American businessman watching the rats observed: "The Japs have got what they have been planning for these many moons and it is clear that Roosevelt played into their hands when he posed as the great peacemaker of the 20th century."[13]

PERHAPS NO EMPIRE'S BEGINNING had been sanctioned as thoroughly by other nations. In 1906, Roosevelt deleted the word *Korea* from the U.S. government's Record of Foreign Relations and placed it under the heading "Japan." Korea would end up providing Japan with most of the two hundred thousand young sex slaves for Japanese troops in World War II. Most of these little Korean girls never benefited from Roosevelt's plan to have the Japanese inculcate them with Anglo-Saxon values. After being raped hundreds of times, most of the Korean girls died.

Korea was only the first victim of Japan's Roosevelt-sanctioned westering. Ba Maw, the president of Burma during the Japanese occupation in World War II, observed, "There was only one way to do a thing, the Japanese way; only one goal and interest, the Japanese interest; only one destiny for the East Asian countries, to become so many...Koreas tied forever to Japan."[14]

ON DECEMBER 8, 1941, President Franklin Roosevelt entered the Capitol building in a wheelchair as a shocked nation awaited his words. The secretary of state, Cordell Hull, had urged FDR to recite the litany of broken Japanese promises over the past decades. Roosevelt instead gave us this eternal narrative:

> Yesterday, December 7, 1941—a date which will live in infamy—the United States of America was suddenly and deliberately attacked by naval and air forces of the Empire of Japan.... Always will we remember the character of the onslaught against us.[15]

The U.S. National Park Service is responsible for preserving the day of infamy's memory at Pearl Harbor. Their official version of why America went to war in the Pacific ignores whole chapters from the historical record:

> The attack on Pearl Harbor was the culmination of a decade of deteriorating relations between Japan and the United States over the status of China and the security of Southeast

Asia. The breakdown began in 1931 when Japanese army extremists, in defiance of government policy, invaded and overran the northern-most Chinese province of Manchuria. Japan ignored American protests, and in the summer of 1937 launched a full-scale attack on the rest of China.[16]

Even this more detailed explanation has Japan suddenly—jack-in-the-box-like—expanding westward, much to America's surprise. (Among Japan's earliest conquests in World War II: Teddy's beloved U.S. Navy citadel at Subig Bay in the Philippines.) Lost in the telling is General LeGendre, who wrote the script for the Greater East Asia Co-prosperity Sphere, and Theodore Roosevelt, who anointed Japan as Asia's civilizer. A new generation of Americans remembered only the photos of the burning hulks at Pearl Harbor. But again, there was a lot that did not appear in the frame.

ROOSEVELT NEVER KEPT HIS promise to publicly endorse the Japanese Monroe Doctrine for Asia, as Kaneko explained:

When President Roosevelt completed his term, he went to shoot big game in Central Africa.

Then he re-entered American politics in the movement to form the Progressive Party. The six years between his retirement and the World War were full of striking events in which Colonel Roosevelt played a part, and Japan's relations with her neighbouring countries in Asia were relatively unimportant. No occasion arose to prompt the publication of the opinion which President Roosevelt had uttered in our talk at Sagamore Hill.[17]

Two years after Roosevelt's death, the former Japanese ambassador to the United States Kikujuiso Ishii told a dinner audience of Americans and Japanese in Tokyo that the United States and Japan would go to war "if Japan attempted to interfere unduly in the Western Hemisphere and if the United States attempted to become dominant in Asia or sought to prevent Japan from her pacific and natural expansion in this part of the world."[18] A decade later, immediately after Japan expanded into Manchuria, the head of the U.S. State Department's Far East Division wrote the secretary of state, Henry Stimson, "For nearly twenty years, Japanese statesmen and writers have been speaking of a 'Japanese Monroe Doctrine for Asia.' Some years ago they were given to comparing the position of Japan vis-à-vis China with that of the United States vis-à-vis Mexico. More recently they have insisted that

Japan's relationship to Manchuria is essentially that of the United States toward weak countries of the Caribbean."[19] Japanese leaders were not shy about discussing the parallel. In 1932, *Time* magazine quoted a top member of Japan's parliament, who explained that their "national policy is that of a Far Eastern Monroe Doctrine."[20] The Japanese minister of war added, "The countries of eastern Asia are objects of oppression by the white people.... The United States loudly professes to champion righteousness and humanity, but what can you think when you review its policy toward Cuba, Panama, Nicaragua and other Latin American nations?"[21] *Time* magazine elaborated that leaders in Japan spoke of a "Japanese Monroe Doctrine claiming the right to protect all Asia...and that the originator to be cited for this idea was none other than the late great Theodore Roosevelt."[22]

That same year, the author Katsuji Inahara—who had studied American history at Stanford and Harvard—wrote, "As long as the United States maintains the Monroe Doctrine—that is, a 'closed door policy'—and still insists on enforcing the Open Door policy [in China], it is only natural and should not be objectionable at all that Japan, acting on the principle of equality, should establish an Asian Monroe Doctrine—that is, 'a closed door policy'—and further demand that the Open Door policy be applied to Central and South America."[23]

Also in 1932, Baron Kaneko wrote an article for *Contemporary Affairs* magazine entitled "A Japanese Monroe Doctrine and Manchuria," in which he recalled what Roosevelt had told him on the porch at Sagamore Hill on July 8, 1905:

All the Asiatic nations are now faced with the urgent necessity of adjusting themselves to the present age. Japan should be their natural leader in that process, and their protector during the transition stage, much as the United States assumed the leadership of the American continent many years ago.[24]

In the same article, Baron Kaneko lamented that Roosevelt wasn't alive to defend Japan:

Now when Japan's policy in Manchuria is much criticized by foreign Powers, it is a matter of the greatest regret to me and to Japan that he died unexpectedly without having uttered in public speech his views on a "Japanese Monroe Doctrine" in Asia. This opinion, held by one of the greatest statesmen of our time, would have been of high importance, had he lived to announce it himself at the present moment, when Manchuria is once more a burning international question.[25]

The next year, the prestigious American journal *Foreign Affairs* summed up the understanding: "The idea of a Monroe Doctrine for Asia arose in Japan shortly after the Russo-Japanese War [and] the intent of the Japanese Government to claim the rights of a Monroe Doctrine for the Far East is perfectly clear."[26]

In 1940, the foreign minister of Japan, Yosuke Matsuoka, coined the phrase "Greater East Asia Co-prosperity Sphere," asking, "If the United States could rely upon the Monroe Doctrine to support its preeminent position in the Western Hemisphere in order to sustain American economic stability and prosperity, why could not Japan do the same with an Asian Monroe Doctrine?"[27] The name Greater East Asia Co-prosperity Sphere caught on quickly among the Japanese in the 1940s—no great surprise given the intellectual roots planted so many years before by General LeGendre and Theodore Roosevelt.

The problem was that when Roosevelt granted Japan a Monroe Doctrine, he assumed they'd be compliant Honorary Aryans and expand westward only as far as he'd allow. Roosevelt had imagined that the Russians would moderate the Japanese expansion, and he had accepted the many promises of his Japanese Harvard buddies to respect the Anglo-American Open Door. But by 1941 the Slav was focused on

Hitler's threat in Europe. The Honorary Aryans had tired of the Anglo-Saxons' "White Is Right" mentality and thought that Japan could and should be the country to civilize Asia. The Land of the Rising Sun had its own sun-following ideas, which were clear from Japan's December 7, 1941, note to the U.S.:

> It is impossible not to reach the conclusion that the American Government desires to maintain and strengthen, in coalition with Great Britain and other powers, its dominant position it has hitherto occupied not only in China but in other areas of East Asia. It is a fact of history that the countries of East Asia for the past hundred years or more have been compelled to observe the status quo under the Anglo-American policy of imperialistic exploitation and to sacrifice themselves to the prosperity of the two nations. The Japanese Government cannot tolerate the perpetuation of such a situation.[28]

When, thirty-six years earlier, Japan had set out to civilize Asia along Anglo-Saxon lines, Roosevelt had seen it as a grand progressive experiment: because Teddy considered Japan "the only nation in Asia that understands the principles and methods of Western civilization," he felt that Japan should lead and protect its neighbors. Teddy would not live to see his benevolent intentions lead over thirty million victims to early graves. Roosevelt never imagined that the sun he wanted the United States to follow could also burn.

Chapter 13

FOLLOWING THE SUN

Many good persons seem prone to speak of all wars of conquest as necessarily evil. This is, of course, a shortsighted view. In its after effects a conquest may be fraught either with evil or with good for mankind, according to the comparative worth of the conquering and conquered peoples. . . . The world would have halted had it not been for the Teutonic conquests in alien lands; but the victories of Moslem over Christian have always proved a curse in the end.
—THEODORE ROOSEVELT, 1896
THE WINNING OF THE WEST

Secretary Taft returned to San Francisco on September 27 aboard the *Korea*—a ship named after a country whose existence he had just terminated.

The Roosevelt administration's most detailed commentary on the imperial cruise was the briefing Taft gave friendly reporters in San Francisco. Big Bill was his usual ebullient self as he artfully employed an array of cheerful words while conveying very little. Taft explained that any Filipino disgruntlement with their American masters was due to "the distressing agricultural situation." Taft was firm about freedom for Pacific Negroes: "Some of the younger men of education have been advocating immediate independence. It therefore became necessary to state with considerable emphasis [that] there was no possible hope for independence short of a generation." Mostly Taft focused on the sunny side: In some provinces, hemp production was up. American tax dollars were hard at work to "make Manila harbor as convenient as any in the Orient."[2]

There were no questions from the White Christian newsmen as to why Chinese traded freely with all countries in the world *except* the United States, or why Roosevelt's daughter had been depicted insultingly in posters plastered on Chinese walls, or why Taft had skulked to Canton under cover of darkness, or why Chinese officials had refused to dine with him. Instead, Taft assured the newspapermen that "the President's proclamation and assurance that justice would be done to the Chinese had an excellent effect."[3]

With their bumbling diplomacy, Roosevelt and Taft had accomplished the seemingly impossible: they gave Korea to Japan and at the same time turned Japanese sentiment against America. But Taft maintained that there had been no anti-American riots and that the Japanese still loved Roosevelt and all Americans.

In December of 1905, the president informed Congress that peace reigned in the Muslim southern part of the Philippines. By then, many observers had lost count of the number of times he had declared the end of hostilities. Just three months later, in March of 1906, word came that the U.S. Army had massacred approximately one thousand Muslim men, women, and children who had cowered in the shallow bowl of an extinct volcano. An outraged Mark Twain called it a "slaughter [by] Christian butchers."[4] Roosevelt cabled the commander, "I congratulate you and the officers and men of your command upon the brilliant feat of arms wherein you and they so well upheld the honor of the American flag."[5]

Meanwhile, Alice decided she had to marry Nick. She later wrote, "I felt I had to get away from the White House and my family."[6] Alice remembered that she broke the news to Edith in the First Lady's bathroom "while she was brushing her teeth, so that she should have a moment to think before she said anything."[7] Nick informed Teddy in the White House

The Moro Massacre, March 1906. President Roosevelt called it a "brilliant feat of arms" that "upheld the honor of the American flag." Mark Twain called it a "slaughter [by] Christian butchers." (National Archives)

study downstairs. Congressman Longworth's well-known reputation as a boozing womanizer apparently didn't faze the president. Nick was well born, wealthy, and a fellow member of Harvard's exclusive Porcellian Club. (Roosevelt wrote to friends, "Nick and I are both members of the Porc, you know."[8])

When the press asked Congressman Longworth if he had asked Alice for her hand while on the cruise, Nick was less than gallant: "I don't really know. I've been in what you might call a trance for so long that I am somewhat mixed as to dates. . . . I

Nicholas Longworth, Alice Roosevelt Longworth, and Theodore Roosevelt, the White House, February 17, 1906. Alice later wrote, "I felt I had to get away from the White House and my family." At the end of the day, Alice's stepmother, Edith Roosevelt, told her, "I want you to know that I am glad to see you leave. You have never been anything but trouble." (Stringer/Hulton Archive/Getty Images)

did not know officially that I was engaged until the announcement."[9]

Alice and Nick were married in the East Room of the White House on February 17, 1906. "Trinkets," Alice had answered when asked about her preference for wedding presents. "Preferably *diamond* trinkets."[10] Guests marveled at the gifts that overflowed the Blue Room. There were costly items from everyone who sought the president's favor, plus extravagant baubles from foreign friends: a solid gold jewelry box with a diamond-encrusted lid from King Edward VII, a Gobelin tapestry from France, a lifetime supply of silk from China, a stunning pearl necklace from Cuba.

At the end of her big day, the bride said good-bye to her stepmother. "Mother," declared Alice, "this has been quite the nicest wedding I'll ever have. I've never had so much fun."

Edith responded, "I want you to know that I am glad to see you leave. You have never been anything but trouble."[11]

While steaming across the Pacific the previous summer, Alice had written of Nick in her diary: "He will go off and do something with some horrible woman and it will kill me off."[12] Years later, the longtime doorkeeper of the House of Representatives called Congressman Longworth "one of the greatest womanizers in history on Capitol Hill."[13] By 1912, Alice contemplated divorce. "He hates me and I him,"[14] she wrote. Twelve years later, forty-year-old Alice found herself pregnant with the child of her own illicit lover, Senator William Borah. Her best friend wrote in her diary, "Poor Alice. She feels humiliated about the baby and dreads what people will say."[15]

Alice gave birth to Paulina Longworth on February 14, 1925, exactly forty-one years to the day Alice's mother and grandmother had died. The *New York Times* caption under a photo of Nick holding Paulina mocked, "Longworth Poses as Fond Father."[16] Nicholas Longworth would later die at the age of sixty-two on April 9, 1931, in the home of one of his lovers, who then traveled to his funeral on a train with another of his mistresses.

As she grew into a shy, awkward girl, Paulina disappointed her outgoing mother. Alice often finished her daughter's sentences. Alice's brother Kermit referred to Paulina as "Sister's competition."[17] Paulina tried to kill herself a number of times and received shock therapy in mental institutions. On January 27, 1957, Paulina fatally swallowed too many sleeping pills. Alice denied it was suicide.

In her old age, Alice was one of Washington's supreme hostesses, known for her biting wit. The pillow on her living room couch was embroidered with "If you haven't got anything nice to say about anybody come sit next to me."

February played a special role in Alice Roosevelt's

life. In that month over the years she had been born, her mother and grandmother had died, she had married Nick, and she had given birth. Alice died at the age of ninety-six on February 20, 1980. She was buried wearing the pearl necklace given to her seventy-four years earlier by American-ruled Cuba when she had been a young bride named Princess Alice.

AN IMPORTANT TEST OF any chief executive is how well he chooses and grooms his successor. Five months before the election of 1908, Roosevelt wrote the British historian George Otto Trevelyan that "always excepting Washington and Lincoln, I believe that Taft as President will rank with any other man who has ever been in the White House."[18] Writing to Taft, Roosevelt was even more effusive: "I have always said you would be the greatest President, bar only Washington and Lincoln, and I feel mighty inclined to strike out the exceptions!"[19]

Roosevelt was more confident than Taft was. Years earlier, Taft had written to one who encouraged him to be president, "I have no ambition in that direction. Any party which would nominate me would make a great mistake."[20]

Taft possessed none of Roosevelt's public-relations genius. During the 1908 presidential campaign, an irritated Teddy chided his friend: "I am convinced that the prominence that has been given to your golf playing has not been wise, and from now on I hope that your people will do everything they can to prevent one word being sent out about either your fishing or your playing golf.... I never let friends advertise my tennis, and never let a photograph of me in tennis costume appear."[21]

Taft pleased his wife and Roosevelt by becoming president, but—as he had predicted—he was all thumbs as a chief executive. "The honest greenhorn at the poker table," the *New York Times* called him.[22]

Roosevelt's decision to oppose Taft in 1912 for the presidency was a disaster: it ruined the Roosevelt-Taft friendship, divided old loyalties (Alice supported her father while Nick supported Taft), and guaranteed victory for the Democratic candidate, Woodrow Wilson.

In 1921, President Warren Harding appointed Taft to be chief justice of the Supreme Court, where he served up until a month before he died on March 8, 1930, at the age of seventy-seven. William Howard Taft is the only president besides John F. Kennedy buried at Arlington National Cemetery.

ROOSEVELT'S FRONTIER HEROES HAD triumphed in North America because, through immigration and extermination, they had eventually outnumbered the continent's Indians. No such glorious result would manifest itself in the Philippines. After cheerleading the expenditure of millions of taxpayer dollars and hundreds of thousands of lives, Roosevelt eventually threw in the towel and admitted the islands' strategic and economic worthlessness. On August 21, 1907, Roosevelt wrote Taft, "I don't see where they are of any value to us....the Philippines form our heel of Achilles. They are all that makes the present situation with Japan dangerous."[23] And later as ex-president, Roosevelt wrote, "I do not believe that America has any special beneficial interest in retaining the Philippines."[24] But such private conclusions would not find their way into his big stick proclamations regarding the Aryan role in Asia.

The United States would free the Philippines after World War II, only to leave it under the rule of descendants of the entrenched oligarchy that William Howard Taft had taught democracy's masquerade.

NOTHING WOULD SHAKE ROOSEVELT'S belief that what was good for White Christian males was good for the world. In his postpresidency, Roosevelt delivered exuberant speeches with titles such as "Expansion of the White Races," in which he repeated the ideas that had earned him his Harvard degree and propelled his rise to best-selling author and president:

It is undoubtedly true that the Indian population of America is larger today than it was
when Columbus discovered the continent, and
stands on a far higher plane of happiness and
efficiency.... Doubtless occasional brutalities
have been committed by white settlers but these
brutalities were not an appreciable factor in the
dying out of the natives.

Of course, the best that can happen to any
people that has not already a high civilization of
its own is to assimilate and profit by American
or European ideas, the ideas of civilization and
Christianity,... the prerequisite condition to
the moral and material advance of the peoples
who dwell in the darker corners of the earth.

I am sure that when international history
is written, from the standpoint of acclaiming
international justice, one chapter will tell with
heartiest praise what our people have done in
the Philippines.[25]

Roosevelt never lost his belief in the need for the
White man to retain his barbarian virtues through
righteous war—where the Whites would triumph
over the dark Others. In 1907, Andrew Carnegie
scolded Roosevelt: "Disputants are both seeking righteousness, both feel themselves struggling for what
is just. Who is to decide? No one. According to you

they must then go to war to decide not what is right but who is strong."[26]

Professor Burgess of Columbia had taught young Teddy that only those Whites with Teutonic blood were fit to rule. In 1910, Roosevelt wrote Burgess: "Your teaching was one of the formative influences in my life. You impressed me more than you'll ever know."[27]

If Theodore Roosevelt traveled from Manhattan to his Sagamore Hill estate today, he probably would not be pleased by what he would see on the drive. Many Koreans live in that part of Long Island, and numerous signs in the Korean language dot the landscape. Roosevelt believed the Koreans to be an uncivilized, dying race. How would he deal with the fact that the average Korean immigrant in the United States often has a higher family income than a White native-born American?

And Roosevelt continued to see Hawaii as America's racial bulwark in the Pacific, recommending the importation of "tens of thousands of Spaniards, Portuguese or Italians or of any of the other European races...in order that the islands may be filled with a white population of our general civilization and culture."[28]

In a 1910 speech at Oxford University, Roosevelt pointed out that the White races had overspread much of the world, but unlike the Aryans, Teutons, and Anglo-Saxons, the modern-day conquerors had allowed the captive races to survive. Therefore, the White gains might be temporary. He told Oxford's White Christian males that "all of the world achievements worth remembering are to be credited to the people of European descent...the intrusive people having either exterminated or driven out the conquered peoples." Roosevelt termed this salutary process "ethnic conquest."[29]

ROOSEVELT WON ACCLAIM AS an author with his interpretation of America's westward expansion as the continuation of an inherited civilizing instinct. As president he cut through complex questions of foreign affairs by tallying who had longest followed the sun. No analysis of Roosevelt's worldview makes sense unless one first gazes through Teddy's race lenses at his galaxy of Aryans, Teutons, Anglo-Saxons, wops, dagos, Huns, Chinks, Japs, and a distasteful assortment of Negroes. According to Roosevelt, China would crumble and the obedient Honorary Aryans would help the English and the Americans pick up the shards. Instead, he failed to recognize the 1905 spark of Chinese patriotism that would leap to 1911 and be a raging fire by 1949. Roosevelt could not imagine the rise of third-world nationalism. It would contradict his belief that patriotism pulsed only in

White veins. So Roosevelt ignored China and linked the future of the United States in Asia with Britain just before the British Empire collapsed. And instead of a White band of civilization that would bring peace to Asia, over two hundred thousand Americans and millions of Asians died battling each other in places like Zamboanga, Iwo Jima, Incheon, and Khe Sanh.

Roosevelt's Japanese buddies had repeatedly assured him that their nation would help the United States penetrate the China market, but after 1905, America's Open Door demands drove Japan into Russia's arms. In 1907 and 1910, Russia and Japan renegotiated the Treaty of Portsmouth and divided Manchuria between them. The Japanese diplomats, businessmen, and military men who flowed into Manchuria spoke among themselves of the Japanese Monroe Doctrine for Asia.

In 1905, when he green-lit Japanese expansion, Roosevelt was forty-six years old and Baron Kaneko was fifty-two. Roosevelt would be dead fifteen years later, while Kaneko would live to hear Franklin Roosevelt criticize Japan for doing what Theodore Roosevelt had recommended.[30] Americans in 1905 clearly understood that Japan was going to expand onto the Asian continent. After the Battle of Tsushima, the famous American minister's sermon had been "Japan's Victory—Christianity's Opportunity," and readers of the *New York Times* nodded in

agreement when they read about Prime Minister Katsura announcing that Japan would soon force "upon
Korea and China the same benefits of modern development that have been in the past forced upon us."[31]
Would the history of the twentieth century be different if the American Aryan had not made the Honorary Aryan his civilizing surrogate in Asia? Maybe my
father didn't have to suffer through World War II in
the Pacific. Maybe the world would be more peaceful
if Teddy hadn't initiated an American foreign policy
that relied primarily on a benevolent big stick.

AS I BEGAN WRITING *The Imperial Cruise,* I realized that the Theodore Roosevelt most of us know
is a character that Teddy had created and historians
have accepted and passed on. As a best-selling author
from his early years, he had long experience in pro-
jecting imagery for public consumption. With his
Ranchman and Rough Rider poses in photo studios,
he created his own legend. In his diplomatic white
vest, the warmonger masqueraded as a man of peace.
Even his private correspondence to his children—
called posterity letters—were self-consciously written
to enhance his historical legacy. After studying his life
for twenty-seven years, the author Kathleen Dalton
wrote in *Theodore Roosevelt: A Strenuous Life,* "Thrown
off the trail by their hero's careful presentation of

himself, too many writers have accepted at face value his explanation of his own behavior."[32]

Most books on Theodore Roosevelt mention his biases but often employ obscure coded phrases and euphemisms. Probably the best-known biography is the Pulitzer Prize–honored *The Rise of Theodore Roosevelt* by Edmund Morris. In his acknowledgments, Morris praises one author and one book:

> To Carleton Putnam, a man I have never met, I express gratitude and admiration for his *Theodore Roosevelt: The Formative Years* (Scribner's, 1958), an essential source for students of Theodore Roosevelt's youth. It is a tragedy of American biography that this grave, neglected masterpiece was never followed by other volumes.[33]

Carleton Putnam wrote another book, entitled *Race and Reason: A Yankee View.* The book's genesis was Putnam's letter to President Dwight Eisenhower protesting the recent integration of America's public schools. Putnam lectured Eisenhower that the Black man was three thousand years behind the White man and that it was dangerous to allow the races to mix. Putnam told Eisenhower to heed the wisdom of a past president:

As Theodore Roosevelt wrote... Teutonic [and] English blood is the source of American greatness: Our American Republic, with all its faults, is, together with England, the fine flower of centuries of self-discipline and experience in free government by the English speaking branch of the white race.[34]

So many still follow the sun.

ACKNOWLEDGMENTS

"There are many humorous things in the world; among them, the white man's notion that he is less savage than the other savages."[1]
—Mark Twain

A heartfelt thank-you to Gaea Anonas, Donald Belanger, Susan Buckheit, Chris Cannon, David Carvalho, John Dower, Max Eisikovic, Robert Eskildsen, Tony Estrada, Jerry Finin, Peggy Freudenthal, Norihasa Fujita, Richard Gordon, Wayne Kabak, Preston Lurie, Lynnette Matsushima, Liese Mayer, Gary McManus, Tina Miao, Hirohiko Nakafuji, Ambeth Ocampo, Maritza Pastor, Bob Rapoport, Jo Ann Rerek, Amanda Robinson, Barbara Russo, the Rye Free Reading Room, Margaret Shannon,

ACKNOWLEDGMENTS

Eric Simonoff, Ge Shuya, Yoshikuni Taki, Richard Wheeler, Fei Xu, Ni Yang, and Mr. Zhu.

I especially want to thank my children—Michelle, Alison, Ava, and Jack—for their understanding and support.

I am fortunate to be represented by the world's finest literary agent, Owen Laster, who christened this voyage and provided invaluable guidance throughout.

My biggest thank-you is to Geoff Shandler, who edited this book. While on this six-year journey across an ocean of cultures and centuries, I periodically found myself washed up on the rocks. Geoff always showed me the way forward, and I will be forever grateful.

Theodore Roosevelt wrote, "Peace may only come through war." In my lifetime the United States has benevolently spent trillions of dollars trying to prove that erroneous notion. In the twentieth century, America extended its military to Asia. Now it's time to work on the human links between cultures. For the past ten years, the James Bradley Peace Foundation and Youth For Understanding have sent American students to live with families overseas. Perhaps in the future when we debate whether to fight it out or talk it out, one of these Americans might make a difference.

James Bradley
September 15, 2009

NOTES

CHAPTER 1: ONE HUNDRED YEARS LATER

CAPTION:
Taft: TR to Taft, August 7, 1908. TR Papers, PLB83, series 2, box 29.

1. TR to John Barrett, October 29, 1900, TR mss as cited in Howard K. Beale, *Theodore Roosevelt and the Rise of America to World Power* (Baltimore: Johns Hopkins University Press, 1956), 174.
2. TR to Benjamin Ide Wheeler, June 17, 1905. TR Papers, Library of Congress, series 2, reel 338.
3. TR to John Barrett, October 29, 1900, TR mss as cited in Beale, *Theodore Roosevelt and the Rise of America to World Power*, 174.
4. *Manila Times*, August 12, 2005, and August 13, 2005.
5. Ibid., August 12, 2005.
6. Stuart Creighton Miller, *Benevolent Assimilation: The American Conquest of the Philippines, 1899–1903* (New

Haven, CT: Yale University Press, 1982), 254. Miller writes: "Chaffee was opening a full scale offensive against the Moros on Mindanao and Jolo."

7. Enclosure in Allen to John Sherman, September 13, 1897, File Microcopies, NO 134 Roll 13, Despatches Korea.

8. TR to Hermann Speck von Sternberg, August 28, 1900, Elting Morison and John Blum, eds., *The Letters of Theodore Roosevelt*, 8 vols. (Cambridge, MA: Harvard University Press, 1951–54), 2:1394.

9. Herbert Croly, *Willard Straight* (New York: Macmillan Company, 1924), 188.

CHAPTER 2: CIVILIZATION FOLLOWS THE SUN

CAPTIONS:

Edith Roosevelt: Edmund Morris, *Theodore Rex* (New York: Random House, 2001), 450.

Alice Roosevelt: Sylvia Jukes Morris, *Edith Kermit Roosevelt: Portrait of a First Lady* (New York: Modern Library, 2001), 273.

TR chopping wood: Mark Sullivan, *Our Times: America at the Birth of the Twentieth Century,* ed. Dan Rather (New York: Scribner's, 1996), 282.

TR, age eleven: TR, *Winning of the West,* 4 vols. (New York: G. P. Putnam's Sons), 4:200.

Burgess: Edward Wagenknecht, *The Seven Worlds of Theodore Roosevelt* (New York: Longmans, Green & Co., 1958), 163.

1. TR: *The Winning of the West,* 1:24.

2. Alice Roosevelt Longworth, *Crowded Hours* (New York: Charles Scribner's Sons, 1933), 69, 70, 73.

3. Ibid., 70.

4. Ibid., 74.

5. *San Francisco Examiner*, May 19, 1905.

6. Nicholas Roosevelt, *Theodore Roosevelt: The Man as I Knew Him* (New York: Dodd Mead & Company, 1967), 25.

7. Carol Felsenthal, *The Life and Times of Alice Roosevelt Longworth* (New York: St. Martin's Press, 1988), 39.

8. Nicholas Roosevelt, *Theodore Roosevelt*, 25.

9. Michael Teague, *Mrs. L.: Conversations with Alice Roosevelt Longworth* (Garden City, NY: Doubleday & Company, 1981), 4, 5.

10. Morris, *Theodore Rex*, 450.

11. Teague, *Mrs. L.*, 36–37.

12. Felsenthal, *Life and Times,* 97.

13. From Alice Roosevelt Longworth's White House Diaries, quoted in Sylvia Jukes Morris, *Edith Kermit Roosevelt,* 273; Teague, *Mrs. L.,* 109.

14. *Washington Star,* October 22, 1967.

15. Longworth, *Crowded Hours*, 62.

16. Ibid., 64.

17. Quoted in Morris, *Edith Kermit Roosevelt,* 273.

18. Howard Teichmann, *Alice: The Life and Times of Alice Roosevelt Longworth* (Englewood Cliffs, NJ: Prentice-Hall, 1979), 6.

19. Natalie A. Naylor, Douglas Brinkley, John Allen Gable, *Theodore Roosevelt, Many-Sided American* (Interlaken, NY: Heart of the Lakes Publishing, 1992), 354.

20. From Alice Roosevelt Longworth's White House Diaries, quoted in Morris, *Edith Kermit Roosevelt,* 274.

21. Naylor, *Theodore Roosevelt,* 354.

22. Ibid.
23. Alice Roosevelt Longworth Diary, June 26, 1905.
24. Stacy A. Cordery, *Alice: Alice Roosevelt Longworth, from White House Princess to Washington Power Broker* (New York: Viking, 2007), 100.
25. Longworth, *Crowded Hours,* 72.
26. "San Francisco Welcomes President's Daughter," *San Francisco Chronicle,* July 5, 1905.
27. Ibid.
28. Naylor, *Theodore Roosevelt,* 355.
29. *San Francisco Chronicle,* July 8, 1905.
30. *San Francisco Bulletin,* July 5, 1905.
31. *San Francisco Chronicle,* July 5, 1905.
32. Stanley Karnow, *In Our Image* (New York: Ballantine Books, 1989), 231.
33. *San Francisco Chronicle,* July 7, 1905.
34. *San Francisco Call,* July 8, 1905.
35. Ibid.
36. *San Francisco Call,* July 7, 1905.
37. *Manila Times,* May 1, 1905.
38. *San Francisco Chronicle,* July 8, 1905.
39. Reginald Horsman, *Race and Manifest Destiny: The Origins of American Racial Anglo-Saxonism* (Cambridge, MA: Harvard University Press, 1981), 12.
40. Ibid.
41. Ibid., 18.
42. Thomas F. Gossett, *Race: The History of an Idea in America* (New York: Schocken Books, 1970), 85–86.
43. John Nicholas Norton, *The Life of Bishop Berkeley* (Charleston, SC: BiblioBazaar, LLC, 2008), 133.

44. Donald S. Lutz, "The Relative Influence of European Writers on Late Eighteenth-Century American Political Thought," *American Political Science Review* 78, 1 (March 1984), 189–197.

45. Gossett, *Race,* 86.

46. Horsman, *Race and Manifest Destiny,* 84.

47. A Summary View of the Rights of British America by Thomas Jefferson. http://libertyonline.hypermall.com/Jefferson/Summaryview.html. Accessed August 21, 2009.

48. Horseman, *Race and Manifest Destiny,* 22.

49. Charles Francis Adams, ed., *Familiar Letters of John Adams and His Wife Abigail Adams during the Revolution* (New York: Hurd and Houghton, 1875), 211.

50. Alan Stoskopf, *Race and Membership in American History: The Eugenics Movement* (Brookline, MA: Facing History and Ourselves National Foundation, 2002), 40.

51. Horsman, *Race and Manifest Destiny,* 90.

52. Ibid., 86.

53. Actual wording of poem ("Facing West from California's Shores" by Walt Whitman):

> *Facing west, from California's shores,*
> *   Inquiring, tireless, seeking what is yet unfound,*
> *I, a child, very old, over waves, towards the house of*
> *   maternity, the land of migrations, look afar,*
> *Look off the shores of my Western sea, the circle almost*
> *   circled;*
> *   For, starting westward from Hindustan, from the vales of*
> *   Kashmere,*

*From Asia—from the north—from the God, the sage, and
  the hero,
From the south, from the flowery peninsulas, and the spice
  islands;
Long having wander'd since—round the earth having
  wander'd,
Now I face home again—very pleas'd and joyous;
  (But where is what I started for, so long ago? And why
  is it yet unfound?)*

54. Charles Darwin, *The Descent of Man, and Selection in
    Relation to Sex* (New York: D. Appleton & Co., 1871),
    172–173.
55. Ralph Waldo Emerson, *English Traits* (Boston: Phillips,
    Sampson, & Company, 1857), 27.
56. Ibid., 144.
57. Robert E. Bieder, *Science Encounters the Indian, 1820–1880*
    (Norman: University of Oklahoma Press, 1986), 61.
58. Ibid., 98.
59. Gossett, *Race*, 74.
60. Horsman, *Race and Manifest Destiny*, 130.
61. Josiah Clark Nott, *Two Lectures on the Natural History of
    the Caucasian and Negro Races* (Mobile, AL: Dade and
    Thompson, 1844), 16, 28–35.
62. Ibid., 137, 155.
63. *De Bows Review* 10 (March 1851), 331.
64. Horsman, *Race and Manifest Destiny*, 279.
65. Lewis H. Morgan, *Ancient Society, or Researches in the Lines
    of Human Progress from Savagery through Barbarism to
    Civilization* (New York: Henry Holt & Co., 1877), 553.

66. Edmund Morris, *The Rise of Theodore Roosevelt* (New York: Coward, McCann, and Geoghegan, 1979), 36.
67. Matthew Frye Jacobson, *Barbarian Virtues: The United States Encounters Foreign Peoples at Home and Abroad, 1876–1917* (New York: Hill & Wang, 2000), 3.
68. John B. Judis, *The Folly of Empire: What George W. Bush Could Learn from Theodore Roosevelt and Woodrow Wilson* (New York: Lisa Drew/Scribner, 2004), 53.
69. TR, *New York* (New York: Longmans, Green, 1891), 188.
70. Kathleen Dalton, *Theodore Roosevelt: A Strenuous Life* (New York: Vintage Books, 2004), 37.
71. Ibid., 52.
72. Ibid., 45.
73. Ibid., 64.
74. Morris, *Rise,* 83.
75. Thomas G. Dyer, *Theodore Roosevelt and the Idea of Race* (Baton Rouge: Louisiana State University, 1960), 5.
76. Warren Zimmerman, *First Great Triumph: How Five Americans Made Their Country a World Power* (New York: Farrar, Straus and Giroux, 2002), 36.
77. Gossett, *Race,* 95.
78. Zimmerman, *First Great Triumph,* 35, 458.
79. John Milton Cooper Jr., *The Warrior and the Priest: Woodrow Wilson and Theodore Roosevelt* (Cambridge, MA: Belknap Press/Harvard University Press, 1983), 6.
80. Carleton Putnam, *Theodore Roosevelt: The Formative Years 1858–1886,* vol. I (New York: Charles Scribner's Sons, 1958), 324.
81. TR, *The Naval War of 1812* (New York: Modern Library, 1999), xvii.

82. Ibid., 21.

83. Ibid., 19.

84. "C250 Celebrates Columbians Ahead of Their Time," http://c250.Columbia.edu/c250_celebrates/remarkable_ Columbians/john_burgess.html, accessed August 1, 2009.

85. Putnam, *Theodore Roosevelt,* 219.

86. Gossett, *Race,* 114.

87. I. A. Newby, *Jim Crow's Defense: Anti-Negro Thought in America, 1900–1930* (Baton Rouge: Louisiana State University Press, 1965), 46.

88. Dyer, *Theodore Roosevelt and the Idea of Race,* 47.

89. Dalton, *A Strenuous Life,* 87.

90. Ibid.

91. Gail Bederman, *Manliness & Civilization: A Cultural History of Gender and Race in the United States, 1880–1917* (Chicago: University of Chicago Press, 1995), 170.

92. Louis S. Warren, *Buffalo Bill's America: William Cody and the Wild West Show* (New York: Knopf, 2005), ix.

93. Ibid., 223, 241.

94. Ibid., 223.

95. *New York Tribune,* July 28, 1884.

96. TR, *The Winning of the West,* 1:xiv.

97. Ibid., 176.

98. Cooper, *Warrior,* 30.

99. Dalton, *A Strenuous Life,* 95.

100. White, *Eastern Establishment,* 126–127.

101. Hermann Hagedorn, *Roosevelt in the Badlands* (Boston: Houghton Mifflin Company, 1921), 101–102.

102. Cooper, *Warrior,* 31.

103. White, *Eastern Establishment,* 84.

104. Morris, *Rise,* 350.

105. TR, *The Winning of the West,* 1:1.

106. Ibid., 1:24.

107. Ibid., 55.

108. Ibid., 20.

109. Ibid., 18.

110. Ibid., 4:55.

111. Ibid., 1:82.

112. *San Francisco Call,* July 9, 1905.

113. *San Francisco Chronicle,* July 9, 1905.

114. *San Francisco Call,* July 9, 1905.

115. *Des Moines Chronicle,* July 8, 1905.

116. *San Francisco Bulletin,* July 9, 1905.

CHAPTER 3: BENEVOLENT INTENTIONS

CAPTIONS:

General Emilio Aguinaldo: James H. Blount, *American Occupation of the Philippines, 1898–1912* (New York: Knickerbocker Press, 1913), 58.

The Philippine Islands (map): Stanley Karnow, *In Our Image* (New York: Random House, 1989), 100.

1. The Teller Amendment, First and Fourth paragraphs. http://www.etsu.edu/cas/history/docs/teller/htm, accessed August 26, 2009.

2. Sam W. Haynes, *James K. Polk and the Expansionist Impulse* (New York: Longman, 1997), 95.

3. Norman A. Graebner, *Empire on the Pacific: A Study in American Continental Expansion* (Claremont, CA: Regina Books, 1983), 63.

4. Ibid., 38.
5. Howard Zinn, *A People's History of the United States, 1492–Present* (New York: HarperCollins, 2003), 155.
6. Haynes, *James K. Polk,* 171.
7. Miguel E. Soto, "The Monarchist Conspiracy and the Mexican War" in *Essays on the Mexican War,* ed. Wayne Cutler (College Station: Texas A&M University Press, 1986), 66–67.
8. Reginald Horsman, *Race and Manifest Destiny: The Origins of American Racial Anglo-Saxonism* (Cambridge, MA: Harvard University Press, 1981), 241.
9. *Congressional Globe,* 29th Congress, 2nd Sess., February 10, 1847, p. 191.
10. Dee Brown, *Bury My Heart at Wounded Knee: An Indian History of the American West* (New York: Henry Holt and Company, 1970), 168.
11. John F. Marszalek, *Sherman: A Soldier's Passion for Order* (New York: Free Press, 1993), 379.
12. TR, *Report of Hon. Theodore Roosevelt to the United States Civil Service Commission, upon a visit to certain Indian Reservations and Indian Schools in South Dakota, Nebraska, and Kansas* (Philadelphia: Indian Rights Association, 1893), 18–19.
13. Frederick Jackson Turner, "The Problem of the West," *The Atlantic Monthly,* September 1896.
14. Frederick Jackson Turner, *The Frontier of American History* (New York: Dover Publications, 1996), 38.
15. John B. Judis, *The Folly of Empire: What George W. Bush Could Learn from Theodore Roosevelt and Woodrow Wilson* (New York: Lisa Drew/Scribner, 2004), 59–60.

16. Kristin L. Hoganson, *Fighting for American Manhood: How Gender Politics Provoked the Spanish-American and Philippine-American Wars* (New Haven, CT: Yale University Press, 2000), 11–12.

17. Warren Zimmerman, *First Great Triumph: How Five Americans Made Their Country a World Power* (New York: Farrar, Straus and Giroux, 2002), 152.

18. William Appleman Williams, *The Tragedy of American Diplomacy* (New York: W. W. Norton & Company, 1988), 32.

19. Henry H. Graff, *American Imperialism and the Philippine Insurrection, Testimony of the Times: Selections from Congressional Hearings* (Boston: Little, Brown and Company, 1969), viii.

20. H. W. Brands, *The Reckless Decade: America in the 1890s* (New York: St. Martin's Press, 1995), 294.

21. Hoganson, *Fighting for American Manhood*, 49.

22. Gerald F. Linderman, *The Mirror of War: American Society and the Spanish-American War* (Ann Arbor: University of Michigan Press, 1974), 129.

23. Marcus M. Wilkerson, *Public Opinion and the Spanish-American War: A Study in War Propaganda* (Baton Rouge: Louisiana State University, 1932), 71.

24. Ibid., 121–122.

25. TR to Anna Roosevelt Cowles, June 28, 1896, Elting Morison and John Blum, eds., *The Letters of Theodore Roosevelt*, 8 vols. (Cambridge, MA: Harvard University Press, 1951–54), 1:545.

26. Edmund Morris, *The Rise of Theodore Roosevelt* (New York: Coward, McCann, and Geoghegan, 1979), 555.

27. Ibid., 559.
28. Henry F. Cabot Lodge and TR, *Selections from the Correspondence of Theodore Roosevelt and Henry Cabot Lodge* (New York: C. Scribner's Sons, 1925), 253.
29. *New York World,* April 9, 1897.
30. Morris, *Rise,* 562.
31. Brands, *The Reckless Decade,* 312.
32. Morris, *Rise,* 571.
33. Ibid., 577.
34. Henry F. Pringle, *Theodore Roosevelt: A Biography* (New York: Harcourt, Brace and Company, 1931), 171.
35. TR to Francis V. Greene, September 23, 1897, TR mss.
36. Ambeth R. Ocampo, *The Centennial Countdown* (Philippines: Orogem International Publishing), 15.
37. Ibid., 75.
38. Wilkerson, *Public Opinion and the Spanish-American War,* 92.
39. *New York Journal,* February 9, 1898.
40. In 1935, President Franklin D. Roosevelt sent the Spanish government a Navy Department statement absolving Spain of all suspicion.
41. Linderman, *The Mirror of War,* 29.
42. Morris, *Rise,* 610.
43. The Teller Amendment. First, second, and fourth paragraphs.
44. Morris, *Rise,* 632.
45. Fitzhugh Lee, Joseph Wheeler, Theodore Roosevelt, and Richard Wainright, *Cuba's Struggle Against Spain with the Causes for American Intervention and a Full Account of the Spanish American War, Including Final Peace Negotiations* (New York: American Historical Press, 1899), 645.

46. Linderman, *The Mirror of War*, 138.

47. Ibid., 137.

48. *Editorial Enterprise*, June 30, 1898.

49. Gail Bederman, *Manliness & Civilization: A Cultural History of Gender and Race in the United States, 1880–1917* (Chicago: University of Chicago Press, 1995), 190.

50. TR, *American Ideals* (New York: G. P. Putnam, 1920), 279.

51. Louis A. Perez, *Cuba Between Empires, 1878–1902* (Pittsburgh: University of Pittsburgh Press, 1998), 349.

52. Leon Wolff, *Little Brown Brother: America's Forgotten Bid for Empire Which Cost 250,000 Lives* (London: Longmans, Green and Co., 1960), 35.

53. Karnow, *In Our Image*, 100.

54. H. H. Kohlsaat, *From McKinley to Harding: Personal Recollections of Our Presidents* (New York: Scribner's Sons, 1923), 68.

55. Don Emilio Aguinaldo y Famy, *True Version of the Philippine Revolution* (Philippine Islands: Tarlak, 1899).

56. Ibid.

57. Ibid. Original quote reads: "...there was no necessity for entering into a formal written agreement because the word of the Admiral and of the United States Consul were in fact equivalent to the most solemn pledge that their verbal promises and assurance would be fulfilled to the letter and were not to be classed with Spanish promises or Spanish ideas of a man's word of honour. The Government of North America is a very honest, just and powerful government."

58. Ocampo, *The Centennial Countdown*, 97.

59. William P. Leeman, "America's Admiral: George Dewey and American Culture in the Gilded Age," *The Historian,* March 22, 2003.

60. Ibid.

61. Winston Churchill, "Admiral Dewey: A Character Sketch," *American Monthly Review of Reviews* 17 (June 1898), 682.

62. TR, "Admiral Dewey," *McClure's Magazine,* October 1899.

63. George Dewey, *Autobiography of George Dewey: Admiral of the Navy* (New York: Charles Scribner's Sons, 1913), 287.

64. Leeman, "America's Admiral."

65. Ibid., Pears' Soap advertisement, circa 1899.

66. Aguinaldo, *True Version of the Philippines Revolution.*

67. Karnow, *In Our Image,* 110, 114.

68. Transcript of PBS's *Crucible of Empire: The Spanish-American War,* 21. http://www.pbs.org/crucible/frames/_sitemap.html, accessed August 17, 2009.

69. Ocampo, *The Centennial Countdown,* 109.

70. Ibid.

71. Blount, *American Occupation,* 31.

72. Wolff, *Little Brown Brother,* 28.

73. Quoted in *Literary Digest* 22 (April 20, 1901), 468.

74. Blount, *American Occupation,* 58.

75. Ibid., 4. Original quote reads: "The governor-general arranged with me that I was to go up and fire a few shots and then I was to make the signal, 'Do you surrender?' and he would hoist the white flag and then the troops would march in; but he was fearful that the Filipinos would get in."

76. Ocampo, *The Centennial Countdown,* 187.

Chapter 4: Pacific Negroes

Captions:

Filipino dead at Santa Ana: TR to William Bayard Cutting, April 18, 1899 in Elting Morison and John Blum, eds., *The Letters of Theodore Roosevelt*, 8 vols. (Cambridge, MA: Harvard University Press, 1951–54), V:254.

General Jake Smith: Joseph L. Schott, *The Ordeal of Samar* (Indianapolis: Bobbs-Merrill, 1964), 76.

1. Actual quote reads: "...we come not to make war upon the people of the Philippines nor upon any party or *faction* among them, but to protect them in their homes, in their employments, and in their personal and religious rights." McKinley's Message to the Secretary of War at the Cession of War, July 13, 1898, as seen in *A Compilation of the Messages and Papers of the Presidents,* ed. James Daniel Richardson (Bureau of National Literature & Art, 1907), 344.

2. Robert E. Austill to Herbert Welsh, June 17, 1902, Herbert Welsh Collection, Correspondence, Box A, Historical Society of Pennsylvania.

3. Walter L. Williams, "United States Indian Policy and the Debate over Philippine Annexation: Implications for the Origins of American Imperialism," *The Journal of American History* 66, no. 4 (March 1980), 810–31.

4. Ibid.

5. Ibid.

6. Eric T. L. Love, *Race Over Empire: Racism and U.S. Imperialism, 1865–1900* (Chapel Hill: University of North Carolina Press, 2004), 188.

7. TR, *The Winning of the West,* 4:200.

8. Matthew Frye Jacobson, *Barbarian Virtues: The United States Encounters Foreign Peoples at Home and Abroad, 1876–1917* (New York: Hill & Wang, 2000), 228.

9. Stuart Creighton Miller, *Benevolent Assimilation: The American Conquest of the Philippines, 1899–1903* (New Haven, CT: Yale University Press, 1982), 15.

10. Kristin L. Hoganson, *Fighting for American Manhood: How Gender Politics Provoked the Spanish-American and Philippine-American Wars* (New Haven, CT: Yale University Press, 2000), 160.

11. Rudyard Kipling, *Complete Verse: Definitive Edition* (New York: Anchor Books, 1940), 321–23.

12. James Blount, *American Occupation of the Philippines, 1898–1912* (New York: Knickerbocker Press, 1913), 117.

13. It came to light only a year and half later on February 26, 1900, after the Senate passed a resolution demanding it from the Executive Branch.

14. Moorfield Storey and Julian Codman, *Secretary Root's Record "Marked Severities" in Philippine Warfare: An Analysis of the Law and Facts bearing on the Action & Utterances of President Roosevelt and Secretary Root* (Boston: Geo. H. Ellis Co., 1902), 31.

15. Miller, *Benevolent Assimilation,* 61.

16. Blount, *American Occupation,* 187. See General Hughes's testimony before Senate Committee, 1900, *Senate Document* 331, p. 508.

17. Stanley Karnow, *In Our Image* (New York: Ballantine Books, 1989), 140.

18. Miller, *Benevolent Assimilation,* 68–69.

19. Ibid., 30.

20. George Dewey, *Autobiography of George Dewey: Admiral of the Navy.* (New York: Charles Scribner's Sons, 1913), 284.

21. *Letters of Henry Adams, 1892–1918,* ed. Worthington Chauncey Ford (Boston: Houghton Mifflin Co., 1938), 208.

22. Richard W. Welch Jr., "American Atrocities in the Philippines: The Indictment and the Response," *Pacific Historical Review* 43 (May 1974), 9.

23. Ibid., 8.

24. Hoganson, *Fighting for American Manhood,* 187.

25. MacArthur had been awarded the Medal of Honor for charging Confederate forces in 1863 when he was nineteen years old. Later he chased Geronimo through New Mexico. He sailed to the Philippines in 1898, fought in the initial battles, and would serve as Military Governor of the Philippines from 1899 to 1901. His son Douglas would help lead America's Pacific operations in World War II and Korea.

26. Henry H. Graff, *American Imperialism and the Philippine Insurrection, Testimony of the Times: Selections from Congressional Hearings* (Boston: Little, Brown and Company, 1969), 136.

27. Miller, *Benevolent Assimilation,* 88.

28. Ibid., 94.

29. Richard Drinnon, *Facing West: The Metaphysics of Indian-Hating and Empire-Building* (Norman: University of Oklahoma Press, 1997), 320.

30. Glenn Anthony May, *Battle for Batangas: A Philippine Province at War* (New Haven, CT: Yale University Press, 1991), 147, 149.

31. Karnow, *In Our Image*, 154.
32. TR, *Public papers of Theodore Roosevelt, Governor, 1899[–1900]*, vol. 2 (Albany, NY: Brandow Printing Company, 1899), 293–307.
33. Miller, *Benevolent Assimilation*, 179.
34. Jacobson, *Barbarian Virtues*, 245.
35. Storey and Codman, *Secretary Root's Record*, 22.
36. Miller, *Benevolent Assimilation*, 189.
37. TR, *The Strenuous Life* (New York: The Century Co., 1905), 28.
38. Leon Wolff, *Little Brown Brother: America's Forgotten Bid for Empire Which Cost 250,000 Lives* (London: Longmans, Green and Co., 1960), 294.
39. Miller, *Benevolent Assimilation*, 100.
40. Ibid., 101.
41. Storey and Codman, *Secretary Root's Record*, 78.
42. Judith Icke Anderson, *William Howard Taft: An Intimate History* (New York: W. W. Norton & Company, 1981), 174.
43. Ibid., 169.
44. Ibid., 69.
45. Oscar Alfonso, *Theodore Roosevelt and the Philippines* (Quezon City: University of the Philippines Press, 1970), 44.
46. John Morgan Gates, *Schoolbooks and Krags: The United States Army in the Philippines, 1898–1902* (Westport, CT: Greenwood Press, 1973), 148.
47. Miller, *Benevolent Assimilation*, 102.
48. Hermann Hagedorn, ed., *Works of Theodore Roosevelt* (New York: Charles Scribner's Sons, 1925), 16:537–60.

49. Robert E. Austill to Herbert Welsh, June 17, 1902, Correspondence, Box A, Herbert Welsh Collection, Historical Society of Pennsylvania.
50. Miller, *Benevolent Assimilation,* 150.
51. Wolff, *Little Brown Brother,* 346.
52. Miller, *Benevolent Assimilation,* 171.
53. Ibid., 174.
54. Blount, *American Occupation,* 373.
55. Anderson, *William Howard Taft,* 76.
56. Karnow, *In Our Image,* 230.
57. Glenn Anthony May, *Social Engineering in the Philippines: The Aims, Execution, and Impact of American Colonial Policy, 1900–1913* (Westport, CT: Greenwood Press, 1980), 93.
58. Karnow, *In Our Image,* 205.
59. Ibid.
60. Ibid., 191.
61. Ibid.
62. Rep. Thomas J. Selby, CR 35, pt. 1, January 22, 1902, 881.
63. Hoganson, *Fighting for American Manhood,* 184.
64. TR, Message to Congress, December 3, 1901, Source: UCSB American Presidency Project, http://www.polsci.ucsb.edu/projects/presproject/idgrant/site/state.html.
65. Blount, *American Occupation,* 414.
66. *New York Times,* January 15, 1902.
67. Alfonso, *Theodore Roosevelt and the Philippines,* 100.
68. Kathleen Dalton, *Theodore Roosevelt: A Strenuous Life* (New York: Vintage Books, 2004), 228.

69. Graff, *American Imperialism and the Philippine Insurrection*, 92.

70. Miller, *Benevolent Assimilation*, 213.

71. Graff, *American Imperialism and the Philippine Insurrection*, 95.

72. Miller, *Benevolent Assimilation*, 213.

73. Schott, *The Ordeal of Samar*, 165.

74. Graff, *American Imperialism and the Philippine Insurrection*, 65.

75. U.S. Congressional record, 57th Cong, 1st sess, XXXV, part 5, 4673.

76. "...horror of the water torture." Welch, *American Atrocities in the Philippines*, 1.

77. Schott, *The Order of Samar*, 244–45.

78. Speech of Roosevelt at Arlington Cemetery, May 30, 1902, TR Papers, Series 5A. Speeches, B1. B.2.

79. Speech given by Theodore Roosevelt at Arlington National Cemetery, May 30, 1902, *Theodore Roosevelt Papers,* Library of Congress, Manuscript Division, Series 5A, Speeches and Executive Orders, 1899–1918.

80. Karnow, *In Our Image*, 194–95.

81. Ibid., 194.

82. Robert W. Rydell, *All the World's a Fair: Visions of Empire at American International Expositions, 1876–1916* (Chicago: University of Chicago Press, 1984), 162.

83. Ibid.

84. Sharra L. Vostral, "Imperialism on Display: The Philippine Exhibition at the 1904 World's Fair," *Gateway Heritage* 13:4 (1993), 19.

85. Beverly K. Grindstaff, "Creating Identity: Exhibiting the Philippines at the 1904 Louisiana Purchase Exposition," *National Identities*, vol. 1, no. 3, 1999.
86. Rydell, *All the World's a Fair*, 177.
87. Tony Smith, *America's Mission: The United States and the Worldwide Struggle for Democracy in the Twentieth Century* (Princeton, NJ: Princeton University Press, 1995), 44.
88. Seth M. Scheiner, "President Theodore Roosevelt and the Negro, 1901–1908," *The Journal of Negro History*, vol. 47, no. 3 (July 1962), 169–82.
89. Rydell, *All the World's a Fair*, 176.

CHAPTER 5: HAOLES

CAPTION:
John Stevens: Rich Budnick, *Stolen Kingdom: An American Conspiracy* (Honolulu: Aloha Press, 1992), 129.

1. TR, *American Ideals* (New York: G. P. Putnam, 1920), 280.
2. Stacy A. Cordery, *Alice: Alice Roosevelt Longworth, from White House Princess to Washington Power Broker* (New York: Viking, 2007), 117.
3. *Des Moines Chronicle*, August 1, 1905.
4. Alice Roosevelt Longworth, *Crowded Hours* (New York: Charles Scribner's Sons, 1933), 69.
5. *Des Moines Chronicle*, July 31, 1905.
6. Stephen Hess, "Big Bill Taft," *American Heritage* 17, no. 6 (October 1966), 6–32.
7. Judith Icke Anderson, *William Howard Taft: An Intimate History* (New York: W. W. Norton & Company, 1981), 89.

8. Ibid., 86.
9. Ibid., 86, 89.
10. Henry F. Pringle, *The Life and Times of William Howard Taft* (Norwalk, CT: Easton Press, 1986), 272.
11. Butt, Letters, January 5, 1909, as cited in Michael L. Bromley, *William Howard Taft and the First Motoring Presidency, 1909–1913* (Jefferson, NC: McFarland, 2003), 42.
12. Hess, "Big Bill Taft."
13. Anderson, *William Howard Taft*, 55.
14. Hess, "Big Bill Taft."
15. "...to be president of the United States," ibid., 48–49; "...brilliant parties and meeting all manner of charming people," Helen Herron Taft, *Recollection of Full Years* (New York: Dodd, Mead & Co., 1914), 6; "...that she fantasized becoming first lady herself... 'vowed to marry a man destined to be president of the United States,'" Philip Weeks, *Buckeye Presidents: Ohioans in the White House* (Kent, OH: Kent State University Press, 2003), 215.
16. Ibid., 53.
17. Ibid., 95.
18. "...of work I wished him to do," ibid., 58; "rather overwhelming" and "an awful groove," Anderson, *William Howard Taft*, 58; interruption...in our peaceful existence" and "very glad because it gave Mr. Taft an opportunity for exactly the kind of work I wished him to do," Carl Sferrazza Anthony, *Nellie Taft: The Unconventional First Lady of the Ragtime Era* (New York: HarperCollins, 2005), 95.

19. Anderson, *William Howard Taft*, 66.

20. Taft, *Recollections of Full Years*, 32.

21. Weeks, *Buckeye Presidents*, 218.

22. Ibid.

23. Pringle, *William Howard Taft*, 167.

24. Lewis L. Gould, *American First Ladies: Their Lives and Their Legacy* (New York: Taylor & Francis, 2001), 218.

25. Taft to H. C. Hollister, September 21, 1903, cited in Pringle, *William Howard Taft*, 236.

26. Longworth, *Crowded Hours*, 76.

27. *Pacific Commercial Advertiser*, July 15, 1905.

28. Ibid.

29. Ibid.

30. Ibid.

31. Ibid.

32. Longworth, *Crowded Hours*, 77.

33. *Pacific Commercial Advertiser*, July 15, 1905.

34. Cordery, *Alice*, 117–18.

35. *Pacific Commercial Advertiser*, July 15, 1905.

36. David E. Stannard, *Before the Horror: The Population of Hawaii on the Eve of Western Contact* (Honolulu: University of Hawaii Press, 1989), 73.

37. Ibid., 61.

38. Ibid., 70.

39. Stannard, *Before the Horror*, 73.

40. O. A. Bushnell, *The Gifts of Civilization: Germs and Genocide in Hawaii* (Honolulu: University of Hawaii Press, 1993), 16.

41. Linda McKee, "Mad Jack and the Missionaries," *American Heritage* (April 1971), 33.

42. Rufus Anderson, *The Hawaiian Islands: Their Progress and Condition Under Missionary Labors* (Boston: Gould & Lincoln, 1864), 276.

43. Amy S. Greenberg, *Manifest Manhood and the Antebellum American Empire* (New York: Cambridge University Press, 2005), 248.

44. Eric T. L. Love, *Race Over Empire: Racism and U.S. Imperialism, 1865–1900* (Chapel Hill: University of North Carolina Press, 2004), 86.

45. Stephen Kinzer, *Overthrow: America's Century of Regime Change from Hawaii to Iraq* (New York: Henry Holt, 2006), 12.

46. John R. Proctor, "Hawaii and the Changing Front of the World," *Forum* 24 (September 1897), 34–35.

47. Jacob Adler, *Clause Spreckels: The Sugar King in Hawaii* (Honolulu: University of Hawaii Press, 1966), 100.

48. Ibid., 61.

49. Blount Report, U. S. House of Representatives, 53rd Congress, 3rd Session, Ex. Doc. 1, Part 1, Appendix II, *Foreign Relations of the United States, 1894: Affairs in Hawaii* (Washington, D.C.: Government Printing Office, 1895). Digital copy available at http://hdl.handle.net/10524/984.

50. Blain to Harrison, August 10, 1891, Kuykendall, vol. III, 486, as quoted in Rich Budnick, *Stolen Kingdom: An American Conspiracy* (Oahu, HI: Aloha Press, 1992), 87.

51. Kinzer, *Overthrow*, 23.

52. Ibid., 22.

53. Budnick, *Stolen Kingdom*, 111.

54. Cornwell Statements, April 24, 1893, Blount Report, 495.

55. Budnick, *Stolen Kingdom*, 129.

56. Ibid., 132.

57. Report of U.S. Special Commissioner James H. Blount to Secretary of State Walter Q. Gresham Concerning the Hawaiian Kingdom Investigation, www .hawaiiankingdom.or/blounts-report.html. Accessed September 22, 2009.

58. The January 20 inaugurations did not go into effect until 1937.

59. Thomas J. Osborne, *Annexation Hawaii: Fighting American Imperialism* (Waimanalo, HI: Island Style Press, 1998), 4.

60. Ibid., 33.

61. Ibid., 31.

62. Budnick, *Stolen Kingdom*, 152.

63. Ibid., 155.

64. Love, *Race Over Empire*, 119.

65. Sanford Dole to John Burgess, December 18, 1894, quoted in Henry Miller Madden, "Letters of Sanford B. Dole and John W. Burgess," *The Pacific Historical Review* (March 1936), 75.

66. Walter A. McDougall, *Let the Sea Make a Noise: A History of the North Pacific from Magellan to MacArthur* (New York: HarperCollins, 1993), 391.

67. Budnick, *Stolen Kingdom*, 170.

68. McDougall, *Let the Sea Make a Noise*, 392.

69. Budnick, *Stolen*, 172; Osborne, *Annexation Hawaii*, 34.

70. Thomas G. Dyer, *Theodore Roosevelt and the Idea of Race* (Baton Rouge: Louisiana State University, 1960), 141.

71. Osborne, *Annexation Hawaii*, 129.

72. Ibid., 134.

73. Love, *Race Over Empire,* 157.

74. Charles Callan Tansill, *The Foreign Policy of Thomas F. Bayard, 1885–1891* (New York: Fordham University Press, 1940), 409.

75. Howard Teichmann, *Alice: The Life and Times of Alice Roosevelt Longworth* (Englewood Cliffs, NJ: Prentice-Hall, 1979), 42; "It was considered just a little indelicate," Longworth, *Crowded Hours,* 77.

76. *Pacific Commercial Advertiser,* July 15, 1905.

77. Ibid.

78. Longworth, *Crowded Hours,* 78.

CHAPTER 6: HONORARY ARYANS

CAPTIONS:

Matthew Perry: Peter Booth Wiley, *Yankees in the Land of the Gods: Commodore Perry and the Opening of Japan* (New York: Penguin Books, 1990), 490.

Emperor Gojong and son: Yur-Bok Lee and Wayne Patterson, eds., *Korean-American Relations, 1866–1997* (Albany: State University of New York Press, 1999), 45; TR to Sternberg, August 8, 1900, in Elting Morison and John Blum, eds., *The Letters of Theodore Roosevelt,* 8 vols. (Cambridge, MA: Harvard University Press, 1951–54), 2:1394.

1. Okakura Kakuzo, *The Book of Tea* (New York: Fox Duffield & Co., 1906), 7.

2. Alice Roosevelt Longworth, *Crowded Hours* (New York: Charles Scribner's Sons, 1933), 78.

3. Ibid.

4. *Japan Weekly Mail*, July 29, 1905.

5. *New York Times,* July 27, 1905.

6. Lloyd C. Griscom, *Diplomatically Speaking* (New York: Literary Guild of America, 1940), 258.

7. *Tokyo Asahi Shimbun,* July 25, 1905.

8. Peter Booth Wiley, *Yankees in the Land of the Gods*, 490.

9. Bob Tadashi Wakabayashi, *Anti-foreignism and Western Learning in Early-modern Japan: The New Theses* [sic] *of 1825* (Cambridge, MA: Harvard University Press, 1992), 90.

10. Amy S. Greenberg, *Manifest Manhood and the Antebellum American Empire* (New York: Cambridge University Press, 2005), 261.

11. U.S. Congress. Senate, *Documents relative to the Empire of Japan,* 32nd Congress, 1st Sess, 1852. Sen. Ex. Doc. 59.

12. Thomas Hart Benton, "America's Pathway to the Orient," in *Manifest Destiny and the Imperialism Question*, Charles L. Sanford, ed. (New York: John Wiley & Sons, 1974), 44.

13. Arthur Walworth, *Black Ships off Japan: The Story of Commodore Perry's Expedition* (New York: Knopf, 1946), 39.

14. William Neumann, *America Encounters Japan: From Perry to MacArthur* (Baltimore: Johns Hopkins Press, 1963), 30.

15. Senate, *Documents relative to the Empire of Japan,* Sen. Ex. Doc. 59.

16. Michael Frederick Rollin, *The Divine Invasion: Manifest Destiny and the Westernization of Japanese Nationalism in the Late Tokugawa and Meiji Periods, 1853–1912* (master's thesis, University of Texas at San Antonio, 2002), 33.

17. Ibid., 34.

18. Wiley, *Yankees in the Land of the Gods,* 81.

19. Rollin, *The Divine Invasion*, 53.
20. Walter A. McDougall, *Let the Sea Make a Noise* (New York: HarperCollins, 1993), 276.
21. Lee Yong-ju, "The Path from a Theory of Civilization to Escape of Asia: Yukichi Fukuzawa's Perception of Asia and 'Mission to Civilize,' " *Sungkyun Journal of East Asian Studies* 3, no. 2 (2003), 146.
22. John Dower, *Japan in War and Peace: Selected Essays* (London: HarperCollins/Hammersmith, 1995), 2.
23. Foster Rhea Dulles, *Yankees and Samurai: America's Role in the Emergence of Modern Japan, 1791–1900* (New York: Harper & Row, 1965), 201.
24. McDougall, *Let the Sea Make a Noise*, 354.
25. Robert W. Rydell, *All the World's a Fair: Visions of Empire at American International Expositions, 1876–1916* (Chicago: University of Chicago Press, 1984), 30.
26. Ibid.
27. Kiyozawa Kiyoshi, *Gaiseika to shite no Okubo Toshimichi* (Tokyo: Chuo Koronsha, 1942), 55–56, as cited in Masakazu Iwata, *Okubo Toshimichi: The Bismarck of Japan* (Berkeley: University of California Press, 1964), 188–89.
28. Sandra Carol Taylor Caruthers, "Charles LeGendre, American Diplomacy, and Expansionism in Meiji Japan" (PhD thesis, University of Colorado, 1963), 59.
29. *New York Times,* September 3, 1873.
30. Charles E. Delong to Hamilton Fish, November 6, 1872, in *Foreign Relations of the United States, Col. 1, 1873–1874* (Washington, D.C., Government Printing Office, 1873–1874), 553–54.

31. *Dictionary of American Biography*, p. 146; *Far East* (1877), 93–94.

32. Caruthers, "Charles LeGendre, American Diplomacy, and Expansionism in Meiji Japan," 62.

33. Ibid.

34. Sophia Su-fei Yen, *Taiwan in China's Foreign Relations, 1836–1874* (Hamden, CT: Shoe String Press, 1965), 196.

35. Ibid., 196.

36. Robert Eskildsen, ed., *Foreign Adventurers and the Aborigines of Southern Taiwan, 1867–1874* (Nankang, Taipei: Institute of Taiwan History, Academic Sinica, 2005), 209.

37. Ibid.

38. Donald Keene, *Emperor of Japan: Meiji and His World, 1852–1912* (New York: Columbia University Press, 2002), 228.

39. Carmen Blacker, *The Japanese Enlightenment: A Study of the Writings of Fukuzawa Yukichi* (Cambridge: Cambridge University Press, 1964), 124–36.

40. F. Hilary Conroy, *The Japanese Seizure of Korea, 1868–1910: A Study of Realism and Idealism in International Relations* (Philadelphia: University of Pennsylvania Press, 1960), 18.

41. Akira Iriye, ed., *The Chinese and the Japanese: Essays in Political and Cultural Interactions* (Princeton, NJ: Princeton University Press, 1980), 45.

42. Lee and Patterson, *Korean-American Relations*, 12.

43. Ibid., 17.

44. Ibid., 13.

45. Alexis Dudden, *Japan's Colonization of Korea: Discourse and Power* (Honolulu: University of Hawaii Press, 2005), 84.
46. Jongsuk Chay, *Diplomacy of Asymmetry: Korean American Relations to 1910* (Honolulu: University of Hawaii Press, 1990), 105.
47. Ibid.
48. James L. McClain, *Japan: A Modern History* (New York: W. W. Norton & Company, 2002), 299.
49. Keene, *Emperor of Japan*, 510.

CHAPTER 7: PLAYING ROOSEVELT'S GAME

1. TR to Theodore Roosevelt Jr., February 10, 1904, Elting Morison and John Blum, eds., *The Letters of Theodore Roosevelt*, 8 vols. (Cambridge, MA: Harvard University Press, 1951–54), 4:724.
2. Kengi Hamada, *Prince Ito* (Tokyo: Sanseido Co., 1936), 116.
3. Walter A. McDougall, *Let the Sea Make a Noise* (New York: HarperCollins, 1993), 386.
4. TR, "A Nation of Pioneers, September 2, 1901," in May Williamson Hazeltine, *Masterpieces of Eloquence: Famous Orations of Great World Leaders from Early Greece to the Present Time* (New York: P. F. Collier & Son, 1905), 25: 10889–92.
5. Kenneth C. Davis, *Don't Know Much About History* (New York: Avon Books, 1990), 224–27.
6. Dexter Perkins, *The Monroe Doctrine, 1867–1907* (Baltimore: Baltimore Press, 1937), 333.
7. TR to White, September 13, 1906, Roosevelt Papers, Library of Congress.

8. TR Annual Message to Congress, December 6, 1904, in *Foreign Relations of the United States, 1904* (Washington, D.C.: U.S. Government Printing Office, 1904), 41.

9. Ibid.

10. Ibid.

11. Roosevelt described his style of foreign policy as "the exercise of intelligent forethought and of decisive action sufficiently far in advance of any likely crisis." TR, *Theodore Roosevelt: An Autobiography* (New York: Macmillan Press Company, 1913), 516.

    Elihu Root served TR as his personal attorney and as both secretary of war and secretary of state. Root wrote that Roosevelt's approach to foreign relations was to view "each international question against the background of those tendencies through which civilization develops and along which particular civilizations advance or decline." Gail Bederman, *Manliness & Civilization: A Cultural History of Gender and Race in the United States, 1880–1917* (Chicago: University of Chicago Press, 1995), 196.

12. Thomas F. Gossett, *Race: The History of an Idea in America* (New York: Schocken Books, 1970), 312.

13. Morison, *Letters*, 4:1327.

14. Albert J. Beveridge, *The Russian Advance* (New York: Harper & Brothers, 1903), 109.

15. Ibid., 122.

16. TR to Hermann Speck von Sternberg, August 28, 1900, Morison, *Letters*, 2:1394.

17. TR to David Bowman Schneder, June 19, 1905, Morison, *Letters*, 4:1240–41.

18. George E. Mowry, *The Era of Theodore Roosevelt and the Birth of Modern America, 1900–1912* (New York: Harper & Row, 1958), 183.

19. John Hay to TR, April 25, 1903, Papers of John Hay, Library of Congress, Manuscript Division, Box 5.

20. Hay to TR, April 23, 1903, Hay Papers.

21. TR to Hay, May 22, 1903, Morison, *Letters,* 3:478.

22. Shumph Okamoto, *The Japanese Oligarchy and the Russo-Japanese War* (New York: Columbia University Press, 1970), 87.

23. Lloyd Griscom to John Hay, January 21, 1904, Despatches from U.S. States Ministers to Japan, 78, National Archives, RG 59.

24. Frederick F. Travis, *George Kennan and the American-Russian Relationship, 1865–1924* (Athens: Ohio University Press, 1990), 252.

25. Sylvia Jukes Morris, *Edith Kermit Roosevelt: Portrait of a First Lady* (New York: Modern Library, 2001), 276.

26. Sophia Su-fei Yen, *Taiwan in China's Foreign Relations, 1836–1874* (Hamden, CT: Shoe String Press, 1965), 196.

27. TR to Sternberg, February 6, 1904, in Howard K. Beale, *Theodore Roosevelt and the Rise of America to World Power* (Baltimore: Johns Hopkins University Press, 1956), 291.

28. Horace N. Allen to Hay, August 31, 1900, Despatches from U.S. Ministers to Korea, 1883–1905, National Archives, RG 59, M134, No. 275.

29. Frederick A. McKenzie, *Korea's Fight for Freedom* (New York: Fleming H. Revell, 1920), 77–78.

30. Oscar Straus to TR, February 11, 1904, Morison, *Letters,* 4:24.

31. Elihu Root to TR, February 15, 1904, ibid., 4:73

32. TR to Theodore Roosevelt Jr., February 10, 1904, ibid., 4:724.

33. Bōei Chō Bōei Kenkyūsho Senshi-shitsu [National Defense Agency, National Defense Institute, War History Office], *Hawai sakusen* [The Hawaii Operation], Senshi Sōsho [War History Series] [Tokyo: Asagumo Shinbunsha, 1967], 84, quoted in Aizawa Kiyoshi, "Differences Regarding Togo's Surprise Attack on Port Arthur," in *The Russo-Japanese War in Global Perspectives,* 2:8.

34. TR to Cecil Spring-Rice, July 24, 1905, in Morison, *Letters,* 4:1283.

Chapter 8: The Japanese Monroe Doctrine for Asia

Caption:
Taft Group: *Tokyo Asahi Shimbun,* July 25, 1905.

1. Viscount Kentaro Kaneko, LL.D., "A 'Japanese Monroe Doctrine' and Manchuria," *Contemporary Japan* 1, no. 1, June 1932.

2. Robert B. Valliant, "The Selling of Japan: Japanese Manipulation of Western Opinion, 1900–1905," *Monumenta Nipponica* 29, no. 4 (Winter 1974). Stable URL: http://www.jstor.org/stable/2383894.

3. Lloyd Griscom to John Hay, February 23, 1904, Papers of John Hay, Library of Congress, Manuscript Division.

4. Valliant, "Selling."

5. *The American Review of Reviews, An International Magazine,* ed. Albert Shaw (July–December 1904).

6. *New York Times*, April 29, 1904.

7. Valliant, "Selling."

8. TR to Kaneko, September 11, 1905, as cited in Tyler Dennett, *Roosevelt and the Russo-Japanese War* (Gloucester, MA: Peter Smith, 1959), 36. Roosevelt wrote: "You have rendered me invaluable assistance by the way in which you have enabled me to know, and also by the way in which you have enabled me to convey to your own government certain things which I thought it desirable to have known and which I hardly cared to forward through official channels."

9. Kentaro Kaneko, "The Yellow Peril Is the Golden Opportunity for Japan," *The North American Review* 179, no. 626 (November 1904).

10. Kentaro Kaneko, "Japan's Position in the Far East," *Annals of the American Academy of Political and Social Science* (Sage Publications, 1905), vol. 26, 77–82.

11. Kentaro Kaneko, "The Russo Japanese War: Its Causes and Its Results," *The International Quarterly* 10, no. 1 (October 1904), 51.

12. Kaneko, "Japan's Position in the Far East."

13. Kaneko, "The Russo Japanese War," 53.

14. Hay diary, March 26, 1904, Hay Papers.

15. Raymond Esthus, *Theodore Roosevelt and Japan* (Seattle: University of Washington Press, 1966), 40.

16. Ibid., 41.

17. Allen to Hay, April 14, 1904, U.S. Department of State.

18. TR to Taft, April 20, 1905, Roosevelt Papers (LC).

19. TR to Cecil Arthur Spring-Rice, June 13, 1904, Elting Morison and John Blum, eds., *The Letters of Theodore*

Roosevelt, 8 vols. (Cambridge, MA: Harvard University Press, 1951–54), 4:833.

20. Ibid.
21. Ibid.
22. Ibid.
23. Ibid.
24. Ibid.
25. Ibid.
26. Esthus, *Theodore Roosevelt and Japan*, 44.
27. Ibid.
28. Hay diary, June 23, 1904, Hay Papers.
29. TR to Hay, July 26, 1904, Morison, *Letters*, 4:865.
30. Carol Christ, "Japan's Seven Acres: Politics and Aesthetics at the 1904 Louisiana Purchase Exposition," *Gateway Heritage* 71:2 (1996), 10.
31. Ibid., 11.
32. Dennett, *Roosevelt and the Russo-Japanese War*, 40, 168.
33. Donald Keene, *Emperor of Japan: Meiji and His World, 1852–1912* (New York: Columbia University Press, 2002), 612.
34. Allen to Hay, December 24, 1904, Hay Papers.
35. TR to Hay, September 2, 1904, Morison, *Letters*, 4:917.
36. TR to Spring Rice, December 27, 1904, ibid., 4:1082.
37. Hay diary, December 24, 1904, Hay Papers.
38. Hay diary, December 6, 1904, Hay Papers.
39. TR to Edward VII, March 9, 1905, Morison, *Letters*, 4:1136.
40. Robert T. Oliver, *Syngman Rhee: The Man Behind the Myth* (New York: Dodd Mead, 1955), 73–87.

41. Esthus, *Theodore Roosevelt and Japan*, 62.

42. Dennett, *Roosevelt and the Russo-Japanese War*, 110.

43. Rockhill to Allen, February 29, 1904, Rockhill Papers.

44. www.dartmouth.edu/~upne/1-928825-001.html.

45. Richard Drinnon, *Facing West: The Metaphysics of Indian-hating and Empire-building* (Norman: University of Oklahoma Press, 1997), 120.

46. Sylvia Jukes Morris, *Edith Kermit Roosevelt: Portrait of a First Lady* (New York: Modern Library, 2001), p. 283.

47. TR to Theodore Roosevelt Jr., March 5, 1904, TRP (PL), Box 147, Bk. No. 15, pp. 335–36.

48. Keene, *Emperor of Japan*, 611.

49. Esthus, *Theodore Roosevelt and Japan*, 65.

50. Keene, *Emperor of Japan*, 612.

51. *New York Times*, April 3, 1905.

52. Keene, *Emperor of Japan*, 612.

53. Shumpei Okamoto, *The Japanese Oligarchy and the Russo-Japanese War* (New York: Columbia University Press, 1970), 119.

54. *New York Times*, June 5, 1905.

55. TR to William Howard Taft, May 31, 1905, as cited in Morison, *Letters*, 4:1198.

56. Esthus, *Theodore Roosevelt and Japan*, 71.

57. Howard K. Beale, *Theodore Roosevelt and the Rise of America to World Power* (Baltimore: Johns Hopkins University Press, 1956), 334.

58. Walter A. McDougall, *Let the Sea Make a Noise* (New York: HarperCollins, 1993), 453.

59. TR to Henry Cabot Lodge, June 5, 1905, Morison, *Letters*, 4:1202–05.

60. TR to Whitelaw Reid, June 5, 1905, ibid., 4:1206.

61. TR to Kermit Roosevelt, June 11, 1905, ibid., 4:1210, 1229, 1232.

62. TR to Benjamin Ide Wheeler, June 17, 1905, TR Papers, Library of Congress, series 2, reel 3.

63. TR to Lodge, June 16, 1905, Morison, *Letters,* 4:1221–33.

64. Raymond Esthus, *Double Eagle and Rising Sun: The Russians and Japanese at Portsmouth in 1905* (Chapel Hill, NC: Duke University Press, 1988), 50, 223.

65. Ibid., 50.

66. Loomis to Reid, telegram, June 15, 1905, Roosevelt Papers.

67. TR to William Howard Taft, July, 3, 1905, Morison, *Letters,* 4:1259–60.

68. Philip C. Jessup, *Elihu Root* (New York: Dodd, Mead and Company, 1938), 2:4.

69. TR to Cecil Spring Rice, July 24, 1905, Morison, *Letters,* 4:1283

70. Kentaro Kaneko, "A 'Japanese Monroe Doctrine' and Manchuria," 176–84.

71. Ibid.

72. Ibid.

73. Ibid.

74. Ibid.

75. Saturday, July 15, 1905 Sagamore Hill –
Conference with Minister Takahira
Letters:

    T.R. to Lloyd Griscom: "The American Government and the American people at large have not the slightest sympathy with the outrageous agitation against the Japanese in certain small sections along

the Pacific slope... [Make known to the Japanese
that] while I am President" there will be no
discrimination. (With permission from the Theodore
Roosevelt Association, Oyster Bay, NY)

76. *New York Times,* July 24, 1905.

77. *New York Times,* July 23, 1905.

78. Lloyd C. Griscom, *Diplomatically Speaking* (New York:
Literary Guild of America, 1940), 259.

79. *San Francisco Chronicle*, July 7, 1905.

80. *Japan Weekly Mail*, July 29, 1905.

81. Tyler Dennett, "President Roosevelt's Secret Pact with
Japan," *Current History* 21, no. 1 (October 1924). See
http://www.icasinc.org/history/katsura.html.

82. TR to Taft, telegram July 31, 1905, in Morison, *Letters,*
4:1293.

83. Alice Roosevelt Longworth, *Crowded Hours* (New York:
Charles Scribner's Sons, 1933), 85.

84. *Tokyo Asahi Shimbun*, July 30, 1905.

85. *New York Times*, July 30, 1905.

86. Kaneko to TR, July 31, 1905, in Dennett, *Russo-Japanese,*
298.

87. *New York Times*, August 2, 1905.

CHAPTER 9: THE IMPERIAL CRUISE

1. Mrs. Campbell Dauncey, *An Englishwoman in the
Philippines* (New York: E. P. Dutton and Company, 1906),
326. Actual quote reads: "I am not come to give you your
Independence, but to study your welfare. You will have your
Independence when you are ready for it, which will not be

in this generation—no, nor in the next, nor perhaps for a hundred years or more." Author has made capitalization changes and omitted the phrase "but to study your welfare."

2. William Manners, *TR & Will: A Friendship That Split the Republican Party* (New York: Harcourt, Brace & World, 1969), 11.

3. Michael Teague, *Mrs. L.: Conversations with Alice Roosevelt Longworth* (Garden City, NY: Doubleday & Company, 1981), 76.

4. Alice Roosevelt Longworth, *Crowded Hours* (New York: Charles Scribner's Sons, 1933), 88.

5. James H. Blount, *American Occupation of the Philippines, 1898–1912* (New York: Knickerbocker Press, 1913), 520.

6. Dauncey, *An Englishwoman in the Philippines*, 86.

7. *Manila Times*, August 5, 1905.

8. Ibid., August 7, 1905.

9. Ibid., August 9, 1905.

10. Dauncey, *An Englishwoman in the Philippines*, 323.

11. *Manila Times*, August 9, 1905.

12. "Remarks of the Secretary of War at the Chamber of Commerce Banquet in Manila at the National Theatre, August 8, 1905," National Archives, RG 350, Entry 5, Box 659, File 12277-11.

13. Dauncey, *An Englishwoman in the Philippines*, 309.

14. Blount, *The American Occupation of the Philippines*, 610.

15. "Speech of Secretary Taft on Friday evening August 11, 1905, at the Hotel Metropole, at a Dinner Given by Filipinos," National Archives, RG 350, Entry 5, Box 659, File 12277-1.

16. *Washington Post,* August 6, 1905, sec. 4, 6.

17. *Manila Times*, August 14, 1905.

18. Ibid., May 19, 1905.

19. Dauncey, *An Englishwoman in the Philippines,* 320.

20. Ibid., 321.

21. Ibid., 320, 322.

22. Ibid., 324.

23. Ibid., 325.

24. Ibid., 326.

25. Ibid. Actual quote reads: "I am not come to give you your Independence, but to study your welfare. You will have your Independence when you are ready for it, which will not be in this generation—no, nor in the next, nor perhaps for a hundred years or more." Author has made capitalization changes and omitted the phrase "but to study your welfare."

26. Ibid.

27. Ibid., 334–40.

28. "Remarks of Secretary Taft at the Filipino Banquet at Cebu on August 22, 1905," National Archives, RG 350, Entry 5, Box 659, File 12277-1.

29. *Manila Times,* August 24, 1905.

30. Resil B. Mojares, *The War Against the Americans: Resistance and Collaboration in Cebu, 1899–1906* (Manila, Philippines: Ateneo e Manila University Press, 1999), 151–52.

31. Blount, *American Occupation of the Philippines,* 356.

32. Ibid., 357.

33. *Manila Times,* August 31, 1905.

CHAPTER 10: ROOSEVELT'S OPEN AND CLOSED DOORS

1. Delber [*sic*] L. McKee, *Chinese Exclusion Versus the Open Door Policy, 1900–1906: Clashes Over China Policy in the Roosevelt Era* (Detroit: Wayne State University Press, 1977), 114.

2. Imperial Mandate of Emperor Qianlong to King George III, in Edmund Backhouse and J.O.P. Bland, *Annals and Memoirs of the Court of Peking: From the 16th to the 20th Century* (Boston: Houghton Mifflin, 1914), 322–34.

3. Carl A. Trocki, *Opium, Empire, and the Global Political Economy: A Study of the Asian Opium Trade, 1750–1950* (New York: Routledge, 1999), 42.

4. Ibid., 94.

5. Ibid., 52.

6. Ibid., 98.

7. Martin Booth, *Opium: A History* (New York: St. Martin's Press, 1996), 136.

8. Stephen E. Ambrose, *Nothing Like It in the World: The Men Who Built the Transcontinental Railroad, 1863–1869* (New York: Simon & Schuster, 2000), 162.

9. Ibid.

10. Ibid.

11. Ibid., 150.

12. Jack Chen, *The Chinese of America* (San Francisco: Harper & Row, 1980), 153.

13. Wesley S. Griswold, *A Work of Giants: Building the First Transcontinental Railroad* (New York: McGraw Hill, 1962), 144.

14. Text of Burlingame-Seward Treaty in Charles I. Bevans, comp., *Treaties and Other International Agreements of the United States of America, 1776–1949* (Washington, D.C., Government Printing Office, 1971), 6:680–84.

15. Ambrose, *Nothing Like It in the World*, 164.

16. Sin-Kiong Wong, *China's Anti-American Boycott Movement in 1905: A Study in Urban Protest* (New York: Peter Lang Publishing, 2002), 19.

17. Matthew Frye Jacobson, *Barbarian Virtues: The United States Encounters Foreign Peoples at Home and Abroad, 1876–1917* (New York: Hill & Wang, 2000), 78.

18. Eric T. L. Love, *Race Over Empire: Racism and U.S. Imperialism, 1865–1900* (Chapel Hill: University of North Carolina Press, 2004), 95. Actual quote reads: "who eat beef and bread and drink beer cannot labor alongside of those who live on rice, and if the experiment [in Asian immigration] is attempted on a large scale, the American Laborer will have to drop his knife and fork and take up the chopsticks."

19. Thomas F. Gossett, *Race: The History of an Idea in America* (New York: Schocken Books, 1970), 291.

20. Jacobson, *Barbarian Virtues*, 194.

21. Ibid., 79.

22. Roger Daniels, *Coming to America: A History of Immigration and Ethnicity in American Life* (New York: HarperCollins, 2002), 271.

23. Thomas G. Dyer, *Theodore Roosevelt and the Idea of Race* (Baton Rouge: Louisiana State University, 1960), 140.

24. Isham Dell, *Rock Springs Massacre 1885* (Lincoln City, OR: Dell Isham & Associates, 1985), 52.

25. TR, "National Life and Character," in *American Ideals, And Other Essays, Social and Political* (New York: G. P. Putnam's Sons, 1897), 1:111–12.

26. Kenton J. Clymer, *John Hay* (Ann Arbor: University of Michigan Press, 1975), 156.

27. Austria-Hungary, France, Germany, Italy, Japan, Russia, the U.K. and the U.S.

28. Terence V. Powderly, "Exclude Anarchist and Chinaman!" *Collier's Weekly* 28 (December 14, 1901).

29. McKee, *Chinese Exclusion Versus the Open Door Policy*, 59.

30. Ibid., 64.

31. Ibid., 68.

32. Ibid., 114.

33. TR to Cortelyou, January 25, 1904, in Elting Morison and John Blum, eds., *The Letters of Theodore Roosevelt*, 8 vols. (Cambridge, MA: Harvard University Press, 1951–54), 3:709.

34. *New York Tribune*, June 29, 1905.

35. Sin-Kiong Wong, "Mobilizing a Social Movement in China: Propaganda of the 1905 Boycott Campaign," *Chinese Studies* (Taipei) 19:1 (June 2001), 375–408.

36. Ibid.

37. Lay to Loomis, August 16, 1905, Canton Dispatches.

38. Chester Holcombe, "The Question of Chinese Exclusion," *Outlook* 80 (July 8, 1905), 619.

39. *New York Times*, June 28, 1905.

40. TR to Taft in Hong Kong, September 3, 1905, Taft papers, series 4, Taft-TR.

41. Sin-Kiong Wong, "Die for the Boycott and Nation: Martrydom and the 1905 Anti-American Movement

in China," *Modern Asian Studies* 35, no. 3 (Cambridge: Cambridge University Press, 2001).

42. *Washington Post*, September 1, 1905; *New York Times*, September 4, 1905.

43. Stacy A. Cordery, *Alice: Alice Roosevelt Longworth, from White House Princess to Washington Power Broker* (New York, Viking 2007), 123.

44. *New York Times*, September 28, 1905.

45. *Washington Post*, September 7, 1905.

46. Lay to Loomis, September 12, 1905, Canton Dispatches.

47. Lay to Loomis, October 30, 1905, Canton Dispatches.

48. Charles Chaile-Long, "Why China Boycotts U.S.," *World Today* 10 (March 1906), 314.

49. Michael Teague, *Mrs. L.: Conversations with Alice Roosevelt Longworth* (Garden City, NY: Doubleday & Company, 1981), 99.

50. Ibid., 89, 95.

51. Ibid., 98.

52. W. W. Rockhill to James L. Rodgers, September 18, 1905, Rockhill Papers.

53. "The Rising Spirit in China," *Outlook* 81 (October 7, 1905): 316.

54. *New York Tribune*, August 30, 1905.

CHAPTER 11: INCOGNITO IN JAPAN

CAPTION:

Emperor Gojong: Enclosure in Allen to John Sherman, September 13, 1897, File Microcopies, no. 134, roll 13, Despatches Korea.

1. Michael Teague, *Mrs. L.: Conversations with Alice Roosevelt Longworth* (Garden City, NY: Doubleday & Company, 1981), 84–86.

2. Mark Sullivan, *Our Times: America at the Birth of the Twentieth Century*, ed. Dan Rather (New York: Scribner's 1996), 282.

3. John Edward Wilz, "Did the United States Betray Korea?" *Pacific Historical Review* 54, no. 3 (1985), 251.

4. His visitors were Syngman Rhee and Pastor Yuu P'yong-Ku.

5. TR to Spring Rice, Nov. 1, 1905, Elting Morison and John Blum, eds., *The Letters of Theodore Roosevelt*, 8 vols. (Cambridge, MA: Harvard University Press, 1951–54), 5:61.

6. Steven Ericson and Allen Hockley, eds., *The Treaty of Portsmouth and Its Legacies* (Hanover, NH: Dartmouth College Press, published by University Press of New England, 2008), 57.

7. TR to Kaneko, August 23, 1905, Morison, *Letters,* 4:1312.

8. TR to Mortimer Durand, British ambassador to the United States, August 23, 1905, ibid., 4:1310–11.

9. British documents, IV, 105, as cited in Raymond Esthus, *Theodore Roosevelt and Japan* (Seattle: University of Washington Press, 1966), 85.

10. Tyler Dennett, *Roosevelt and the Russo-Japanese War* (Gloucester, MA: Peter Smith, 1959), 262; Ericson and Hockley, *Treaty of Portsmouth*, 60.

11. Walter A. McDougall, *Let the Sea Make a Noise* (New York: HarperCollins, 1993), 455.

12. Raymond Esthus, *Double Eagle and Rising Sun: The Russians and Japanese at Portsmouth in 1905* (Chapel Hill: Duke University Press, 1988), 167.
13. Ibid., 171.
14. Andrew Gordon, "The Crowd and Politics in Imperial Japan: Tokyo, 1905–1918," *Past and Present* 121, no. 121 (November 1988), 141–70.
15. Lloyd C. Griscom, *Diplomatically Speaking* (New York: Literary Guild of America, 1940), 262.
16. Ibid.
17. Griscom to TR, September 21, 1905, Roosevelt Papers.
18. TR to Hermann Speck von Sternberg, September 6, 1905, Morison, *Letters,* 5:14–15.
19. William W. Rockhill to Taft, telegram, September 14, 1905, NARA, RG 59, M77 (Diplomatic Instructions of the Department of State, 1801–1906), roll 43, frames 117–18.
20. Raymond Esthus, *Theodore Roosevelt and Japan* (Seattle: University of Washington Press, 1966), 41.
21. Esthus, *Double Eagle and the Rising Sun*, 174.
22. Saturday, September 2, 1905, Sagamore Hill. Letters: TR to Alice: If the belligerents had not met at Portsmouth "they would not have made peace." (With permission of the Theodore Roosevelt Association, Oyster Bay, NY)
23. Teague, *Mrs. L.,* 106.
24. Ibid., 108.
25. Ibid.
26. Willard Straight to Frederick Palmer, October 3, 1905, Willard Straight Papers, Cornell University Rare and Manuscript Collections.
27. Ibid.

28. Esthus, *Theodore Roosevelt and Japan,* 108.
29. Longworth, *Crowded Hours,* 104.
30. TR to Rockhill, telegram September 17, 1905, NARA, RG 59, M92 (Despatches from U.S. Ministers to China, 1843–1906), roll 129.

> TELEGRAM RECEIVED September 17ᵀᴴ, 1905
>
> Rockhill,
> Peking.
> Further investigation satisfies me that Miss Roosevelt's contemplated trip with her party incognity? (incognita) to Japan can be quite safely made. It would be wise however as you suggest for Newlands to communicate with Griscom by cable before coming.
>
> Taft.
> [Author Note: "Incognita" is the feminine Latin version of "incognito." Classically educated Taft was referring to a female, Alice Roosevelt.]

31. Teague, *Mrs. L.,* 87.
32. Longworth, *Crowded Hours,* 106; "Not a banzai to be heard," Teague, *Mrs. L.,* 87.

CHAPTER 12: SELLOUT IN SEOUL
1. Enclosure in Allen to John Sherman, September 13, 1897, NARA, RG 59, M77 (Diplomatic Despatches to Korea), 13.
2. TR to Hermann Speck von Sternberg, August 8, 1900. Elting Morison and John Blum, eds., *The Letters of Theodore*

Roosevelt, 8 vols. (Cambridge, MA: Harvard University Press, 1951–54), 2:1394.

3. Monday, October 30, 1905, en route to Washington D.C. on the U.S.S. *West Virginia*. Letters: Edith to Kermit: Alice is looking very careworn and troubled about something. She will not say what is wrong. (With permission of the Theodore Roosevelt Association, Oyster Bay, NY)

4. *Kokumin Newspaper*, November 4, 1905.

5. TR to Taft, October 5, 1905, Morison, *Letters*, 5:46.

6. Raymond Esthus, *Theodore Roosevelt and Japan* (Seattle: University of Washington Press, 1966), 105.

7. Jongsuk Chay, *Diplomacy of Asymmetry: Korean American Relations to 1910* (Honolulu: University of Hawaii Press, 1990), 146.

8. Tyler Dennett, *Roosevelt and the Russo-Japanese War* (Gloucester, MA: Peter Smith, 1959), 305.

9. Esthus, *Theodore Roosevelt and Japan*, 61.

10. Ibid., 111.

11. "The treaty rested on the false assumption that Korea could govern herself well. It had already been shown that she could not in any real sense govern herself at all." TR, *America and the World War* (New York: Charles Scribner's Sons, 1915), 29.

    In his *Autobiography*, Roosevelt wrote that he approved of Japan taking over Korea because Korea "had shown herself utterly impotent either for self-government or self-defense (and) was in actual fact almost immediately annexed to Japan." *Theodore Roosevelt, An Autobiography* (New York: Macmillan Co., 1913), 545.

12. Herbert Croly, *Willard Straight* (New York: Macmillan Company, 1924), 188.

13. Howard K. Beale, *Theodore Roosevelt and the Rise of America to World Power* (Baltimore: Johns Hopkins University Press, 1956), 322.

14. Joyce C. Lebra, *Japan's Greater East Asia Co-Prosperity Sphere in World War II: Selected Readings and Documents* (New York: Oxford University Press, 1975), 157.

15. Franklin D. Roosevelt's Address to the nation in light of the Japanese attack on Pearl Harbor. www.nationalcenter. org/FRooseveltDateInfamy1941.html, accessed August 22, 2009.

16. www.nps.gov/history/nr/twhp/wwwlps/ lessons/18arizona/18facts1.htm, accessed August 22, 2009.

17. Kentaro Kaneko, "A 'Japanese Monroe Doctrine' and Manchuria," *Contemporary Japan* 1, no. 1 (June 1932).

18. "Monroe Doctrine for Japan Stirs American Criticism," *Washington Star,* July 4, 1921.

19. Stanley Hornbeck memorandum, January 14, 1932, "Manchuria…for Asia," in Justus D. Downecke, comp., *The Diplomacy of Frustration: The Manchurian Crisis of 1931–1933 as Revealed in the Papers of Stanley K. Hornbeck* (Palo Alto, CA: Hoover Institution Press, 1981), 127.

20. Kaku Mori, leader of the Seiyukai Party, quoted in "Japan: Fissiparous Tendencies," *Time,* September 5, 1932.

21. Ibid.

22. Ibid.

23. Kiyoshi K. Kawakami, *American-Japanese Relations: An Inside View of Japan's Policies and Purposes* (New York: Fleming H. Revell, 1912).
24. Kaneko, "A 'Japanese Monroe Doctrine' and Manchuria."
25. Ibid.
26. George H. Blakeslee, "The Japanese Monroe Doctrine," *Foreign Affairs* 11, issue 4 (July 1933), 671–81.
27. Kimitada Miwa, "Japanese Images of War with the United States," in Akira Iriye, ed., *Mutual Images: Essays in American-Japanese Relations* (Cambridge, MA: Harvard University Press, 1975), 133.
28. *Department of State Bulletin* 5, no. 129 (December 13, 1941).

CHAPTER 13: FOLLOWING THE SUN

CAPTIONS:

Moro Massacre: Samuel Clemens, "Comments on the Moro Massacre" (March 12, 1906), in Howard Zinn and Anthony Arnove, eds., *Voices of a People's History of the United States* (New York: Seven Stories Press, 2004), 248–51.

Wedding: Michael Teague, *Mrs. L.: Conversations with Alice Roosevelt Longworth* (Garden City, NY: Doubleday & Company, 1981), 128, 129.

1. TR, *The Winning of the West* (New York: G. P. Putnam's Sons, 1894), vol. 1: *From the Alleghanies to the Mississippi, 1769–1776*, x, xi.
2. *New York Times*, September 9, 2008.
3. Ibid.
4. Clemens, "Comments on the Moro Massacre."

5. Ibid.

6. Teague, *Mrs. L.,* 129.

7. Carol Felsenthal, *The Life and Times of Alice Roosevelt Longworth* (New York: St. Martin's Press, 1988), 85.

8. Ibid., 98.

9. Ibid.

10. Edmund Morris, *Theodore Rex* (New York: Random House, 2001), 436.

11. Teague, *Mrs. L.,* 128.

12. Alice Roosevelt Longworth, Diary entry, July 27, 1905, Papers of Alice Roosevelt Longworth, Library of Congress.

13. William "Fishbait" Miller and Francis Spatz Leighton, *Fishbait* (Englewood Cliffs, NJ: Prentice Hall, 1977), 103–104.

14. Stacy A. Cordery, *Alice: Alice Roosevelt Longworth, from White House Princess to Washington Power Broker* (New York: Viking, 2007), 231.

15. Ibid., 312.

16. *New York Times,* May 16, 1955.

17. Cordery, *Alice,* 423.

18. TR to Trevelyan, June 19, 1908, Elting Morison and John Blum, eds., *The Letters of Theodore Roosevelt,* 8 vols. (Cambridge, MA: Harvard University Press, 1951–54), 6:1805.

19. TR to Taft, August 7, 1908. TR Papers, PLB 83, series 2, Box 29.

20. Henry F. Pringle, *The Life and Times of William Howard Taft* (Norwalk, CT: Easton Press, 1986), 102.

21. TR to William Howard Taft, September 5, 1908. Morison, *Letters*, 6:1209–10; Henry F. Pringle, *Theodore Roosevelt: A Biography* (New York: Harcourt, Brace and Company, 1931), 504.

22. Stephen Hess, "Big Bill Taft," *American Heritage Magazine* 17, no. 6 (October 1966).

23. TR to William Howard Taft, August 21, 1907, in Morison, *Letters*, 5:761.

24. Richard H. Collin, *Theodore Roosevelt, Culture, Diplomacy, and Expansion: A New View of American Imperialism* (Baton Rouge: Louisiana State University Press, 1985), 151.

25. Theodore Roosevelt, "Expansion of the White Races," in Hermann Hagedorn, ed., *National Edition: The Works of Theodore Roosevelt*, vol. 18 (New York: Charles Scribner's Sons, 1926), 348.

26. Edward Wagenknecht, *The Seven Worlds of Theodore Roosevelt* (New York: Longmans, Green & Co., 1958), 163.

27. Howard K. Beale, *Theodore Roosevelt and the Rise of America to World Power* (Baltimore: Johns Hopkins University Press, 1956), 460.

28. Roosevelt to Philander Knox, February 8, 1909. Morison, *Letters*, 6: 1512–13.

29. Theodore Roosevelt, "Biological Analogies in History," *The Romanes Lecture delivered before the University of Oxford, June 7, 1910* (New York: Oxford University Press, 1910), 31.

30. Baron Kaneko died in Tokyo at the age of eighty-nine, seven months after his countrymen attacked Pearl Harbor.

31. *New York Times*, July 30, 1905.

32. Kathleen Dalton, *Theodore Roosevelt: A Strenuous Life* (New York: Vintage Books, 2004), 35.

33. Edmund Morris, *The Rise of Theodore Roosevelt* (New York: Coward, McCann, and Geoghegan, 1979), 743.

34. Carleton Putnam, *Race and Reason: A Yankee View* (Washington, DC: Public Affairs Press, 1961), 41.

ACKNOWLEDGMENTS

1. Theodore Roosevelt, *The Strenvous Life, Essays and Addresses* (New York: The Century Co., 1905), 28.

ABOUT THE AUTHOR

"Just because you wrote a few books, the world is not going to change. You will find that you will go to sleep and awaken as the same son-of-a-bitch you were the day before."
—JAMES MICHENER

James Bradley is a son of John Bradley, who helped raise the American flag on Iwo Jima. He is the author of *Flags of Our Fathers* and *Flyboys* and is the president of the James Bradley Peace Foundation.